TRADE AND DEVELOPMENT

Also by V. N. Balasubramanyam

CURRENT ISSUES IN DEVELOPMENT ECONOMICS (*editor with Sanjaya Lall*)
TOPICS IN POLICY APPRAISAL: VOLUME 2

Also by D. Greenaway

CURRENT ISSUES IN INTERNATIONAL TRADE: THEORY AND POLICY (*editor*)
CURRENT ISSUES IN MACROECONOMICS (*editor*)
ECONOMIC DEVELOPMENT AND INTERNATIONAL TRADE (*editor*)
GLOBAL PROTECTIONISM (*editor with Robert C. Hine, Anthony P. O'Brien and Robert J. Thornton*)
INTERNATIONAL TRADE POLICY: FROM TARIFFS TO THE NEW PROTECTIONISM
PIONEERS OF MODERN ECONOMICS IN BRITAIN: VOLUMES 1 AND 2 (*editor with John R. Presley*)
TRADE AND FISCAL ADJUSTMENT IN AFRICA (*with David Bevan, Paul Collier and Norman Gemmell*)
TRADE AND INDUSTRIAL POLICY IN DEVELOPING COUNTRIES: A MANUAL OF POLICY ANALYSIS (*with Chris Milner*)

Trade and Development

Essays in Honour of Jagdish Bhagwati

Edited by

V. N. Balasubramanyam
Professor of Development Economics
Lancaster University

and

D. Greenaway
Pro-Vice-Chancellor and Professor of Economics
University of Nottingham

382
B57 tr

First published in Great Britain 1996 by
MACMILLAN PRESS LTD
Houndmills, Basingstoke, Hampshire RG21 6XS
and London
Companies and representatives
throughout the world

A catalogue record for this book is available
from the British Library.

ISBN 0–333–65616–4

First published in the United States of America 1996 by
ST. MARTIN'S PRESS, INC.,
Scholarly and Reference Division,
175 Fifth Avenue,
New York, N.Y. 10010

ISBN 0–312–16146–8

Library of Congress Cataloging-in-Publication Data
Trade and development : essays in honour of Jagdish Bhagwati / edited
by V. N. Balasubramanyam and D. Greenaway.
p.   cm.
Includes index.
ISBN 0–312–16146–8
1. International trade.   2. International economic relations.
I. Balasubramanyam, V. N.   II. Greenaway, David.   III. Bhagwati,
Jagdish N., 1934–   .
HF1379.T688   1996
382—dc20   96–7690
                                                                    CIP

10   9   8   7   6   5   4   3   2   1
05   04   03   02   01   00   99   98   97   96

Printed and bound in Great Britain by
Antony Rowe Ltd, Chippenham, Wiltshire

Contents

PART FOUR   COUNTRY-SPECIFIC STUDIES

Acknowledgements

We gratefully acknowledge the generous financial support for the conference on Trade and Development in honour of Jagdish Bhagwati provided by Mr Ivan Wheatley of the Management Development Division of the Management School, Lancaster University and the Economic and Social Research Council of the UK. We would also like to thank Carol Barlow for her assistance with the organisation of the conference and her editorial assistance for this volume.

Notes on the Contributors

V.N. Balasubramanyam is Professor of Development Economics, Lancaster University.

Subrata Ghatak is Senior Lecturer in Economics, University of Leicester.

David Greenaway is Pro-Vice-Chancellor and Professor of Economics, University of Nottingham.

Vijay Joshi is Fellow of Merton College, Oxford University.

Homi Katrak is Reader in Economics, University of Surrey.

Sajal Lahiri is Professor of Economics, University of Essex.

Ian Little is Emeritus Professor, Oxford University.

Alasdair MacBean is Emeritus Professor, Lancaster University.

Andrew McKay is Lecturer in Economics, University of Nottingham.

Chris Milner is Professor of International Economics, University of Nottingham.

Oliver Morrissey is Senior Lecturer in Economics, University of Nottingham.

Carlo Perroni is Lecturer in Economics, University of Warwick.

Pascalis Raimondos is Associate Professor, Economic Policy Research Unit, Copenhagen Business School.

M.A. Salisu is Research Fellow, Lancaster University.

David Sapsford is Professor of Economics, Lancaster University.

Oded Stark is Professor of Economics, University of Oslo.

Utku Utkulu is Research Fellow, University of Leicester.

John Whalley is Professor of Economics, University of Warwick.

Martin Wolf is Deputy Editor, *The Financial Times*, London.

Conference Participants

The following participants attended the conference held on 9 and 10 December 1994 at Lancaster House Hotel, to celebrate Jagdish Bhagwati's sixtieth birthday:

Karim Abouzahr, New College, Oxford University
Melinda Acutt, Lancaster University
V.N. Balasubramanyam, Lancaster University
Maya Balasubramanyam, Imperial College of Science
Rajeev Balasubramanyam, Oriel College, Oxford University
Carol Barlow, Lancaster University
Jagdish Bhagwati, Columbia University
Peter Buckley, University of Bradford
Neil Corless, Lancaster University
Inés Galsasò, New College, Oxford University
Subrata Ghatak, Leicester University
David Greenaway, CREDIT and University of Nottingham
Vijay Joshi, Merton College, Oxford University
Homi Katrak, University of Surrey
Sajal Lahiri, University of Essex
Ian Little, Nuffield College, Oxford University
Alasdair MacBean, Lancaster University
Andrew McKay, CREDIT and University of Nottingham
Chris Milner, CREDIT and University of Nottingham
Oliver Morrissey, CREDIT, University of Nottingham
Sheila Page, ODI
Mohammed Salisu, Lancaster University
David Sapsford, Lancaster University
Nick Snowdon, Lancaster University
Oded Stark, University of Oslo
Vivek Tandon, University College London and British Telecom
Subidey Togan, Bilkent University, Turkey
John Whalley, University of Warwick
Martin Wolf, *The Financial Times*, London

Introduction

V.N. Balasubramanyam and David Greenaway

Anyone who lives long enough can reach the age of 60, a wit is supposed to have said. True, but very few reach the age of 60 in such style and attain such stature in their chosen profession as Jagdish Bhagwati. His vast number of articles on international economics and development, republished in five collected volumes, his 16 books, many of which have been translated in several languages, his ceaseless refutation of protectionism and advocacy of free trade, both in the popular press and professional journals, and his influential work as policy adviser to international institutions have all earned him wide acclaim. Regarded by many as a star in the constellation of influential economic thinkers and opinion-makers today, Jagdish Bhagwati is widely admired.

The 11 essays, written by Jagdish Bhagwati's admirers and students in this Festschrift volume were presented at a conference, jointly convened by the Centre for Research on Economic Development and International Trade (CREDIT) of Nottingham University and the Department of Economics, Lancaster University, to celebrate Jagdish Bhagwati's sixtieth birthday. Each of the essays analyses major issues in trade and development on which Bhagwati has written extensively. The 11 papers can be grouped into four categories: international factor movements, trade policy, international institutions, and country-specific studies relating to India and China.

I INTERNATIONAL FACTOR MOVEMENTS

Chapter 1 by V.N. Balasubramanyam, M. Salisu and David Sapsford (Lancaster) on foreign direct investment, chapter 2 on food aid by Sajal Lahiri (Essex) and Pascalis Raimondos (Copenhagen), chapter 3 on return migration by Oded Stark (Harvard and Oslo), and chapter 4 on the choice between imported and in-house technologies by Homi Katrak (Surrey) belong in this group.

Balasubramanyam, Salisu and Sapsford attempt an empirical verification of a hypothesis concerning the relationship between trade policy regimes and the efficacy of foreign direct investment (FDI) in developing countries, enunciated by Bhagwati. The hypothesis suggests that productive efficiency of FDI, identified by its impact on the growth rate, tends to be higher in countries pursuing an export promotion (EP) strategy of development than in countries pursuing an import substitution (IS) strategy of development. Balasubramanyam, Salisu and Sapsford draw upon the *new growth theory* to substantiate further Bhagwati's hypothesis and test it, utilising data on FDI and growth rates for a sample of 46 developing countries. The tests, grounded in sophisticated statistical techniques, ratify Bhagwati's hypothesis.

Lahiri and Raimondos's paper analyses the long-standing hypothesis (belief) in the literature that food aid to developing countries depresses domestic food production in the recipient countries. Bhagwati has written extensively on this question, putting it into the theoretical framework of the transfer problem while at the same time challenging the equation of the distinct issues of the positive and the normative impacts of food assistance. Lahiri and Raimondos construct and use two theoretical models. The first is built on the assumption that food aid is contingent upon the reduction of tariffs on imports of manufactures in the countries receiving aid, and the second is built around the assumption that the proceeds of food aid are spent on R&D in agriculture. This paper not only lends support to Bhagwati's long-standing advocacy of liberal trade regimes, but also demonstrates that under certain circumstances food aid need not depress domestic food production in the recipient countries.

The third paper in this group, by Oded Stark, extends Bhagwati's work on migration to investigate the conditions and circumstances which give rise to return migration. What are the factors that influence migrants to return home? Stark's thesis is that return migration is not induced by inter-country wage differentials, but may be prompted by other factors, such as a reduced need for insurance at home, higher purchasing power of savings at home than in the country to which labour has migrated, and information asymmetries concerning skill levels of workers who migrate.

Homi Katrak analyses the impact of differing types of trade policy regimes on the choice of entrepreneurs between home-grown and imported technologies. Following a succinct discussion of the benefits and costs of these two types of technology in both the EP and IS trade regimes, Katrak arrives at the agnostic conclusion that the type of trade policy regime pursued may tilt the choice between imported and home-produced technologies either way, and that it is impossible to predict the choice between the two.

II TRADE POLICY

The papers by Chris Milner and Andrew MacKay (Nottingham and CREDIT), Subrata Ghatak and Utku Utkulu (Leicester) and Martin Wolf

(*Financial Times*) address issues of trade policy, past and present. In chapter 5 Milner and MacKay extend Bhagwati's definition and conceptualisation of IS and EP policy regimes to include the presence of a non-tradeables sector in addition to the export and import substitution or tradeables sectors of the economy. On the basis of theoretical models they proceed to show that in the presence of a non-tradeables sector a country may optimally pursue a mixed strategy with elements of Bhagwati's definition of IS and EP strategies. They extend their theoretical analysis to an empirical examination of the experience of developing countries such as Barbados.

Ghatak and Utkulu, in chapter 6, examine the impact of trade policy on growth in the context of the *new growth theory*. They formulate a theoretical model of the relationship between different types of trade policy regimes and growth, incorporating key elements of the new growth theory such as human capital. This model is then tested with data from India, Turkey and Malaysia. On the basis of these statistical tests they conclude that a liberal trade policy has a positive impact on growth and that accumulation of both physical and human capital is central to growth.

In the final chapter of Part Two, Martin Wolf provides a lucid critique of arguments for intervention in free trade, based on the need to preserve the environment and labour standards. Wolf does not deny the need to protect the environment and preserve and promote the interests of labour. Trade policy, however, is not the ideal instrument for achieving these objectives. Wolf's closely argued paper exposes the moral incoherence and the economic fallacies underlying the arguments for protection, which are ostensibly cast in terms of the need to preserve the environment and protect labour. The paper succeeds in its objective of reviewing and extending the recent work of Jagdish Bhagwati in this area.

III INTERNATIONAL INSTITUTIONS

David Greenaway and Oliver Morrissey (Nottingham and CREDIT), in chapter 8, evaluate the role of international institutions such as the World Bank and the GATT in the recent trade liberalisation strategies of developing countries and speculate on how these roles may evolve in the post-Uruguay Round setting. Their paper provides a detailed review of the nature and extent of trade liberalisation in a number of developing countries, including the factors that have influenced liberalisation, as a prelude to the discussion of the role of international institutions in the observed liberalisation efforts. It also provides a critical review of theoretical models such as the strategic organisational approach designed to analyse the nature of organisations and their role in liberalisation. The paper concludes by identifying the areas in which the international institutions can co-ordinate their activities, including promotion and monitoring of trade liberalisation. Especially relevant in this context are their suggestions concerning the role institutions such as UNCTAD and the World Bank can play in facilitating the negotiation of foreign direct investment projects between developing countries and multinational enterprises.

John Whalley and Carlo Perroni (Warwick) discuss the role of competition policy in the newly established World Trade Organisation (WTO) and its implications for the trade and welfare of developing countries. This paper, on a novel theme, examines the interrelationship between competition policy and trade policy and presents a case of international co-ordination of competition policy. Preliminary estimates made by the authors suggest that harmonisation of competition policy across countries could be of considerable importance to developing countries, almost of the order of 5 - 6 per cent of national income. Thus the authors argue that competition policy negotiation may be potentially more significant to developing countries than the whole of the trade discipline achieved in the Uruguay Round.

IV   COUNTRY-SPECIFIC STUDIES

India and China are the focus of chapters 10 and 11 by Vijay Joshi and Ian Little (Oxford) and Alasdair MacBean (Lancaster). Joshi and Little provide a succinct analysis of the objectives and instruments of macroeconomic policy in developing countries and review the course of macroeconomic policies in India over the past 40 years. Their paper, which draws on their important recent book on India, underscores the need for fiscal discipline, drawing upon various episodes in India's recent economic history. The main lesson is that in the absence of fiscal discipline, trade liberalisation may be futile. Their essay provides a valuable lesson for the proponents of the economic reforms introduced in India since 1991 on the need for which Bhagwati has written extensively since the mid-1960s.

Alasdair MacBean's paper provides a succinct review of China's economic policy reforms and achievements in recent years and also underscores the need for fiscal discipline and effective management of public sector enterprises. The two papers on India and China complement one another in their analysis of economic policy reforms pursued by two of the most populous developing countries in the world.

It is our hope that the diversity and quality of the essays in this volume will provide a small but fitting tribute to such a distinguished scholar and influential economist as Jagdish Bhagwati.

Part One
International Factor Movements

1 Foreign Direct Investment, Trade Policy and Economic Growth

Selected LDC's

O19 -

F21

F13

F43

V.N. Balasubramanyam, M.A. Salisu and David Sapsford

I INTRODUCTION

The factors that determine the magnitude of foreign direct investment (FDI) in various developing countries and the role that FDI plays in the growth process have for long been topics of intense debate. Jagdish Bhagwati's work has provided major insights into these two issues, and in this chapter we test empirically the twin hypotheses concerning FDI propounded by Bhagwati. Bhagwati has argued persuasively that both the magnitude and the effectiveness of FDI in promoting economic growth are higher in those countries that pursue an export promotion (EP) trade policy than in those countries that adopt an import substitution (IS) policy orientation.

In essence, this chapter will analyse the relationship between trade policy, FDI and the rate of economic growth in a sample of developing countries. The chapter is organised as follows. Section II outlines the arresting hypothesis advanced by Jagdish Bhagwati, which links trade strategy to both the amount of FDI that individual developing countries are able to attract and its efficacy in promoting growth; section III describes our model and empirical findings; while section IV provides a summary and offers concluding remarks.

II THE HYPOTHESIS

Bhagwati (1978) has hypothesised that the volume and efficacy of incoming FDI will vary according to whether a country is following an export promoting (EP) or an import substituting (IS) strategy. Specifically, he defines an EP strategy as one which equates the average effective exchange rate on exports to the average effective exchange rate on imports. Thus defined, an EP strategy is trade-neutral or bias-free. In contrast, the IS strategy is one where the effective exchange rate on imports exceeds the effective exchange rate on exports and is biased in favour of import substitution activities.[1]

Bhagwati then argues that, on balance, given all other factors influencing FDI flows and their efficacy, an EP strategy is likely both to attract a higher volume of FDI and promote more efficient utilisation thereof than is an IS strategy. The essential feature of the EP strategy being its *neutrality*, the EP trade regime does not provide artificial and transitory incentives to FDI. The major incentive for FDI that the regime provides is 'simply the conjunction of cheaper costs and the EP orientation' (Bhagwati, 1985). In contrast, the IS regime is entirely policy-driven. As Bhagwati (1985) puts it, 'the IS strategy, on both domestic investments and FDI, has been cut from the same cloth: protect your market and attract home based investments to serve the market.' The magnitude of IS-induced FDI would not be as large as EP-oriented FDI simply because it would be limited by the character of the host-country market which induces it in the first place. Again, EP-induced FDI is likely to be much more efficient in promoting growth simply because it is allowed to operate in a distortion-free environment. The Bhagwati hypothesis therefore has two components: first, that EP countries attract a greater volume of FDI, and second, that they enjoy greater efficiency (social returns) therefrom. Section III reports evidence relating to both the former (or *volume* effect) and the latter (or *efficiency* effect) component of Bhagwati's hypothesis.

Magnitude of FDI in EP and IS Countries

At first sight the proposition that EP countries are likely to attract larger volumes of FDI than IS countries appears to run counter to conventional wisdom. The usual presumption is that tariffs and quotas on imports induce so-called *tariff-jumping* FDI, which also enjoys the added advantage of protection from import competition. Bhagwati does not deny the influence of protection on inflows of FDI. In his incisive Esmée Fairbairn lecture, delivered at Lancaster University in 1985, he acknowledged the influence of protection on FDI. The essence of Bhagwati's argument though is that, ultimately, IS-induced FDI will neither be as large as EP-induced FDI nor will it be sustained over time. The IS strategy is likely to result in a mere relocation of investment from the home countries of investors to that of the host countries with little by way of additions to the existing volume of FDI in the world economy. IS-induced FDI is driven by short-term policy measures whereas EP-induced FDI is driven by considerations of comparative advantage and market forces and is therefore likely to be sustained over time. Moreover, IS-induced FDI is likely to compound the inefficiencies inherent in IS policies, whereas EP-induced FDI is likely to nurture and promote comparative advantage in production and trade which the host countries possess.

New Growth Theory and FDI

Bhagwati's hypothesis concerning the efficiency effect of FDI is grounded in an extensive and detailed analysis of IS-induced inefficiencies. The inefficiencies which such a trade regime imposes on the economy run to a long list; its heavy reliance on tariffs and quotas on trade as the principal instruments of the strategy introduces widespread distortions in factor and product markets; it encourages the adoption of production techniques widely at variance with the factor endowments of the economy. In addition, it provides widespread incentives for rent-seeking and directly unproductive profit-seeking (DUPE) activities (Bhagwati, 1994); it contributes to the growth of income disparities; and it not only promotes misallocation of resources but also encourages X-inefficiency (Bhagwati and Srinivasan, 1975, 1979; Kreuger, 1975; Bhagwati, 1978; Greenaway and Nam, 1988). The immiserisation of growth that might occur as a consequence of protection-induced inflows of FDI into an import competing industry has also been extensively analysed (Bhagwati, 1973; Brecher and Diaz-Alejandro, 1977).

The principal virtue of the EP strategy, with its emphasis on neutrality of policy between the import and export sectors of the economy, is that it allows for a free play of market forces and the allocation of resources on the basis of comparative advantage. Furthermore, because of the neutrality of its policy orientation it offers none of the incentives for rent-seeking and DUPE which the IS policy provides. The competition it allows for from both international trade and domestic sources encourages R&D and investment in human capital. Allocation of resources on the basis of comparative advantage and market forces also promotes specialisation and scale economies.

These are also the factors that new growth theory emphasises, albeit in a novel fashion. It is thus that new growth theory has significant implications for the hypotheses concerning the efficiency of FDI in EP relative to IS countries. The concern of new growth theories is with endogenising the growth rate of GDP, which in turn requires the rate of investment to be endogenised, for ultimately it is factor accumulation which accounts for growth. But for factor accumulation to grow, the return to the capital stock in the aggregate should not diminish, although returns to single acts of investment may diminish. In other words, the social rate of return to investment must exceed the private rate of return. Such a discrepancy between the private and social rates of return occurs because individual acts of private investment add to the stock of knowledge and hence to the productivity of the capital stock. In addition, there are various sorts of knowledge spillover effects and externalities which contribute to growth in the aggregate. A succinct account of this idea is given by Romer (1986, 1987). Here investment in knowledge or R&D is assumed to be subject to diminishing returns, but the utilisation of such knowledge in production activity results in increasing returns. Also, while the product which embodies new knowledge can be protected through patents, the knowledge itself which generates the product cannot thus be protected. New growth theory also emphasises learning by doing and, in the presence of these growth-promoting ingredients, the input of capital may not experience diminishing returns. In sum, externalities, human capital and learning by doing form the mainsprings of endogenous growth theory.

Many of the growth-promoting factors identified by new growth theory can be initiated and nurtured by FDI. FDI has long been recognised as a major source of technology and know-how to developing countries. Indeed, it is the ability of FDI to transfer not only production know-how but also managerial skills that distinguishes it from all other forms of investment, including portfolio capital and aid. Externalities, or spillover effects, have also been recognised as a major benefit accruing to host countries from FDI. It is widely recognised that technical progress accounts for a relatively low proportion of the growth experienced by developing countries in general (Shaw, 1992). This is because most of these countries are endowed with a relatively low volume of *human* capital. Because of disparities in the initial endowments of human capital between the developed and developing countries, the latter are constrained from undertaking investments in R&D which would result in the generation of new knowledge, with its attendant spillover effects. This gap in skills can be bridged through FDI. The knowledge created in developed countries with their relatively high endowments of human capital can be transferred to developing countries through FDI. Admittedly, the knowledge transferred to developing countries is likely to be the preserve of the foreign entity undertaking the investment. But knowledge and technology could spill over from the foreign firms to the domestic firms through the training of labour and indigenous management and through links between foreign firms and local suppliers of components. In addition, local firms can *learn by watching*. Moreover, the very presence of foreign-owned firms in the economy, with their superior endowments of technology, may compel locally owned firms to invest in learning, if only to keep abreast of the competition. In turn, increased competition from locally owned firms through their investments in innovation may compel foreign firms to bring in superior quality technology and know-how. In sum, imported skills enhance the marginal productivity of the capital stock in the host countries and thereby promote growth (Wang and Blomstrom, 1992).

New growth theory, therefore, provides powerful support for the thesis that FDI could be a potent factor in promoting growth. The exploitation of this potential, however, requires a conducive economic climate. In the absence of such a climate FDI may be counterproductive: it may thwart rather than promote growth, and may serve to enhance the private rate of return to investment by foreign firms while exerting little impact on social rates of return in the recipient economy. Because of all the inefficiencies it generates, an IS policy is unlikely to provide an economic climate conducive to the efficient operations of foreign firms. The pervasive factor and product market distortions that it introduces may bias investment away from activities in which the country possesses a comparative advantage.

In contrast, for reasons stated earlier, the EP policy, with its emphasis on neutrality of policy, the free play of market forces and competition, provides an ideal climate for the exploitation of the potential of FDI to promote growth. The absence of artificial policy-imposed barriers to trade promotes the efficient allocation of both imported and domestic resources, and the competition it engenders provides a powerful stimulus for investment in technology and human skills. It also provides a climate for specialisation and the generation of economies of scale.

In this context the distinction between those factors that lift the economy from one level of growth to another and those that generate growth, or change the slope of the production possibilities frontier, is relevant. Lucas (1988, 1990) argues that removal of trade barriers in developing countries merely produces a one-off *level* effect, without altering the slope of the production possibilities frontier. There is, however, no basis in theory for this assertion. Even in the traditional Harrod–Domar model of growth, a change in efficiency which permanently reduces the capital–output ratio will, with the savings rate fixed, increase the growth rate of the economy. Efficient allocation of resources on the basis of comparative advantage is likely to promote efficiency in more ways than one. It promotes both allocative efficiency and technological efficiency by allowing for a choice of sectors and techniques of production which reflects the factor endowments of the economy. In any case, the infusion of human capital and new technology into a distortion-ridden economy may neither lift the economy to a higher plane nor alter the slope of the production function. It may, instead, merely serve to redistribute income in favour of the new agents of production. This in fact is the conclusion of the research on FDI in the presence of restrictions on trade that was cited earlier.

III   THE MODELS

As the preceding discussion has made clear, there are two separate
dimensions to Bhagwati's hypothesis; the first concerns the *amount* of FDI
attracted by EP as opposed to IS countries, while the second concerns the
growth-enhancing effects of FDI under EP relative to IS regimes. In this
section we test both these dimensions of Bhagwati's hypothesis.

Determinants of FDI Flows

In order to test Bhagwati's hypothesis regarding the determinants of FDI
flows we employ the following estimating equation, originally developed by
Balasubramanyam and Salisu (1991):

$$FDI/P = \beta_0 + \beta_1 GDP/P + \beta_2 GDP/Pg + \beta_3 A/P + \beta_4 WPI + \beta_5 DS + \beta_6 WR + \varepsilon \tag{1}$$

where FDI/P = inflow of foreign direct investment per capita
  GDP/P = per capita real income
  GDP/Pg = growth rate of per capita real income
  A/P = inflows of foreign aid per capita
  WPI = rate of inflation of wholesale prices
  DS = index of development strategy pursued by the country in
       question
  ε = disturbance term
  WR = real wage rate per person

Model (1) is tested against a cross-section of 38 developing countries, with
the relevant variables being constructed as averages across the period 1970–
80. Details of both data sources and countries included in the sample are
given in the Appendix (p. 19). The type of development strategy (EP or IS)
pursued by the countries is by no means an easy variable to measure. In the
analysis that follows two alternative proxies for DS are employed: first, the
share of imports in *GDP* (*M/GDP*), and second, the composite distortion
index (*DI*) devised by the World Bank. We have to rely on these proxy
variables to represent the type of trade strategy pursued by the countries in
the sample because of the lack of published data on subsidies and quotas
required to estimate the effective exchange rates for exports and imports.

   The first of the proxies we use requires some explanation. It is the
presumption that countries that exhibit a relatively high ratio of imports to
GDP tend to be relatively free of policy-induced distortions, for restrictions
on imports are likely to be the most significant of the distortions that an IS

policy induces. In the presence of a restriction-free import regime there would be little inducement, apart from that provided by the market, for entrepreneurs to invest in import-competing industries. Given that production for the domestic market as opposed to export markets is unlikely to attract policy-induced rents, there would be no need for subsidies to lure entrepreneurs to the export sector. In other words, in countries where imports constitute a high proportion of *GDP* the effective exchange rate for imports is most unlikely to be different from that for exports. Such countries would therefore be pursuing a neutral trade policy. It could be argued that size of countries is likely to influence the volume of imports, with relatively small countries importing a high volume of goods. This may be so. But the variable we utilise takes size into account, since imports are normalised by the *GDP* of countries in the sample. It is also of relevance that size alone may not be a decisive determinant of imports. Large countries which lack domestic resources or well-developed internal networks may be forced to import most of their requirements of intermediates and components. India, for instance, may not possess machinery and component suppliers whereas the United States does. India may, however, choose to follow an IS policy and delimit imports, but this would be a chosen policy and not a consequence of size and endowments of resources.

The other important characteristic of countries pursuing an EP strategy identified by Bhagwati is the availability of cheap labour. The annual average real wage rate per person included in the estimated regression captures the impact of wage rates on FDI. The political stability of countries is yet another variable identified by Bhagwati in his hypothesis. Several studies have attempted to assess the impact of political factors on the inflows of FDI into developing countries (Levis, 1979; Root and Ahmed, 1979; Schneider and Frey, 1985). These studies have employed various sorts of proxy including strikes, number of coups d'état and the political ideology of countries. Such studies arrive at a mixed bag of conclusions concerning the importance of political factors relative to economic factors. Here we take the view that while political factors may be significant determinants of FDI, any attempt to separate out their influence from that of economic factors may be futile. Most variables used to proxy political factors in regression equations are inadequate and the results they yield are correspondingly ambiguous. For these reasons, we argue that economic factors such as per capita income, the growth rate of national product and the rate of inflation suffice to capture the influence of political factors on economic stability and hence on inflows of FDI. We also include foreign aid per capita as an explanatory variable in the equations. This is to assess whether aid complements FDI flows. It is the usual presumption that countries that are hospitable hosts to FDI are also the recipients of increased aid flows from the donors. Real *GDP* per capita and its growth rate are included to assess the influence of market size and economic potential of the recipients of FDI.

Results

The estimated regression equations on balance appear to support Bhagwati's hypothesis. Equation (1.1) in Table 1.1 relates to the estimates incorporating *M/GDP* as a proxy for the type of development strategy pursued by the countries in the sample. The coefficient of the *M/GDP* variable is positive and statistically significant, and fortifies Bhagwati's hypothesis that EP countries are likely to be recipients of a relatively large volume of FDI. All the other coefficients, with the exception of the coefficients of the growth rate and the aid variable, conform to the hypothesis discussed earlier. The coefficient of the growth rate variable is not only negative but also statistically insignificant. This result may be due in part to the observed relatively high correlation between the *M/GDP* variable and the GDP/P_g variable.[2] Deletion of the GDP/P_g variable as a method of correcting for the observed collinearity between GDP/P_g and *M/GDP* did not materially affect

Table 1.1   Estimated Regression Equations (dependent variable, annual average inflows of foreign direct investment per capita for the years 1970–80)

Eq. No.	C	GDP/P	GDP/P_g	A/P	M/GDP	WPI	WR	DI	R^2 adj.	N
1.1	−1.08	0.007*	−0.07	−0.13**	0.12*	−0.05*	−0.02*		0.65	38
	(1.11)	(5.02)	(0.58)	(2.04)	(3.01)	(5.26)	(2.55)			
1.2	7.17	0.010*	−0.61	0.12+		−0.05*	−0.03*	−2.87**	0.58	38
	(2.08)	(5.35)	(1.40)	(1.85)		(2.98)	(2.59)	(2.11)		
1.2a	6.80	0.010*	−0.32	0.21			−0.002*	−3.89+	0.60	38
	(1.32)	(5.65)	(0.78)	(1.04)			(2.51)	(1.64)		
1.3	−1.49	0.008*	−0.004		0.73*	−0.05*	−0.02*		0.63	38
	(1.88)	(5.92)	(0.01)		(2.19)	(5.27)	(3.61)			
1.4	6.13	0.009*	−0.73+			−0.07*	−0.01**	−2.57	0.62	38
	(1.55)	(4.38)	(1.67)			(3.45)	(2.24)	(1.38)		

Notes:
+, **, *, significant at the 10 per cent, 5 per cent and 1 per cent level, respectively. Figures in parentheses are absolute values of *t* ratios of individual coefficients.

the sign and statistical significance of the coefficients of the other variables. The coefficient of the aid variable is negative and statistically significant at the 5 per cent level. This result appears to lend support to our hypothesis discussed earlier that countries exhibiting a relatively poor economic performance receive relatively large amounts of aid, and their poor economic performance also deters inflows of large volumes of FDI. The estimated correlation coefficients between per capita aid and the two income variables and that between FDI/P and A/P appear to support this conjecture.

As noted, the composite distortion index (DI) as an alternative proxy for the type of development strategy pursued by the countries in the sample also ratifies Bhagwati's hypothesis. The coefficient of the distortion index is negative as hypothesised, and is statistically significant. It may be recalled that we have argued earlier that EP countries are likely to provide a relatively distortion-free economic environment and hence attract relatively large amounts of FDI. Most of the estimated coefficients, including that of the wage rate variable, conform to the postulated hypothesis. But as in the case of equation (1.1) the coefficient of GDP/P_g is negative and statistically insignificant. This again may be due to the observed high correlation between the distortion index and GDP/P_g. The coefficient of aid variable, however, is positive and statistically significant at the 10 per cent level. We are unable to provide an explanation for this result, except to suggest that it may be due to the observed correlation between the DI and the other independent variables, especially that between the DI variable and the growth rate variable on the one hand, and the DI variable and the rate of inflation variable on the other. Furthermore, there appears to be a weak but negative relationship between the aid variable and the DI variable. In order to redress the problems posed by the observed multicollinearity between the independent variables, we re-estimated equation (1) by deleting the inflation index variable with which the DI variable is correlated (Table 1.1, equation 1.2a). As stated earlier, the inflation index forms a part of the composite distortion index – hence our decision to delete the inflation index from the estimated equation. The estimated results for equation (1.2a) show that the coefficient of the DI is statistically significant at the 10 per cent level and that it continues to be negative as hypothesised. The coefficient of the aid variable, although positive, turns out to be statistically insignificant. Both the equations explain 60 per cent of the variation in FDI flows into the countries in the sample.

It is frequently argued that a few countries, such as Hong Kong and Singapore, tend to figure prominently in the list of EP countries and that most of the propositions concerning the economic performance of such countries derive their strength from the experience of these special cases. We have attempted a test of this proposition by deleting Hong Kong from the sample

of countries. Scatter diagrams of *FDI/P* on *M/GDP* and *FDI/P* on the
distortion index showed Hong Kong to be the principal outlier. However, the
estimated equations are very similar to the ones that included Hong Kong in
the sample (see Table 1.2). Thus, Bhagwati's hypothesis appears to survive
comfortably even with the deletion of the outlier country from the sample. In
any case it may be perverse and paradoxical to exclude Singapore and Hong
Kong from a statistical analysis designed to test the impact of the EP strategy
on inflows of FDI for the simple reason that they are prime examples of EP
countries! One might equally suggest the exclusion of India, Brazil and
Indonesia, prime examples of countries pursuing the IS strategy, for most of
the time period of our exercise, from the sample.

FDI as a Source of Growth

The second component of Bhagwati's hypothesis may be stated in formal
terms as follows: other things being equal, the partial derivative of the rate of
economic growth with respect to FDI is higher in countries following an EP
strategy than in countries following an IS strategy.

The model we used to test this hypothesis is derived, conventionally, from
a production function in which FDI is introduced as an input in addition to
labour and domestic capital. As stated earlier, FDI is the prime source of

Table 1.2 Estimated Regression Equations (dependent variable, annual average
inflows of foreign direct investment per capita for the years 1970–80)

Eq. No.	C	GDP/P	GDP/P$_g$	A/P	M/ GDP	WPI	WR	DI	R^2 adj.	N
2.1	−0.79	0.007*	−0.08	−0.08**	0.10*	−0.04*	−0.02*		0.62	37
	(0.82)	(4.66)	(0.75)	(2.23)	(2.37)	(5.25)	(2.83)			
2.2	6.14	0.009*	−0.52	0.10$^+$		−0.05*	−0.02*	−2.93**	0.55	37
	(1.97)	(4.91)	(1.22)	(1.60)		(2.93)	(2.54)	(2.00)		
2.3	−0.86	0.008*	−0.07		0.06$^+$	−0.05*	−0.02*		0.60	37
	(0.88)	(5.82)	(0.57)		(1.65)	(5.56)	(3.85)			
2.4	5.91	0.008*	−0.71$^+$			−0.07*	−0.01	−2.43	0.60	37
	(1.47)	(3.72)	(1.50)			(3.78)	(0.94)	(1.33)		

Notes:
+, **, *, significant at the 10 per cent, 5 per cent and 1 per cent level respectively.
Figures in parentheses are absolute values of *t* ratios of individual coefficients.

human capital and new technology to developing countries and this variable is included in the production function in order to capture the externalities, learning by watching and spillover effects associated with FDI. We also introduce exports as an additional input into the production function, following the large number of empirical studies which investigate the export-led growth hypothesis (e.g. Feder, 1983; Balassa, 1985; Ram, 1985; Salvatore and Hatcher, 1991; Greenaway and Sapsford, 1994). Salvatore and Hatcher (1991) provide three reasons for the explicit introduction of exports into the production function. First, they argue that the neutrality of incentives associated with export orientation is likely to lead, *ceteris paribus*, to higher factor productivity because of the exploitation of economies of scale, better utilisation of capacity and lower capital–output ratios. Second, they argue that exports are likely to alleviate serious foreign exchange constraints and thereby provide greater access to international markets. Third, exports like FDI are likely to result in a higher rate of technological innovation and dynamic learning from abroad. In the usual notation the production function can be written as follows:

$$Y = g(L, K, F, X, t)$$

where:

Y = Gross domestic product (GDP) in real terms
L = Labour input
K = Domestic capital stock
F = Stock of foreign capital
X = Exports
t = a time trend, capturing shifts in the production function brought about by technical progress

Assuming the production function to be linear in logs, taking logs and differencing we obtain the following expression describing the determinants of the growth rate of GDP:

$$y = \alpha + \beta l + \gamma k + \psi f + \varphi x + u \tag{2}$$

where lower case letters denote the rates of growth of individual variables, u denotes a disturbance term and the parameters β, γ, ψ and φ are output elasticities of labour, domestic capital, foreign capital and exports, respectively. Alternatively, these parameters may be interpreted as the partial derivatives of the growth rate of GDP with respect to the growth rate of the respective right-hand side variables in the production function.

In view of the well-known and formidable problems associated with attempts to measure the capital stock – especially in the context of less developed countries – we follow the precedent set in numerous previous studies by approximating the rate of growth of the capital stock by the share of investment in GDP. Accordingly, replacing the rates of change in domestic and foreign capital inputs by the share of domestic investment and foreign direct investment in GDP yields the following growth equation:

$$y = \alpha + \beta l + \gamma(I/Y) + \psi(FDI/Y) + \varphi x \qquad (3)$$

In the econometric analysis which follows the parameter ψ, the elasticity of output with respect to foreign capital is of particular interest.

Following Bhagwati's hypothesis we expect the coefficient of the FDI to GDP ratio in the growth equation (3) not only to be positive but also to be numerically greater for the export-oriented countries than for those countries which pursue an import-substituting trade policy. Because of the spillover effects and externalities associated with human capital, and the higher rate of technical innovation associated with foreign direct (as opposed to domestic) investment, it seems reasonable to expect that, at least for the export-oriented group of countries, foreign investment is a more powerful driving force in the growth process than is domestic investment. According to this *supplementary* hypothesis, the elasticity of output with respect to foreign capital is predicted as exceeding that with respect to domestic capital. Looked at from an alternative perspective, this supplementary hypothesis suggests that foreign investment is more important than domestic investment in terms of its individual contribution to the (calculated value of the) growth rate, as the dependent variable in equation (3). In statistical terms such 'importance' may be measured by so-called *beta*, or standardised regression, coefficients (see Goldberger, 1964, pp. 197–8). Accordingly, we expect that at least in the export-oriented group of countries to find that the beta coefficient of the FDI variable will be numerically greater than that associated with domestic investment.

The Evidence

The results which were obtained when model (3) was estimated against annual average data relating to a cross-section of 46 LDCs over the period 1970–85 are reported in Table 1.3. Details of data definitions and sources and of the country composition of the sample are given in the Appendix (p. 19).

The ordinary least squares results set out in equation (3.1) relate to the entire set of 46 countries in our sample. Since Bhagwati's hypothesis is concerned with the differential impact of FDI upon growth in EP as opposed to IS countries, equations (3.2) and (3.3) report the results which were obtained when model (3) was estimated for each separate group of countries. As already noted, one would ideally wish to classify the countries in the sample into EP or IS categories according to the relationship which exists between their average effective exchange rates on exports and imports. Unfortunately, the necessary data on tariff and quota levels and export subsidies relating to the countries in the sample are not available. As a viable alternative we classify countries as either EP or IS according to the taxonomy developed by the World Bank. The World Bank has devoted considerable research effort into developing its own categorisation of countries as either outwardly or inwardly oriented in respect of their trade policy orientation (Greenaway and Nam, 1988; Stopford et al., 1991). Of the 46 countries which make up our sample, 34 fall within the sample considered by the World Bank. If we equate countries classed, in the World Bank's terminology, as either strongly or moderately outwardly oriented with the EP category, and countries classed as either moderately or strongly inwardly oriented with the IS category, we obtain a sample made up of 10 EP and 24 IS countries (Stopford et al., 1991, p. 11). The results obtained when model (3) is estimated for each separate group of countries are set out in equations (3.2) and (3.3). A listing of the countries falling into each category on this system of classification is given in the Appendix.

Considering equation (3.1) we see that, with the exception of the domestic investment variable (which is insignificantly different from zero), all slope coefficients are correctly (positively) signed and significantly different from zero at the 1 per cent level. In overall terms, the diagnostic statistics associated with this equation provide no grounds for concern. Ramsey's RESET test (LM_1) provides no evidence of misspecification of functional form, while the Bera and Jarque test (LM_2) provides no evidence of non-normal residuals. Likewise, the Lagrange multiplier test for heteroscedasticity (LM_3) provides no evidence to suggest a departure from the assumption of homoscedastic disturbances. The estimated parameters in equation (3.1) suggest that, across the sample as a whole, the elasticity of output with respect to foreign capital (1.84) exceeds that with respect to labour input (1.07), which in turn exceeds that with respect to exports (0.22), while that with respect to domestic capital is insignificantly different from zero.

Turning now to the separate results for the EP and IS groups of countries, it can be seen from the diagnostic statistics associated with equations (3.2) and (3.3) that there is no evidence of functional form misspecification, non-normally distributed errors or heteroscedasticity. Comparing the estimated value of ψ, the elasticity of output with respect to foreign capital, as between EP countries and IS countries we see that our results provide strong support

Table 1.3 Cross-Section Regression Analysis of Determinants of Growth Rate of Real GDP, 1970–85 (annual averages). Estimated Coefficients of:

Eq. No.	Sample	Cons	FDI/Y	I/Y	l	x	R^2	LM_1	LM_2	LM_3
3.1	All countries (N = 46)	-0.20 (0.16)	1.84** (3.86)	-0.004 (0.09)	1.07** (2.73)	0.22** (4.74)	0.57	1.27	1.01	0.99
3.2	EP countries (N = 10)	-3.25 (1.66)	1.54* (3.43)	0.06 (0.86)	2.09* (3.83)	0.22 (2.31)	0.90	1.29	0.27	0.62
3.3	IS countries (N = 24)	1.57 (0.83)	-0.14 (0.08)	-0.05 (0.71)	0.90 (1.61)	0.21 (2.02)	0.33	3.88	5.86	0.06

Notes:
Figures in parenthesis are absolute *t* values. A single asterisk denotes an estimated coefficient which is significantly different from zero at the 5 per cent level, while a double asterisk denotes significance at the 1 per cent level. LM_1 denotes Ramsey's RESET test of functional form, LM_2 denotes the Jarque–Bera test for residual normality, LM_3 denotes the Lagrange multiplier test for heteroscedasticity. On the relevant null hypothesis these test statistics are distributed as χ^2 with 1, 2 and 1 degrees of freedom, respectively.

for Bhagwati's hypothesis. The results reported in equation (3.2) indicate that the output elasticity of foreign capital in EP countries is 1.54 (significantly different from zero at the 5 per cent level), which compares to an estimated elasticity in IS countries which is *not* significantly different from zero at anything approaching conventional levels. In essence what these results indicate is that while FDI is a potent driving force in the growth process in EP countries (with the relevant elasticity being to the order of 1.54) it exerts no (significant) influence upon growth in IS countries. This is strong support for Bhagwati's hypothesis.

Turning now to the supplementary hypothesis referred to above (according to which we expect the output elasticity of foreign capital to exceed that of domestic capital) we see from equation (3.2) that our evidence for EP countries offers empirical confirmation, in that the estimated coefficient of the domestic investment term at only 0.06 is insignificantly different from zero. In short, our results suggest that as far as EP countries are concerned, it is FDI and *not* domestic investment which acts as a driving force in the growth process.[3] In terms of the relative magnitudes of output elasticities, the results reported in equation (3.2) indicate that additions to the labour force are most effective in improving growth performance in EP countries, followed by increases in the stock of foreign-owned capital, followed by increased exports. At the bottom of this ranking of growth sources in EP countries according to their effectiveness, seen in terms of relative output elasticities, comes an increase in the stock of domestic capital.[4]

The results in equations (3.1)–(3.3) were obtained using ordinary least squares (OLS). However, in light of the potential problem of simultaneous equation bias which will arise if either the FDI and/or the export growth variable in model (3) is endogenously determined, equations (3.1)–(3.3) were re-estimated using the generalised instrumental variable (GIVE) method of estimation. The results thus obtained[5] tell essentially the same story as their OLS counterparts, with the output elasticity for EP countries being estimated to be to the order of 1.5, which compares with an insignificant (negative) value for IS countries. Likewise the GIVE results for EP countries offer confirmation of the supplementary hypothesis, according to which the output elasticity of foreign capital exceeds that of domestic capital.[6]

IV CONCLUSIONS

This paper has investigated both the factors which determine the flow of FDI to developing countries and the role which FDI itself plays in the growth process in the context of developing countries characterised by differing trade policy regimes. In the first of these contexts, we have elaborated upon Bhagwati's hypothesis that EP countries are likely to attract large volumes of FDI relative to IS countries. Using two alternative proxies for trade strategy we have put this hypothesis to the statistical test and found it to be supported by the data. Regarding the second issue, the evidence which emerged from our analysis of cross-section data relating to a sample of 46 developing countries offers strong support for the hypothesis advanced by Jagdish Bhagwati, according to which the growth-enhancing effects of FDI are stronger in countries which pursue an EP policy than in those following an IS one.

NOTES

1. The effective exchange rate on exports (EER_x) and the effective exchange rate on imports (EER_m) are defined as follows:
$$EER_x = n(1 + s), \text{ and } EER_m = n(1 + t)$$
where n = the nominal exchange rate, t = average tariff rate on imports, s = average rate of subsidies on exports. It should be noted that t should include all policy instruments, including tariffs and quotas, which bias policy incentives in favour of imports, and s should include all incentives which favour export-oriented activities.

2. See Balasubramanyam and Salisu (1991, p. 203).
3. Since our empirical analysis effectively subdivides the total stock of capital into its separate domestic and foreign components, this finding suggests that the significant coefficient on total capital stock growth found in numerous previous studies of growth (see Greenaway and Sapsford, 1994, for a review) might be misleading in that it disguises the fact that it is increases in foreign, as opposed to domestic, capital which is influencing growth.

   A similar conclusion follows from the beta (standardised regression) coefficients associated with equation (3.2): these being 0.509 and 0.133 for the foreign and domestic capital growth terms, respectively. Since beta coefficients are simply the relevant regression coefficients multiplied by the ratio of the standard deviation of the regressor in question to that of the dependent variable, the latter of these values may be considered as zero.
4. Considering equation (3.3) we see that as far as the IS countries are concerned (bearing in mind that the estimated coefficients of both the FDI and domestic investment ratios are insignificant in this group of countries) additions to the labour force, followed by increased exports, appear as the most potent driving force in the growth process.
5. Available from the authors on request.
6. In addition, it may also be noted that the GIVE results reveal the same ranking of the sources of growth in EP countries according to their importance in the growth process (seen in terms of estimated output elasticities) as was suggested by the OLS results.

REFERENCES

Balassa, B. (1985), 'Exports, Policy Choices, and Economic Growth in Developing Countries After the 1973 Oil Shock', *Journal of Development Economics*, vol. 18, pp. 23–35.

Balasubramanyam, V.N. and Salisu, M.A. (1991), 'EP, IS and Direct Foreign Investment in LDCs', in A. Koekkoek and L.B.M. Mennes, eds, *International Trade and Global Development* (London: Routledge).

Bhagwati, J.N. (1973), 'The Theory of Immiserizing Growth: Further Applications', in Michael B. Connolly and Alexander K. Swoboda, eds, *International Trade and Money* (Toronto: University of Toronto Press).

——— (1978), *Anatomy and Consequences of Exchange Control Regimes*, Vol. 1, Studies in International Economic Relations, No. 10 (New York: National Bureau of Economic Research).

——— (1985), *Investing Abroad* (Esmee Fairbain Lecture: Lancaster University, England).

——— (1994), 'Free Trade: Old and New Challenges', *Economic Journal*, vol. 104, no. 423, pp. 231–46.

Bhagwati, J.N. and Srinivasan, T.N. (1975), *Foreign Trade Regimes and Economic Development: India* (New York: National Bureau of Economic Research).

——— (1979), 'Trade Policy and Development', in R. Dornbusch and J.A. Frenkel, eds, *International Economic Policy: Theory and Evidence* (Baltimore: Johns Hopkins University Press).

Brecher, R.A. and Diaz-Alejandro, C.F. (1977), 'Tariffs, Foreign Capital and Immiserizing Growth', *Journal of International Economics*, vol. 7, pp. 317–22.

Feder, G. (1983), 'On Exports and Economic Growth', *Journal of Development Economics*, vol. 12, pp. 59–73.

Goldberger, A. (1964), *Econometric Theory* (London and New York: John Wiley).

Greenaway, D. and Nam, C.H. (1988), 'Industrialisation and Macroeconomic Performance in Developing Countries Under Alternative Trade Strategies', *Kyklos*, vol. 41, no. 3, pp. 419–35.

Greenaway, D. and Sapsford, D. (1994), 'What Does Liberalisation Do for Exports and Growth?', *Weltwirtschaftliches Archiv*, vol. 130, no. 1, pp. 152–73.

Kreuger, A. (1975), *Foreign Trade Regimes and Economic Development: Turkey* (New York: National Bureau of Economic Research).

Levis, M. (1979), 'Does Political Instability in Developing Countries Affect Foreign Investment Flows? An Empirical Examination', *Management International Review*, vol. 19.

Lucas, R.E. (1988), 'On The Mechanics of Economic Development', *Journal of Monetary Economics*, vol. 22, pp. 3–42.

———— (1990), 'Why Doesn't Capital Flow from Rich to Poor Countries?', *American Economic Review*, Papers and Proceedings, vol. 80, pp. 92–6.

Ram. R. (1985), 'Exports and Economic Growth. Some Additional Evidence', *Economic Development and Cultural Change*, vol. 33, pp. 415–25.

Romer, P.M. (1986), 'Increasing Returns and Long-Run Growth', *Journal of Political Economy*, vol. 94, no. 4–6, pp. 1002–37.

———— (1987), 'Growth Based on Increasing Returns Due to Specialization', *American Economic Review*, Papers and Proceedings, vol. 77, pp. 56–62.

Root, F. and Ahmed, A. (1979), 'Empirical Determinants of Manufacturing Direct Foreign Investment in Developing Countries', *Economic Development and Cultural Change*, vol. 27.

Salvatore, D. and Hatcher, T. (1991), 'Inward Oriented and Outward Oriented Trade Strategies', *Journal of Development Studies*, vol. 27, pp. 7–25.

Schneider, F. and Frey, B.S. (1985), 'Economic and Political Determinants of Foreign Direct Investment', *World Development* (February).

Shaw, G.K. (1992), 'Policy Implications of Endogenous Growth Theory', *The Economic Journal*, vol. 102, pp. 611–21.

Stopford, J., Strange, S. and Henley, J. (1991), *Rival States, Rival Firms: Competition for World Market Shares* (Cambridge: Cambridge University Press).

Summers, R. and Heston, A. (1988), 'A New Set of International Comparisons of Real Product and Price Levels: Estimates for 130 Countries, 1950–85', *Review of Income and Wealth*, vol. 34, pp. 1–25.

Wang, J. and Blomstrom, M. (1992), 'Foreign Investment and Technology Transfer: A Simple Model', *European Economic Review*, vol. 36, no. 1, pp. 137–55.

APPENDIX

Data Sources: Model (1)

World Bank Tables, OECD Development Co-operation (various years); UNCTAD, *Handbook of International Trade Statistics* (1986 Supplement); International Monetary Fund, *International Financial Statistics Yearbook* (1988).

Data Sources: Model (3)

Real GDP growth data were derived from Summers and Heston (1988), while data relating to domestic investment and import shares and real exports were derived from the International Monetary Fund's *International Financial Statistics* (various editions). Labour force data were obtained from the *World Development Report* (various issues) and FDI data were obtained from various editions of *Transnational Corporations in World Development* (New York: United Nations).

Sample of Countries used in Estimation of Model (1)

1. Argentina	20. Egypt
2. Brazil	21. Ghana
3. Colombia	22. Ivory Coast
4. Costa Rica	23. Malawi
5. Mexico	24. Tunisia
6. Uruguay	25. Chile
7. Peru	26. El Salvador
8. India	27. Haiti
9. Malaysia	28. Honduras
10. Philippines	29. Jamaica
11. Singapore	30. Nicaragua
12. Sri Lanka	31. Paraguay
13. Thailand	32. Trinidad and Tobago
14. South Korea	33. Ethiopia
15. Hong Kong	34. Morocco
16. Sudan	35. Uganda
17. Tanzania	36. Zambia
18. Turkey	37. Indonesia
19. Kenya	38. Nigeria

Sample of Countries Used in Estimation of Model (3)

1. Bangladesh	11. Uganda
2. Nepal	12. Ghana
3. Pakistan	13. Venezuela
4. India	14. Colombia
5. Argentina	15. Turkey
6. Bolivia	16. Sudan
7. Guatemala	17. Ethiopia
8. Brazil	18. Uruguay
9. Ecuador	19. Paraguay
10. Mexico	20. Peru

Sample of Countries Used in Estimation of Model (3) *cont.*

21. Nigeria	34. South Korea
22. Indonesia	35. Honduras
23. Philippines	36. Sri Lanka
24. Panama	37. Ivory Coast
25. Tanzania	38. Costa Rica
26. Thailand	39. Trinidad and Tobago
27. Morocco	40. Tunisia
28. Egypt	41. Zambia
29. Kenya	42. Chile
30. Haiti	43. Jamaica
31. El Salvador	44. Malaysia
32. Nicaragua	45. Hong Kong
33. Malawi	46. Singapore

World Bank Classification of Countries

IS Countries	**EP Countries**
1. Indonesia	25. Singapore
2. Sri Lanka	26. Hong Kong
3. Pakistan	27. South Korea
4. Colombia	28. Malaysia
5. Mexico	29. Thailand
6. Philippines	30. Tunisia
7. Kenya	31. Brazil
8. Honduras	32. Turkey
9. Costa Rica	33. Uruguay
10. Guatemala	34. Chile
11. Ivory Coast	
12. El Salvador	
13. Nicaragua	
14. Bangladesh	
15. India	
16. Ethiopia	
17. Sudan	
18. Peru	
19. Tanzania	
20. Argentina	
21. Zambia	
22. Nigeria	
23. Bolivia	
24. Ghana	

Source: Stopford et al. (1991, p. 11).

019
013
F35

2 Food Aid and Food Production: A Theoretical Analysis
Sajal Lahiri and Pascalis Raimondos

I INTRODUCTION

Given that starvation and malnutrition are pervasive among a significant proportion of the population in many developing countries, aid in the form of food may seem to many to be a very appropriate humanitarian gesture on the part of the developed countries. However, economists have expressed serious doubts about the beneficial effects of food aid. The most common argument against it is that it may have a damaging long-term effect on domestic food production, which may lead to permanent dependence on the donor countries for food.[1]

Food is a very special commodity; nobody can do without it. (This is perhaps the reason why agriculturalists in most developed countries receive so much subsidy from their governments.) Thus, if food aid does indeed have a permanent adverse effect on food production, the case against food aid is beyond any reasonable debate, since there cannot be any arguments in favour of a declining trend in food production in the developing countries. However, there are considerable question marks about the validity, or rather the inevitability, of the so-called disincentive effect of food aid on food production.[2] Is it possible for the donor countries to attach conditions to food aid in order to avoid the possible adverse effect on food production?[3] Or is it possible for the recipient country's government to utilise the additional revenue it generates by selling the food aid for development projects that help raise food production? In this paper we argue, with the help of two theoretical models, that the answers to both these questions are in the affirmative.

The adverse effect of food aid on food production is particularly worrying because the level of food production is already very low in many developing countries for a wide variety of reasons. One of the more important reasons is the relative neglect of the agricultural sector in many developing countries. The governments of most developing countries, in their drive for rapid industrialisation, have protected their manufacturing sectors with the help of tariffs, quotas and industrial licensing policies. The result has been a reduction of the relative price of food.[4] In other words, in most developing countries there is already a bias against the agricultural sector. In the first of the two models that we analyse, we take bias against the food-producing sector in the form of tariffs on imports in the manufacturing sector as our starting point. The effect of food aid on food production is then analysed when such aid is tied to reductions in tariffs in ways that leave government revenue constant at the initial equilibrium values of the variables. This form of tying aid is quite common these days and seems reasonable for at least three reasons:[5] (1) it rectifies the existing distortion in the allocation of resources, (2) it does not affect government revenue and thus development programmes undertaken by the government, and (3) it can be viewed as a form of 'usual marketing requirements' (UMR), whereby the donor country makes sure that aid does not reduce its commercial sales.[6]

The recipient government can, of course, sell the food aid in the domestic market and thus earn some revenue. This revenue may be extremely helpful in carrying out development projects. Singer et al. (1987, p. 199) cite India, Korea, Israel and Greece as countries that have used revenues from large-scale food aid quite successfully to promote vigorous development of local food production. Similar arguments are also made by Rosenstein-Rodan (1961). In the second of our exercises we formalise these stylised facts and analyse the effect of food aid on food production when a part of the revenue from food aid is invested in R&D in food production.

A few remarks on the existing literature on tied aid are in order here. Most of the theoretical literature deals with one form of tied aid only: aid that is tied to more imports from the donor,[7] the only exceptions being Brecher and Bhagwati (1982), who analyse the tying of aid directly to increased food production, and Lahiri and Raimondos (1994a, 1994b), who analyse the tying of aid to trade policy reform. However, in Brecher and Bhagwati (1982) tying aid to increased food production actually introduces a distortion and thus becomes a reason for recipient-immiserising (and donor-enriching) foreign aid. In contrast, in the present paper tying aid to trade policy reform reduces existing distortions and in the process indirectly increases food production. Lahiri and Raimondos (1994a, 1994b) were mainly concerned with the welfare effects of general aid. Bhagwati (1986) and Srinivasan (1991) are the only papers which argue that food aid, even when it is not tied, can be desirable. They show that the disincentive effect of untied food aid can be corrected by the use of appropriate tax/subsidy policies. Their arguments are also applicable to the models developed in this paper.

In the next section we present and analyse a model where food aid is tied to a reduction of tariffs. Section III then considers the situation where the recipient government uses some of the revenue from food aid for R&D in food production. Some concluding remarks are provided in section IV.

II FOOD AID AND TARIFF REFORM

In this section we consider a general equilibrium model of international trade in which two countries – a donor country and a recipient country – trade in two goods. The donor country gives aid in the form of food of the amount T to the recipient country. Food is taken as the numeraire good. The recipient country has in place a tariff (t) on the non-numeraire good, the international price of which is denoted by p. The expenditure functions for the two countries are given by e^α $(1, p, u^\alpha)$ and e^β $(1, p + t, u^\beta)$ where the superscripts α and β refer to the variables and functions specific to the donor country and the recipient country respectively, and u^i is the utility level of the representative consumer in country i(i = α and β). Similarly, the revenue functions of the two countries are given by $r^\alpha(1,p)$ and $r^\beta(1,p + t)$.[8]

Assuming that all the tariff revenues and the foreign aid are distributed to the consumers in a lump-sum fashion, we can write the budget constraints in the countries as:

$$e^\alpha(1,p,u^\alpha) = r^\alpha(1,p) - T \tag{1}$$

$$\text{and} \qquad e^\beta(1,p + t,u^\beta) = r^\beta(1,p + t) + T + tm^\beta \tag{2}$$

where imports in country i, m^i, are given by:[9]

$$m^i = e^i_2(\cdot) - r^i_2(\cdot) \qquad (\text{i} = \alpha, \beta) \tag{3}$$

Finally, the model is completed by presenting the product market clearing condition, viz. that global consumption of the non-numeraire commodity is equal to its global production:

$$e^\alpha_2(\cdot) + e^\beta_2(\cdot) = r^\alpha_2(\cdot) + r^\beta_2(\cdot) \tag{4}$$

As mentioned in the Introduction to this chapter, we assume that aid is tied to the requirement that an increase in T is accompanied by a decrease in tariffs t so as to leave the level of tariff revenue unchanged at the initial level of imports. This way aid can also be viewed as a compensation for the loss of government revenue as a result of the reduction in the rate of tariffs. That is:

$$dT = -m^\beta dt \tag{5}$$

This completes the description of the basic framework of our first model and we turn now to its analysis. Totally differentiating (1)–(4) and using (5) we get:

$$(e_3^\beta - te_{23}^\beta)du^\beta = -(m^\beta - tS^\beta)d(p + t) \qquad (6)$$

$$e_3^\alpha du^\alpha = m^\beta d(p + t) \qquad (7)$$

$$Sm^\beta d(p + t) = -S^\alpha dT \qquad (8)$$

where

$$S = \frac{e_3^\beta S^\beta}{e_3^\beta - te_{23}^\beta} + S^\alpha - \frac{e_{23}^\beta m^\beta}{e_3^\beta - te_{23}^\beta} + \frac{e_{23}^\alpha m^\beta}{e_3^\alpha}$$

For the system to be Walrasian stable, S has to be negative. $S^\alpha = e_{22}^\alpha - r_{22}^\alpha$ and $S^\beta = e_{22}^\beta - r_{22}^\beta$, which are the slopes of the compensated excess demand functions in country α and β respectively, are also assumed to be negative. Furthermore, we assume that $e_3^\beta - te_{23}^\beta$ is positive.[10] These assumptions can be formally stated as:

Assumption 1: $S < 0$, $S^\alpha < 0$, $S^\beta < 0$, and $e_3^\beta - te_{23}^\beta > 0$.

Given assumption 1, it immediately follows from (8) that:

$$\frac{d(p + t)}{dT} < 0 \qquad (9)$$

That is, the relative domestic price of the non-numeraire good unambiguously goes down and thus our type of tied food aid unambiguously raises the relative price of food, which in turn raises food production. This is a very strong result, which says that if food aid is tied to reduction of tariffs in the non-food sector, then such aid will not have any disincentive effect.

Proposition 1: *Any food aid that is tied to a reduction of tariffs on non-food so as to keep government revenue unchanged cannot have an adverse effect on food production.*

The intuition for the result is as follows. Since food price is determined in the world market, and aid in the form of food is a transfer from one country to another, it does not have any direct effect on the aggregate supply of food. However, on the aggregate demand, it has an effect via income if the marginal propensities to spend on food are different in the two countries. This is because food aid increases income in the recipient country and reduces it in the donor country. Furthermore, a reduction in the tariff on non-food increases excess demand for non-food (and thus decreases the same for food) in the recipient country. This would tend to decrease the international price of food. This is the well-known terms of trade effect of tariffs. Reduction of tariff also increases the relative domestic price of food for a given level of the international price. This positive effect on domestic food price dominates the possible negative effect via changes in income and the terms of trade effect.

III FOOD AID AND TECHNOLOGICAL PROGRESS

The model analysed in section II assumes that food is a tradeable good and its price is determined in the world market. This assumption means that food aid does not have any direct effect on the aggregate supply of food. In order to capture the direct effect of food aid on domestic food price and therefore its domestic production, in this section we assume food to be a non-tradeable commodity. In all other respects the recipient country is a small, open economy and the international price of all other goods are exogenously determined.

We consider a two-period model where both the consumers and the government can borrow (save) in period 1 and repay (spend) in period 2. Food aid is received in both periods. For national simplicity we assume that the same amount of food aid, T, is received in both periods. The international prices of traded goods (which include the numeraire good) and food in period i ($i = 1,2$) are denoted by the vectors P^i and p_f^i, respectively. Given the assumption of intertemporal borrowing by the consumers, the aggregate expenditure function for the representative consumer can be represented by e $(P^1, P^2, p_f^1, p_f^2, u)$, where u is the aggregate utility level of the representative consumer.

The government is assumed to use the revenue generated by selling food aid in the domestic market – which is equal to $(p_f^1 + p_f^2) T$ – in R&D activities in period 1. These R&D activities result in technological progress in the production of food in period 2. In this sense, R&D is treated as an investment in a public input, which is produced by the government in the first period using aid revenue and given free of charge to private food producers in the second period. Thus, in describing the production side of this economy in period 1 we need to introduce the restricted revenue function r^1 (P^1, p_f^1, θ), which gives the value of private production given the price levels and the amount of the public input θ.[11] Since the fruits of the R&D activities are only realised in the second period, the partial derivative of the restricted revenue function with respect to θ gives the unit cost of production of the public input, i.e. $-r_3^1(.) = c_\theta$, c_θ being the unit cost. The description of the production technology in period 2 is simpler since the technological advantage due to R&D can easily be incorporated in the standard revenue function as $r^2(P^2, \theta' p_f^2)$, where θ' represents the Hicks-neutral technological parameter and is the sum of θ_0, the initial level of technology, and θ, the output of R&D activities.[12]

Given the assumption of intertemporal borrowing, the budget constraints for the consumer and the government are thus given respectively by:

$$e(P^1, P^2, p_f^1, p_f^2, u) = r^1(P^1, p_f^1, \theta) + r^2(P^2, \theta' p_f^2) + (p_f^1 + p_f^2)T, \quad (10)$$

$$\theta c_\theta = (p_f^1 + p_f^2)T \quad (11)$$

It only remains to describe the market clearing conditions for food in the two periods, and these are given by:

$$e_3(\cdot) = r_2^1(\cdot) + T \quad (12)$$

$$e_4(\cdot) = \theta' r_2^2(\cdot) + T \quad (13)$$

Equations (12) and (13) state that in each period the demand for food in the recipient country is equal to domestic production plus the amount of aid.

Before proceeding to the analysis we may state the initial assumptions that we make. (These assumptions are made to avoid unrewarding complications. The qualitative nature of our results would not change in their absence.) First, we assume the unit cost of producing θ to be constant. This implies that $r_{33}^1 = r_{32}^1 = r_{23}^1 = 0$. We also assume the price of food in one period does not have any effect on the demand for food in the other period, i.e. $e_{34} = e_{43} = 0$. Finally, the initial level of food aid is assumed to be zero, i.e. $T = 0$. With these assumptions, total differentiation of the above equations yields:

$$e_5 du = p_f^2 r_2^2 d\theta \quad (14)$$

$$c_\theta d\theta = (p_f^1 + p_f^2) dT \quad (15)$$

$$S^1 dp_f^1 = \left(1 - \frac{C_Y^1 p_f^2 r_2^2 (p_f^1 + p_f^2)}{c_\theta p_f^1}\right) dT \quad (16)$$

$$S^2 dp_f^2 = \left(1 - \frac{C_Y^2 r_2^2 (p_f^1 + p_f^2)}{c_\theta} + \frac{r_2^2 (1 + \epsilon)(p_f^1 + p_f^2)}{c_\theta}\right) dT \quad (17)$$

where $S^i(< 0)$ is the slope of the demand function for food in period i, C_Y^i is the marginal propensity to spend on food in period $i(i = 1, 2)$, and $\epsilon(> 0)$ is the price elasticity of food supply in period 2.

Finally, denoting by A^i domestic food production in period $i(i = 1, 2)$, and using the above three equations we obtain:

$$\frac{dA^1}{dT} = r_{22}^1 \frac{dp_f^1}{dT}, \tag{18}$$

$$\frac{dA^2}{dT} = \frac{d(\theta' r_2^2)}{dT}$$

$$= \frac{(\theta')^2 r_{22}^2}{S^2}\left(1 - \frac{C_Y^2 r_2^2 (p_f^1 + p_f^2)}{c_\theta}\right) + \frac{r_2^2(1 + \epsilon)(p_f^1 + p_f^2)e_{44}}{S^2} \tag{19}$$

From equations (16) and (18) it is clear that food aid will increase food production in period 1 if the second term on the right-hand side of (16) is sufficiently large, which it would be if either the marginal propensity to spend on food in period 1 is sufficiently large or the unit cost of producing new technology is sufficiently low. It is interesting to note that food aid can increase food production even in period 1 where the gains of new technology do not come into effect. The reason for this result is that the new technology creates additional income in period 2. Since consumers in period 1 can borrow against income in period 2 (because of intertemporal borrowing facilities), consumer demand function in period 1 will shift outward, increasing food prices and production. Increased availability of food in the marketplace because of aid will shift the supply function outward, decreasing food prices and food production in period 1. The first effect via increased income will dominate the second if either the marginal propensity to spend on food is high or the unit cost of producing the new technology is low. Lower cost of producing the technology produces more technology from the given revenue constraint and generates more income.

The same arguments hold as far as the effect of food aid on food production in period 2 is concerned. In addition to the above effects, there is a direct positive effect on food production in period 2 as the effect of technological progress is realised in period 2. Thus the condition which is necessary and sufficient for food aid to have no disincentive on food production in period 1 only becomes a sufficient condition in period 2.

The above result can be stated formally as:

Proposition 2: *Food aid, the revenue from which is used for R&D in food production, increases domestic food production in period 1 if and only if:*

$$c_\theta < \frac{C_Y^1 P_f^2 r_2^2 (p_f^1 + p_f^2)}{c_\theta P_f^1}$$

and in period 2 if:

$$c_\theta < \frac{C_Y^2 r_2^2 (p_f^1 + p_f^2)}{c_\theta}$$

We would like to re-emphasise that the condition for food aid to increase food production in period 2 is only a sufficient condition, i.e. food production may increase even if the condition is not satisfied.

IV CONCLUSION

Over the years foreign aid in general and food aid in particular have come under close academic scrutiny from both development economists and from international trade theorists. It has been said that food aid leads to permanent dependency as it depresses domestic food prices and thus farmers find it profitable to take land out of food production and into more lucrative activities.

In this paper we have developed two alternative scenarios under which the hypothesis about the damaging effect of food aid may not be true. Under the first scenario, we have argued that food production in developing countries is often low due to unfavourable trade policies and if food aid is tied to the removal of bias against the agricultural sector, food aid will not have any disincentive effect on food production. In our second exercise we have argued that the revenue raised by the recipient government by selling aid could be used for R&D in the agricultural production. We have shown that under very reasonable conditions once again food aid will not have an adverse effect on food production.

ACKNOWLEDGEMENT

This paper was first presented at a conference held in honour of Professor Jagdish Bhagwati at the University of Lancaster. The authors are grateful to Professor Bhagwati and other participants of the conference for helpful comments.

Raimondos's research was funded by a grant from the Danish National Research Foundation.

NOTES

1. See Cassen (1988) and Singer et al. (1987) for details.
2. See Singer et al. (1987) for an extensive study of non-emergency food aid. A very strong case in favour of food aid is made in this book.
3. In the literature, food aid that is tied to projects mutually agreed upon by the two parties is called project aid.
4. Chakravarty (1987, pp. 20–2) discusses how the Indian government used the agricultural sector as a 'bargain sector' providing a 'cheap food regime' in the process of industrialisation. More recently, Bhagwati (1993) has provided an analysis of the biased industrial and trade policies in India.
5. See Morrissey (1993) for the evidence on tying of aid to trade policy reforms.
6. See Bhagwati and Srinivasan (1969) for a discussion on UMR.
7. See Kemp (1992) for a survey of this literature.
8. The endowments which do not vary in our analysis are left out of the arguments of the revenue functions.
9. A subscript j to the revenue and expenditure functions refers to the partial derivative of the functions with respect to the jth argument ($j = 1,2,3$).
10. This is known as the Vanek–Bhagwati–Kemp stability condition (see Bhagwati, Brecher and Hatta, 1985). It can be easily verified that if the numeraire good is normal in the recipient country, this condition holds.
11. For detailed properties of restricted revenue functions, see Abe (1992). The use of the restricted revenue function is necessary due to the fact that the R&D activities use up resources in competition with the sectors producing final goods.
12. For the treatment of technological progress in a revenue function, see Dixit and Norman (1980, pp. 137–8).

REFERENCES

Abe, K. (1992), 'Tariff Reform in a Small Open Economy with Public Production', *International Economic Review*, vol. 33, pp. 209–22.
Bhagwati, J.N. (1986), 'Food Aid, Agricultural Production and Welfare', in S. Guhan and M.R. Shroff, eds., *Essays on Economic Progress and Welfare in Honour of I.G. Patel* (New Delhi: Oxford University Press), pp. 19–173.
———— (1993), *India in Transition: Freeing the Economy* (Oxford: Clarendon Press).
Bhagwati, J.N., Brecher, R. and Hatta, T. (1985), 'The Generalized Theory of Transfers and Welfare: Exogenous (Policy-imposed) and Endogenous (Transfer-induced) Distortions', *Quarterly Journal of Economics*, vol. 3, pp. 697–714.
Bhagwati, J.N. and Srinivasan, T.N. (1969), 'Optimum Policy Intervention to Achieve Non-economic Objectives', *Review of Economic Studies*, vol. 36, no. 1, pp. 27–38.
Brecher, R.A. and Bhagwati, J.N. (1982), 'Immiserising Transfers from Abroad', *Journal of International Economics*, vol. 13, pp. 353–64.
Cassen, R. (1988), *Does Aid Work?* (Oxford: Clarendon Press).
Chakravarty, S. (1987), *Development Planning: The Indian Experience* (Oxford: Clarendon Press).

Dixit, A. and Norman, V. (1980), *Theory of International Trade* (Cambridge: Cambridge University Press).

Kemp, M.C. (1992), 'The Static Welfare Economics of Foreign Aid: A Consolidation', in D. Savoie and I. Brecher, eds., *Equity and Efficiency in Economic Development: Essays in Honor of Benjamin Higgins* (Montreal: McGill-Queens University Press), pp. 289–314.

Lahiri, S. and Raimondos, P. (1994a), 'Tying of Aid to Trade Policy Reform and Welfare', Essex Discussion Paper No. 434, University of Essex.

——— (1994b), 'Welfare Effects of Aid under Quantitative Trade Restrictions', *Journal of International Economics*, vol. 39, pp. 297–315.

Morrissey, O. (1993), 'The Mixing of Aid and Trade Policies', *The World Economy*, vol. 16, pp. 69–84.

Rosenstein-Rodan, P.N. (1961), 'International Aid for Underdeveloped Countries', *Review of Economics and Statistics*, vol. 43, pp. 107–38.

Singer, H., Wood, J. and Jennings, T. (1987), *Food Aid: The Challenge and the Opportunity* (Oxford: Clarendon Press).

Srinivasan, T.N. (1991), 'Food Aid: A Cause or Symptom of Development Failure or an Instrument of Success', in U. Lee and I. Nabi, eds., *Transition in Development: The Role of Aid and Commercial Flows* (San Francisco: ICS Press), pp. 373–400.

3 On the Microeconomics of Return Migration

Oded Stark

I INTRODUCTION

Quite often the duration of labour migration is shorter than the duration of the individual's working life. If agents choose where to offer their labour freely, though not necessarily costlessly, in a world consisting of two countries, this statement implies return migration. Why do migrants return? What determines which workers stay and which return?

This paper outlines three models of return migration which are not associated with a reversal of the inter-country wage differential, and it seeks to characterise the returnees.

The theoretical microeconomic literature on labour migration is quite silent on return migration. This is somewhat surprising since the number of migrant workers in any country is just as dependent on departures as on arrivals, and evidence suggests that return migration is of no trivial magnitude. In spite of the difficulties associated with measuring return migration, there are reasons to believe that even in the case of countries ordinarily viewed as countries of destination, not departure, such as the United States and Germany, the numbers involved are quite large. Until 1957 the United States collected information on both the arrival of migrants and on their departure. Between 1908 and 1957, of the 15.7 million migrants admitted to the United States 4.8 million departed – nearly one-third (US, 1960). In Germany, the foreign population in 1988 was no larger than in 1983 (OECD, 1990). During this six-year period, the outflow of foreign population was 2,378,000 (data are based on the Central Registry of Aliens). This outflow includes asylum-seekers whose requests were refused; 389,000 asylum-seekers were received during 1983–8. Obviously, there are lags involved, but even if we subtract *all* the asylum-seekers, we are still left with an outflow of 2 million people. We do not know that these people returned to their country of origin, but all indications suggest that this is largely so.

A considerable reprieve from measurement, estimation and interpretation difficulties is provided by the interesting case of return migration from the United States to Puerto Rico. The usefulness of this particular case arises

32

from the absence of administrative barriers to migration between the two destinations; issues of asylum, work permits, and so on thus do not arise. From the returns of the 1980 Census of the Population of the United States (US, 1983, 1984) we learn that in 1980, approximately 1 million people born in Puerto Rico were resident in the United States. But in the same year 283,000 returned to Puerto Rico after living in the United States between 1970 and 1980.

A recent representative sample of young Irish labour market participants offers a unique micro-data set which provides additional helpful evidence (Reilly, 1994). A December 1987–January 1988 follow-up survey of 1981–2 Irish school leavers contains information on educational qualifications, migration and whether or not the migrant returned. The emphasis on young workers is appropriate because historically they have comprised a sizeable proportion of the outflows. Of 1,299 school leavers, 378 migrated at least once between leaving school and 1988; of these, 117 had returned by 1988. Analysis based on a bivariate probit model reveals that the educational qualifications of the returnees were significantly lower than those of the migrants who remained. Controlling for labour market conditions at destination, return migration is more likely from non-UK EU countries in which employers are said to 'fail to recognise Irish qualifications', than from the UK (or, for that matter, from Australia and New Zealand).

Section II models return migration; section III suggests interactions between models; and section IV offers conclusions.

II MODELLING RETURN MIGRATION

With conventional migration theory attributing migration to a positive wage differential, a conventional explanation of return migration is, not surprisingly, a negative wage differential (Dustmann, 1993, p. 2). While this explanation might be correct, considerable return migration appears to take place in the absence of a reversal of the relative wages of the sending and receiving countries.

Speaking generally, the typical explanations are that migrants return because of failure, or because of success: if reality does not tally with expectations, or the draw from a mixture of good draws and bad draws (random shocks) is bad, migrants may return. Alternatively, migrants whose returns on human or financial capital are higher at home than abroad may find it optimal to return. A recent perceptive study by Borjas and Bratsberg (1996) gives precisely these two reasons for return migration. The possibilities are richer, however, and three additional reasons can be suggested.

Declining Risk

A member of a family may migrate in order to diversify the familial income-earning portfolio. If income away from home and income at home do not covary fully, and there is a post-migration pooling and sharing of income, the family's risk is lowered. Just as bearing one risk makes agents less willing to bear another risk, *not* bearing that one risk makes agents more willing to bear another risk (Pratt and Zeckhauser, 1987; Kimball, 1993). This allows for experimentation at home with a relatively high-risk, high-return option, say, introducing a high-yield seed variety. When such an experiment is successful, the need for migration-provided insurance ceases. Thus, the reason for return migration is not that the migrant accumulated capital with an expected high return at home, but rather that migration facilitated a high-return investment at home by others (Stark, 1991).

Reinstatement of Informational Symmetry

Return migration may take place because a regime of asymmetric information that gives rise to the pooling together at destination of low-skill workers with high-skill workers no longer reigns. Absent pooling, the wage of low-skill workers is lower than the *average* wage of high-skill and low-skill workers. When the skill-specific wage of the low-skill workers at destination falls below their home country wage, they will return-migrate, while the high-skill workers will stay at destination *a fortiori*.

More concretely, consider the following simple model. In a world consisting of two countries – a rich foreign country F and a poor home country H – the net wages in a given occupation for a worker are a function of the worker's skill level θ such that a higher θ fetches a higher wage. Reflecting the fact that F is rich and H is poor, the F country wage is higher than the H country wage for each and every θ. Skills are perfectly transferable across countries. Let k be a discount factor applied by country H workers to country F wages, arising from a preference for H's life-style. If individual skill levels are fully known to all employers (and to the workers themselves), those workers whose k discounted skill-specific wage in F is higher than in H will migrate to F; the rest will stay. However, the skill of each potential migrant may be known in H where he or she has been observed for a while, but unknown in F. When markets (countries H and F) are isolated in the sense that information does not ordinarily flow across them (or does not flow costlessly and freely) an employer (or employers) in one market (country H) may possess information on the productivity of individual workers. Such information may be revealed to the employer over time as a by-product of normal monitoring and co-ordinating activities – but the information is market- (country-) specific.[1] (For the moment, we exclude the possibility that true skill is revealed in F over time.)

Faced with a group of workers whose individual productivity is unknown to the employer (we assume that only the distribution of earnings abilities is known), the wage offered will be the same for all such workers and will be related to the average product of all members of the group. Assume that the actual individual wage offered is equal to the average product of the group and that wage offers are known to all workers. Hence, under asymmetric information, workers whose *average* wage in F is higher than their *skill-specific* wage in H will migrate, while the other workers will stay.

We can consider a very simple case of two skill levels, low skill θ_1 and high skill θ_2, two work periods, and a particular example where under informational symmetry θ_2 migrate while θ_1 do not, while under informational asymmetry both θ_1 and θ_2 migrate. Think of wages 7 and 9 for θ_1 and θ_2 respectively in H; of wages 10 and 20 for θ_1 and θ_2 respectively in F; and of θ_1 and θ_2 constituting $1/2$ each of the group of workers. Let $k = 2/3$. If at the end of the first period of employment employers in F identify costlessly and correctly the skill levels of individual workers and adjust pay accordingly, the θ_1 workers who now will be paid in F less than in H $((2/3) \cdot 10 < 7)$ will return to H, while the θ_2 workers will stay in F. The externality conferred by the high-skill workers facilitates migration by the low-skill workers (as $(2/3) \cdot 15 > 7$) while its waning prompts their return. Interestingly, the wages of the migrant workers who stay will be seen to rise (from 15 to 20), but this takes place not because of an increase in the human capital of individual migrants, but rather as a consequence of an increase in the average level of human capital (skill level) of the group of migrants.

Thus, return migration – indeed, migration dynamics – is explained by a change in the informational environment. Note that the model characterises fully the migrant workers who return (the low-skill workers). A more elaborate version of the model considers the case of several skill levels (Stark, 1995). Basically, as the individually identified (high-skill) θ_2 stayers and (low-skill) θ_1 returnees are removed from the pooling process, migration as above is replicated by yet a higher quality subset of workers (say θ_3 and θ_4); and so on. By migrating, workers constituting the first subset block the migration of workers constituting a higher quality subset(s). But once identified, these workers pave the way for the migration of higher quality workers. Thus, migration proceeds in waves with each wave breaking into workers who stay and workers who return, and within waves the returning migrants are the low-skill workers.

Purchasing Power Differential

Return migration may occur because of the higher purchasing power of savings (generated from work abroad) at home than abroad. While other researchers have been sensitive to the possibility that consumption at home is preferable to consumption abroad, and have incorporated this preference into carefully argued models (Hill, 1987; Djajic and Milbourne, 1988), this section attempts to identify the factors that underlie such a preference, if it exists, and to account for return migration even if that preference is absent. Specifically, it investigates the role of purchasing power parity in rendering given amounts of savings to facilitate different levels of consumption at home and abroad. While earlier work considered the effect of the probability of return migration on migrants' optimal savings (Stark, 1991, chapter 27), this section develops a reverse line of inquiry: how migrants' savings determine the optimal timing of return. *Inter alia*, this section points to a negative relationship between the optimal duration of migration and the purchasing power differential. Further, it shows a negative relationship between the optimal duration of migration and the wage abroad.

Consider the following 'naive model' in which an individual lives for two periods in a two-country world. In the first period the individual works but does not consume; in the second period the individual consumes but does not work. Utility is derived solely from consumption which, in turn, is of a single (composite) consumption good. There are no migration costs and there is no uncertainty. Wage earnings can be moved costlessly across countries. If wages in foreign country F are higher than in home country H, while the price of the consumption good is lower in country H than in country F, the country H individual will migrate to country F (for work) in the first period and return-migrate to country H (for consumption) in the second period. The optimal duration of migration is shorter than the duration of life, and the returns to migration are realised upon return migration. Put differently, optimisation (attainment of maximal utility) mandates return migration.

A less naive, yet very simple model can be constructed by invoking the following assumptions:

1. Consumption per time-period is fixed at a constant baseline consumption level, that is, the income elasticity of consumption is equal to zero, and consumption at home and consumption abroad are equal.

2. The wage in the home country is zero. The wage abroad, W_F, is positive and is higher than consumption abroad, C_F.

3. The life expectancy of individuals is fixed at T.

4. The duration of staying abroad, denoted by $t_F \leq T$, is continuous.
5. Purchasing power at home is E times higher than abroad. This implies that savings are E times higher in value when transferred to the home country.
6. At the end of his or her life the individual leaves zero net wealth; there are no bequests in the model.
7. All else equal, a given level of consumption at home is (marginally) more enjoyable than the same level of consumption abroad.

It follows that consumption at home must be equal to E times savings generated from work abroad, that is

$$(T - t_F) C_F = (W_F - C_F) t_F E. \tag{1}$$

From equation (1), the duration of staying abroad can be expressed as:

$$t_F = \frac{T}{1 + E\left(\frac{W_F}{C_F} - 1\right)}. \tag{2}$$

Equation (2) yields two results:

$$\frac{\partial t_F}{\partial E} = -\frac{T\left(\frac{W_F}{C_F} - 1\right)}{\left[1 + E\left(\frac{W_F}{C_F} - 1\right)\right]^2} < 0, \tag{3}$$

and

$$\frac{\partial t_F}{\partial W_F} = -\frac{T\left(\frac{E}{C_F}\right)}{\left[1 + E\left(\frac{W_F}{C_F} - 1\right)\right]^2} < 0. \tag{4}$$

Thus, an increase in purchasing power at home (equation (3)) and a rise in income abroad (equation (4)) *shorten* the duration of migration. These results deserve comment.

Conventional migration models could have led us to expect that a higher wage at destination increases the destination's relative attraction, presumably prolonging a stay there. Equation (4) predicts the converse. In addition, from equation (3) a new potential policy instrument is identified: the equation suggests that, for example, devaluation of the home country's currency will induce migrants working abroad to bring forward their return home, while appreciation of the home country's currency will have the opposite effect.

An interesting implication of the simple model is the possibility that a migrant may return home even though wages there are zero. But if some portion of the wage earned abroad cannot be saved and transferred home, return migration will not take place.

In related work, Stark, Helmenstein and Yegorov (1996) use the usual concave utility function in a general model that determines the income elasticity of consumption endogenously. (Clearly, perfectly inelastic consumption is a necessary and strong assumption for obtaining the results described above. Relaxing this assumption requires other conditions for determining the optimality of consumption abroad and consumption at home.) Interestingly, the negative relationship between purchasing power parity and the duration of stay abroad (equation (3)) is preserved under the general model. However, the result that a rise in the foreign country's wage shortens the duration of migration (equation (4)) is *reversed* under the general model *if* an interior solution exists, and depending on parameter values is retained or reversed in the case of a border solution.[2]

Consider evidence from Germany pertaining to migrants from Greece, Italy, Yugoslavia, Spain and Turkey (Brecht and Brecht, 1993). The evidence indicates that the distributions of migrants who return to their home country plotted against the duration of their stay in Germany differ considerably across migrant groups. A testable hypothesis then is that holding everything else constant, return occurs earlier to a county in which E is higher, that is, to where the purchasing power of savings generated from work abroad is higher.

III INTERACTIONS

Suppose that migration by a family member arises from the need for investment insurance. Assume that the family has available to it several investments that differ from each other by their high-risk–low-risk span: for example, a relatively high-risk, high-return investment becomes a relatively low-risk investment after several periods, while a relatively low-risk, low-return investment becomes a quite low-risk investment after just one period. Take the case of a family migrant who is a low-skill worker. This migrant receives a higher wage abroad than at home during the one period characterised by informational asymmetry. Subsequently, upon reinstatement of informational symmetry and the adjustment of wages, the migrant returns home; the provision of insurance-cum-migration is thus confined to that one period. Hence the family will be able and willing to bear the risk associated with the second investment, but reluctant to bear the risk associated with the first investment. A connection arises between the expected timing of return migration (the duration of insurance provision) and the type of investment pursued at home. Moreover, since a family whose migrant member is a high-skill worker will enjoy a longer insurance coverage than a family whose migrant member is a low-skill worker, and since riskier investments are more likely to be high-return investments than less risky investments, a positive correlation will be observed between the skill level of the migrant and the family's income, with causality running from the former to the latter.

Another connection may be unravelled upon joint consideration of the second and third reasons for return delineated in section II. We outlined a model that attributes return migration to maximisation of life-time consumption which, in turn, leads to disposition at home of savings accumulated abroad. And we developed the argument that return migration of low-skill workers arises from the reinstatement of symmetric information. These two explanations may be complementary. Presumably, revelation of information is quicker than accumulation of savings. Hence, in a return process that takes a long time to unravel, there will be an initial bout of information-induced return, followed by return induced by consumption maximisation. LaLonde and Topel (1996) report that in the United States, much of the total return migration occurs within a short span of time from arrival, with the rest spread over as much as several decades from the time of arrival (that is, until about one-third of the migrants return).

Upon further reflection, additional interactions may be identified.

IV CONCLUSIONS

An interest in the number of migrants in a country, in their skill composition and in their length of stay entails an interest in return migration and in the reasons underlying it. This paper outlines three models of return migration and provides examples of connections between them. Return migration might be prompted by a declining need for insurance, by a reinstatement of informational symmetry and by the higher purchasing power of savings (generated from work abroad) at home. Just as the set of reasons underlying migration is richer than a response to a positive inter-country wage differential (Stark, 1991), the reasons for return migration go beyond a response to a negative wage differential.

The reasons outlined suggest several novel implications for research and policy. For example, the first model implies that return migration is prompted by a realisation (an *ex post* investment risk) at home, not at destination; the second model implies that migration will not be selective at first, but will be positively selective thereafter; and the third model implies that the standard method for calculating the differential in *real* wages between abroad and home requires revision: the wage abroad should not be deflated in its entirety by the country-of-destination price level – the amount that is saved should be deflated by the price level at the country of *origin*.

The policy implications of the models can be illustrated briefly. The faster the risks of investments at home are reduced, the faster the pace of return migration. Time – an implicit policy tool – will result in the departure of low-skill workers who, under initial asymmetric information, migrated along with high-skill workers. And both the country of origin and the country of destination can affect the value of migrants' savings and thereby return migration through exchange rate policies: either devaluation of the country-of-origin currency or appreciation of the country-of-destination currency is likely to accelerate return migration.

NOTES

1. Perfect competition *within* a market (country) ensures that information in the hands of one employer is information in the hands of all employers.
2. The border solution case arises when optimisation, which requires equal marginal utilities from consumption abroad and consumption at home, results in violation of a constraint that consumption abroad must not fall below a given minimal level.

REFERENCES

Borjas, George J. and Bratsberg, Bernt (1996), 'Who Leaves? The Outmigration of the Foreign Born', *Review of Economics and Statistics*, forthcoming.

Brecht, Beatrix and Brecht, Leo (1993), 'Time-discrete Nonparametric Survival Analysis Using Panel Data', mimeo (University of Konstanz).

Djajic, Slobodan and Milbourne, Ross (1988), 'A General Equilibrium Model of Guest-Worker Migration: A Source-Country Perspective', *Journal of International Economics*, vol. 25, November, pp. 335–51.

Dustmann, Christian (1993), 'Return Intentions of Temporary Migrants', Paper presented at the Seventh Annual Meeting of the European Society for Population Economics, Budapest.

Hill, John K. (1987), 'Immigrant Decisions Concerning Duration of Stay and Migration Frequency', *Journal of Development Economics*, vol. 25, pp. 221–34.

Kimball, Miles S. (1993), 'Standard Risk Aversion', *Econometrica*, vol. 61, May, pp. 589–611.

LaLonde, Robert J. and Topel, Robert H. (1996), 'Economic Impact of International Migration and the Economic Performance of Migrants', in Mark R. Rosenzweig and Oded Stark, eds., *Handbook of Population and Family Economics* (Amsterdam: North-Holland).

OECD (Organisation for Economic Co-operation and Development) (1990), *Directorate for Social Affairs, Manpower and Education. Continuous Reporting System on Migration (SOPEMI)* (Paris: OECD).

Pratt, John W. and Zeckhauser, Richard J. (1987), 'Proper Risk Aversion', *Econometrica*, vol. 55, January, pp. 143–54.

Reilly, Bary (1994), 'What Determines Migration and Return? An Individual Level Analysis Using Data for Ireland', mimeo (University of Sussex).

Stark, Oded (1991), *The Migration of Labor* (Oxford and Cambridge, MA: Basil Blackwell).

———— (1995), 'Return and Dynamics: The Path of Labor Migration when Workers Differ in Their Skills and Information is Asymmetric', *Scandinavian Journal of Economics*, vol. 97, pp. 55–71.

Stark, Oded, Helmenstein, Christian and Yegorov, Yury (1996), 'Migrants' Savings, Purchasing Power Parity, and the Optimal Duration of Migration', mimeo (Institute for Advanced Studies, Vienna).

US Department of Commerce, Bureau of the Census (1960), *Historical Statistics of the United States* (Washington, DC: Government Printing Office).

———— (1983), *General Social and Economic Characteristics, United States, 1980 Census of Population* (Washington, DC: Government Printing Office).

———— (1984), *General Social and Economic Characteristics, Puerto Rico, 1980 Census of Population* (Washington, DC: Government Printing Office).

4 Foreign Trade Policies, Domestic Competition and the Benefits of Imported and In-house Technologies in the Newly Industrialising Countries

Homi Katrak

I INTRODUCTION

The governments of a number of newly industrialising countries have implemented various policies to achieve 'technological self-reliance' (TSR). The precise interpretation of this objective[1] has differed somewhat from one country to another but, as recent studies by Enos (1991) and Forsyth (1989) and also earlier work by UNCTAD (1981) and UNIDO (1981) suggest, TSR policies encourage the development of indigenous technological capabilities and assign only a limited role to imported technologies. The policy measures actually used to promote TSR have included government support for further education in science, engineering and technology, funding of scientific and industrial research institutes, incentives to enterprises to develop in-house technological know-how and restrictions on the imports of technology and on competing import products.

These policies have, however, had rather limited success in some of the countries concerned. Empirical research by Adikibi (1988), Braga and Willmore (1991), Katrak (1989, 1994), Katz (1987) and Lall (1987) suggests that many enterprises have preferred to use foreign technologies rather than develop the technological know-how through in-house efforts: enterprises that have wanted to diversify their product portfolio, move up-market and/or introduce more efficient processes have initially relied on imported technologies and undertaken in-house technological effort mainly to adapt the imported know-how and designs to the local environment.

This tendency of enterprises to rely primarily on imported technologies has been a matter of concern in some countries and has raised an important

42

question. Why is it that notwithstanding government policies to promote TSR, many enterprises have not chosen to develop technologies through in-house efforts?

The purpose of this paper is to examine this question in the context of a country's foreign trade and exchange policies. The reason for adopting the foreign trade context is that some of the countries where these concerns have been voiced have, until recently, followed restrictive foreign trade and exchange policies. India is an obvious case. Tariffs and other barriers to competing imports have increased the profits from domestic market sales while overvaluation of the currency has made it difficult to export. It thus seems worth exploring whether these countries' trade and exchange rate policies could have influenced enterprises' choices between imported and in-house technologies.

Research by Helleiner (1990), Pack (1988) and Rodrik (1991) has shown that protectionist policies may have mixed effects on an enterprise's technological efforts: protection may either discourage or encourage such effort. This paper examines a related question. Even if protectionist policies do not discourage enterprises from introducing a new technology (i.e. a technology that it has not used before), could those policies influence the enterprises to import a new technology rather than develop one through in-house technological efforts?

The influence of import protection may be of particular interest for it not only decreases competition from foreign products, but may also affect the nature of competition between domestic enterprises, and that in turn may further influence enterprises' technological decisions. Some effects of domestic market competition in the newly industrialising countries have previously been considered among others by Katz (1987) and Katrak (1988) and its influence seems worth exploring further here.

The effects of trade liberalisation on enterprises' technological choices may have interesting welfare implications. Bhagwati (1994 and numerous earlier papers) has pointed out that free trade is superior to protection in a wide range of situations. The question for the present analysis is whether the standard welfare gains from trade liberalisation would be enhanced or reduced if that policy also influenced enterprises' choices between imported and in-house technologies.

The plan of this paper is as follows. Section II discusses the relative advantages of imported and in-house technologies. Section III examines how enterprises' choice of those technologies may be affected by the country's foreign trade and exchange policies. Section IV examines some welfare questions arising from the analyses. The Appendix elaborates on some propositions used in the text.

II RELATIVE ADVANTAGES OF IMPORTED AND IN-HOUSE TECHNOLOGIES

Consider a simple scenario where an enterprise that has initially been producing, say, mopeds decides to move up-market and produce, say, cars. The up-market product will require the use of more complex technological know-how, which may be acquired either by licensing a foreign technology or by in-house technological efforts.

The enterprise will want to compare the present discounted value (PDV) of the profits that can be earned with each of the two types of technology. These profits will be affected by (at least) the following factors: pre-production costs, gestation lag and first-mover advantages, uncertainty and product quality, production costs, exclusive rights and domestic market rivalry. Some of these factors will favour the use of an imported technology, while others may have an opposing effect or a mixed influence.

Pre-production Costs

These costs will be relatively lower with the imported technologies: the enterprise will incur the costs of searching for a foreign supplier of suitable technology, negotiating the terms of the technology transfer agreement, solving start-up problems and will perhaps have to make front-end (lump-sum) payments. In comparison, the development of an in-house technology will entail considerable costs of R&D efforts, as well as the costs associated with start-up problems. Thus the pre-production costs are likely to make for relatively lower profits with the in-house technologies.

Gestation Lag and First-mover Advantages

As the R&D efforts may take some time, the in-house technology will have a longer gestation lag and that, in turn, will mean a lower PDV of the subsequent profits.[2] Thus the gestation lag will also give rise to a preference for imported technologies. This influence will be enhanced by the presence of market rivals, as each enterprise will want to set up production ahead of its rivals in order to capture some first-mover advantages.[3]

Uncertainty and Product Quality

The enterprise may face technical uncertainties: it will be concerned that the technology will 'not work', production will be interrupted by breakdowns, etc.; however, this uncertainty will be lower with the imported technology, because that technology will, at least, be 'known to have worked' in the foreign supplier's environment. There will also be commercial uncertainty, i.e. that production will not be sufficiently profitable. This, too, may be lower with the imported technology: the product may have a higher quality and consumers may be familiar with the quality reputation of the foreign supplier of the technology; moreover, products made with the foreign technologies may have an attraction *per se*. Thus the certainty equivalent of the enterprise's profits will be relatively higher with the imported technologies.

Production Costs

The costs of plant and machinery and also those of the variable inputs are likely to be lower with the in-house technologies. This is so for the following reasons. (1) The design of the in-house technology may incorporate the use of suitable low-cost indigenous materials. (2) If production of the up-market product replaces (wholly or partly) that of the initial product, the design of the in-house technology may incorporate some components of the plant and machinery previously used for the initial product. (3) A related point is that an enterprise that designs its own technology will have greater insights into the know-how and know-why and so is more likely to benefit from subsequent learning-by-doing: in comparison, the learning associated with an imported technology may be limited to merely following the blueprints and instructions of the foreign supplier. (4) As the imported technology is likely to be designed for a relatively higher quality product, it will require more complex machinery and better quality variable inputs. (5) The foreign technology supplier may charge a high price for the physical inputs that are specific to the use of that technology. (6) The imported machines and materials may be subject to import duties. Finally (7), the variable costs of using an imported technology will include the production-related royalty payments.

Exclusive Rights

Both types of technology may enable an enterprise to seek exclusive rights to production and sales (at least for a few years). An enterprise that develops an in-house technology may seek a patent right, though some NICs grant patents only for process developments. Correspondingly, an importer of technology may negotiate an exclusive right of sale with the foreign supplier.[4] Thus in general, these arrangements may not confer an advantage to either type of technology. However, as foreign technology suppliers usually grant exclusive rights for domestic sales only, the imported technologies may

Trade and Development

have a relative advantage in protectionist regimes, where enterprises are mainly interested to sell in their domestic markets.

Product Quality and Production Costs

The imported technology produces a relatively higher quality product but also entails higher variable costs. The effects of these differences on the relative profits of the two types of technologies are shown in Figure 4.1. It is assumed that the enterprise sells in the home market only. V_mE_m (extended) and V_hE_h are the enterprise's unit variable costs for its imported and in-house technologies respectively, while B_mE_m and B_hE_h show the corresponding marginal revenue curves; the costs and revenues are greater for the imported technologies, as it produces higher quality products.[5] The operating profits, defined as the excess of revenues over variable costs, are $V_mB_mE_m$ and $V_hB_hE_h$.

The factors determining these profits are further examined in the Appendix (p. 57). In Figure 4.1 the profits are shown to be greater with the imported technology; as we can see, this requires that the excess of marginal revenues over the marginal costs is greater for that technology, for all relevant levels of output.

Market Rivalry

The operating profits may also be affected by the presence of rival enterprises. An interesting possibility is that rivalry could cause the profits to become higher for the in-house technology. The reason is that an enterprise's revenues will now be affected by the output responses of its rivals and, moreover, those responses may depend on the types of technology being used.

Suppose that an enterprise believes that its rival will retaliate against its increase in output, but that its own best strategy is not to match the rival's output responses. This scenario would be likely if the rival were a larger enterprise and able to expand output more quickly. Suppose also that the enterprise expects that the rival's response will be greater the more similar are their products, in terms of quality. Thus, if an enterprise knows that the rival will use an imported technology to produce a high-quality product, it will expect that the rival's response will be greater if it were also to make a high quality product (with some other imported technology). In such a case, the enterprise will expect that its operating profits would be relatively lower with the imported technology, even though, in the absence of rivalry, those profits would be higher with that technology. Formally, this requires that $\pi_m > \pi_h$ but yet:

$$\pi_m + [(\partial\pi_m/\partial Q_{mr})dQ_{mr}] \; < \; \pi_h + [(\partial\pi_h/\partial Q_{hr})dQ_{hr}] \qquad (1)$$

where π_m is the enterprise's profits from an imported technology in the absence of rivalry, dQ_{mr} is the rival's output response, $(\partial\pi_m/\partial Q_{mr})$ is the effect of that response, and the corresponding terms with subscript h pertain to an in-house technology. If the rival is producing a high quality product we expect:

$$dQ_{mr} > dQ_{hr} > 0 \text{ and } (\partial\pi_m/\partial Q_{mr}) < (\partial\pi_h/\partial Q_{hr}) < 0$$

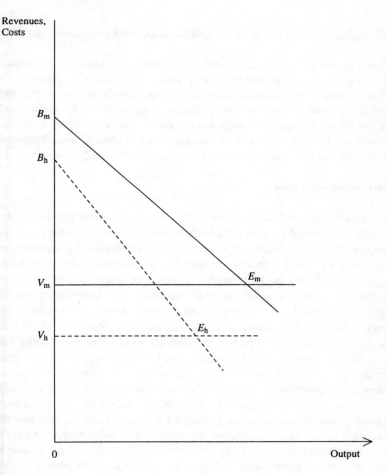

Figure 4.1

So in this scenario, market rivalry could induce an enterprise to make a lower quality-price product with an in-house technology.

Note that this argument applies to enterprises that are smaller than their rivals and that adopt a defensive stance, i.e. do not compete in the rival's product range. In a protectionist regime these arguments cannot apply to all enterprises: some may use imported technologies, while others may adopt the defensive stance and use in-house technologies. However, as we shall see, in a liberalised economy the defensive stance becomes more important for NICs' enterprises.

III   THE EFFECTS OF TRADE LIBERALISATION

What interests us now is how a country's trade and exchange regime may affect the relative advantages of the two types of technology. Suppose that a country initially had restrictions on competing imports and an overvalued domestic currency, and that enterprises wishing to move up-market had usually turned to imported technologies, rather than develop an in-house technology. How would trade liberalisation and exchange rate adjustment affect the costs and revenues of the two types of technology?

Pre-production Costs

The costs of imported technologies will be affected in two opposing ways. First, as an imported technology is likely to require the use of some imported equipment, components, etc., the cut in the import duties and restrictions on such items will mean a decrease in costs to the importer of the technology. On the other hand, the technology supplier may charge higher front-end payments; as the technology supplier may now also have the option of exporting its products to the liberalised economy, licensing its technology would entail forgoing some export earnings and, as Caves et al. (1983) and Contractor (1981) have reported, the supplier would impute a charge for those forgone earnings. Thus these two considerations suggest that the pre-production costs of imported technologies may be either decreased or increased. In comparison, the costs of in-house technologies are more likely to decrease. There are two reasons for expecting this. First, even in-house technologies may require some imported components and so may benefit from a cut in import duties. Second, the trade liberalisation programme may also allow enterprises easier access to international capital markets. In such a case, enterprises undertaking in-house technological effort would earlier have had to fund those expenditures domestically, but may now turn to the international market. Consequently, as interest charges abroad are likely to be lower than in a protected NIC's market, the costs of funding in-house technological effort would be reduced.[6]

Gestation Lag and Exclusive Rights

In a protected economy, where enterprises sell mainly in the domestic market, imported technologies may have an advantage because their shorter gestation lag would help an enterprise to obtain a first-mover advantage over any rivals, which may be developing in-house technologies. However, under a liberalised regime this advantage of imported technologies would be greatly reduced: the NIC's enterprises would be competing with enterprises from the economically advanced countries and it is most likely that the first-mover advantages would be captured by the latter enterprises. (The shorter gestation lag of the imported technologies would, however, still be an advantage vis-à-vis any domestic rivals using in-house technologies.)

Liberalisation may also decrease the likelihood of exclusive rights for an imported technology: a foreign technology supplier, who may now consider exporting some of its products to the liberalised economy, would be less willing to grant an exclusive right of sale to the licensee, or may charge a higher payment for that right.

Most of the preceding arguments suggest that trade liberalisation is likely to decrease the profits of the imported technologies relative to those of an in-house technology. However, there are in addition some further effects to consider; these arise because the quality and cost advantages of the two types of technology are affected by import competition, export opportunities and foreign rivalry.

Product Quality and Production Costs

The products of a NIC's enterprise (with either type of technology) are likely to be differentiated from the competing imports and so the enterprise will face a downward sloping demand curve.[7] However, the demand curve will differ between the two types of technologies and that, in turn, will cause differences in their operating profits. We can see in the Appendix (p. 57) that the profits may be written as:

$$(\pi_m/\pi_h) = (C_m/C_h)^\lambda (Z_m/Z_h)^\beta (Y^\zeta) \tag{2}$$

where subscripts m and h pertain to imported and in-house technologies, π and C denote respectively the operating profits and the unit variable costs

Trade and Development

of production, Z is an index of product quality, Y is consumers' income, $\lambda = (1 + \rho)$ and ρ is the own-price elasticity of demand, β is the demand elasticity with respect to product quality and $\zeta = (\psi - \sigma)$ where ψ and σ are the income elasticities for the products made with the imported and in-house technologies respectively. We expect $C_m > C_h$, $Z_m > Z_h$, $\rho < -1$ and β, ψ and σ are positively signed. Note that the price and quality elasticities are assumed to be the same for the two types of technologies; this assumption is relaxed in the Appendix.

Equation (2) suggests that import competition could affect the relative profits, (π_m/π_h) in a number of opposing ways. To illustrate, if import competition increased the modulus value of the price elasticity, the profits of the imported technology would decrease relative to that of the in-house technology; but if the quality elasticity were increased, (π_m/π_h) would increase. Thus there is no presumption that import competition would favour any particular type of technology. This agnostic conclusion is reinforced by allowing for the possibility that the price and quality elasticities may differ as between the products of the two types of technology and also import competition may have a greater effect on the elasticities for one of those products.[8]

The relative profits may also be affected by increased interest in export markets.[9] First, competition in export markets may also influence the price and quality elasticities. Second, there may be an 'income' effect since consumers in export markets are likely to have higher incomes than those in the NIC: as can be seen from equation (2) an increase in the average income will affect the relative profits (π_m/π_h) if the income elasticities of demand of the two products differ. However, as with import competition, the precise effects of these influences on the choice of technology cannot be determined on an a priori basis.

We see, then, that whereas the arguments about pre-production costs, gestation lag and exclusive rights had suggested that liberalisation may decrease the relative advantage of the imported technologies, the influence of the price, quality and income elasticities makes the picture rather more complex. The overall outcome is thus likely to differ from one situation to another, depending on the quantitative impact of each of the above factors.

However, export opportunities may also have a further, less ambiguous effect. By enlarging the overall market, exports may enable the enterprises to employ both types of technology. An imported technology may be used to make a higher quality product for upper-income consumers while in-house technological effort may be aimed to develop a lower-cost product for lower-income consumers. Thus if, on the basis of all preceding influences, the enterprise had used, say, an imported technology only, it may now also develop an in-house technology. The required condition for this is that $(d\pi/dQ_{hl}) > 0$ and is defined as:

$$(d\pi/dQ_{hl}) = (\partial\pi/\partial Q_{hl}) + (\partial\pi_{mu}/\partial Q_{mu})(dQ_{mu}/dQ_{hl}) \quad (3)$$

where subscripts l and h denote lower- and upper-income groups, $\pi = (\pi_{hl} + \pi_{mu})$, π_{hl} and π_{mu} are respectively the operating profits from using the in-house and imported technologies, Q_{hl} and Q_{mu} are the corresponding levels of output and $(dQ_{mu}/dQ_{hl}) < 0$ as the products are differentiated substitutes. An additional condition is that the operating profit for each product must be large enough to cover the pre-production costs and fixed production costs.

Market Rivalry

In a liberalised regime a NIC's enterprise will be concerned with the output responses of foreign,[10] as well as domestic, rivals. In fact, the foreign responses may be of greater concern as those enterprises will be larger and able to expand output more readily. Now, as the foreign enterprises are likely to be producing relatively high-quality and high-priced products, a NIC's enterprise may decide to avoid rivalry in those product lines and instead make mainly lower-cost products. This, in turn, may be a further inducement to develop in-house technologies. The formal conditions for this would be the same as those of inequality (1) at the end of section II.

IV SOME WELFARE IMPLICATIONS

Suppose now that the balance of the preceding arguments was such that in a protectionist regime an enterprise moving up-market would have preferred an imported technology, but that in a liberalised economy the up-market move would have been made by developing an in-house technology. In such a case trade liberalisation would have helped the government's objective of technological self-reliance. But what would be the welfare implications?

In keeping with the received theory of trade and commercial policy we expect that trade liberalisation *per se* will enhance economic welfare. However, what interests us are the welfare effects of the change in enterprises' technological decisions which are brought about by the liberalisation. These effects may include inappropriable benefits, such as consumer surplus and technological spillover to other enterprises, as well as the increase in profits of those enterprises that revised their technological decisions. Would the inappropriable benefits be enhanced if trade liberalisation induced enterprises to use in-house technologies?

The scope for technological spillover may be greater with in-house technologies: as Cohen and Levinthal (1989) have argued, such spillovers require that enterprises are able to assimilate the know-how that has been developed elsewhere, and that in turn requires that the enterprises have themselves undertaken some related technological effort. On the other hand, imported technologies having a shorter gestation lag may enable consumption at an earlier date and consequently enhance the discounted value of consumer surplus.

A further consideration for consumer surplus is that the products made with imported technologies may have a higher product quality, but may also entail higher marginal costs and so have a higher price. The effect on consumer surplus from using, say, an imported technology may then be written as:

$$(dS/dZ) = (\partial S/\partial Z) + (\partial S/\partial P)(dP/dZ) \qquad (4)$$

where Z, as before, is an indicator of product quality, S and P are respectively consumer surplus and the product price, $(\partial S/\partial Z) > 0$, $(\partial S/\partial P) < 0$ and $(dP/dZ) > 0$. Thus in terms of product price-quality the consumer surplus may be either greater, or less, with the imported technologies.

An interesting implication of equation (4) is that the imported technology may yield a relatively greater consumer surplus the lower are the level of trade restrictions. This is because the lower the degree of protection, the lower will be the extent by which an enterprise can increase its product price (with higher quality) and so the greater will be the consumer surplus from the high quality product.

Figure 4.2 illustrates the preceding arguments. The schedules π_m and π_h show respectively how an enterprise's profits from imported and in-house technologies are affected by the level of trade restrictions.[11] At levels of protection higher (lower) than OT_1 the enterprise would prefer an imported (in-house) technology. The lines W_m and W_h show the corresponding effects on welfare, including consumer surplus, technological spillovers and the enterprise's profits; W_m increases relative to W_h as the level of protection decreases, because of the greater gains to consumer surplus. Now if the level of trade restrictions was higher than OT_1, the enterprise would prefer the imported technology, but welfare would be greater if instead the enterprise had used an in-house technology. Next, if the level of protection was reduced to some level between OT_1 and OT_2, the enterprise would prefer the in-house technology and welfare would also be greater with that technology. And with a further decrease in protection the enterprise would remain with the in-house technology while the level of welfare would increase along W_h.

Thus in this illustrative case, a decrease in trade restrictions may help promote the government's objective of technological self-reliance and enhance welfare. However, the welfare gain would have been even higher if the trade liberalisation had not induced the enterprise to prefer the in-house technology.

An alternative case would be where the positioning of π_m and π_h would be as in Figure 4.2, but the consumer surplus effects would be such that the W_h

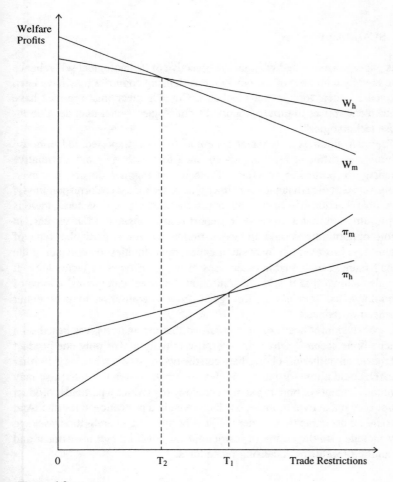

Figure 4.2

schedule was always above W_m. A decrease in trade restrictions below OT_1 would again induce the enterprise to switch to an in-house technology. The welfare gain would correspond to a movement along W_m up till the level of restrictions OT_1 and then as restrictions are further reduced an additional gain along W_h.

Finally, if liberalisation leads to an increase in export opportunities such as to enable an enterprise to produce both types of technology, there would be a further welfare gain as home consumers would have a wider choice of products.

V SUMMARY

This paper has examined whether the objective of technological self-reliance promoted by a number of the newly industrialising countries may have been affected by their foreign trade policies. Could protectionist regimes have induced enterprises to turn to imported technologies, rather than develop in-house technologies?

The main findings of the analysis are as follows. Imported and in-house technologies differ in certain respects such that each may have a relative advantage in particular situations. Protectionist regimes do not, however, create a systematic advantage for either type of technology. Correspondingly, trade liberalisation will have some opposing effects and, in general, there is no presumption that a decrease in import restrictions and/or an increase in export opportunities could induce a preference for a particular type of technology; however, an increase in export opportunities, by enhancing the overall market, may enable enterprises to use both types of technology. It was also shown that if trade liberalisation did affect enterprises' choice of technology, the standard welfare gains from liberalisation may be either enhanced or reduced.

In conclusion, it needs to be recognised that the analysis was based on a rather simple scenario where an enterprise initially makes only one product and makes an 'either/or' choice between the two types of technology. Further research could allow for more complex scenarios, where the enterprise may combine elements of both types of technology to produce a particular product and/or may make two, or more, products even in a protectionist regime. And it would be desirable to consider the possibility that a liberalisation package may include also the easing of restrictions on inward direct investment and relaxation of industrial licensing procedures.

NOTES

1. The expression 'technological self-reliance' is used by UNIDO (1981), while UNCTAD (1981) discusses a broader objective of 'technological transformation'.
2. Imported technologies may also be affected by a gestation lag caused by administrative delays in obtaining government permission, foreign exchange clearance, etc. However, such lags are due to governments' policies, rather than the characteristics of the imported technologies *per se*.
3. The first mover may find it easier to acquire consumer loyalty. In addition, as Patibandla (1992) argues, in countries like India where capital markets are imperfect, a first mover that grows up to some critical size may acquire recognition in the capital market and may be able to raise capital at lower cost.
4. As Chudnovsky (1981) reported, exclusive rights have been negotiated by enterprises in India and in some Latin American countries.
5. The revenues may also be enhanced by a reputation premium earned by products made with imported technologies.
6. This consideration may also apply to imported technologies, but is likely to be of less importance as the pre-production costs associated with those technologies will have been financed by the foreign supplier in its own country.
7. Product differentiation between the NICs' products and the competing imports from the economically advanced countries has been recognised, among others, by Gunasekara and Tyers (1991) and Devarajan and Rodrik (1991). Most likely, the NICs' products may be a technologically older version of the competing imports.
8. Import competition may have a relatively greater impact on the price and quality elasticities of the product made with the imported technology as it is likely to be a closer substitute for the competing imports. However, as this may apply to the price and quality elasticities, the relative profits of that product may either increase or decrease.
9. The interest in exporting will arise because the increased pressures of import competition will push some enterprises to export and/or because the exchange rate adjustment will increase the profitability of exporting.
10. 'Foreign enterprises' are defined as only those that are producing in a foreign location. Local subsidiaries of foreign enterprises are viewed as domestic rivals.
11. It is assumed here that the enterprise produces only one product-quality and uses only one type of technology.

REFERENCES

Adikibi, O.T. (1988), 'The Multinational Corporation and Monopoly of Patents in Nigeria', *World Development*.
Bhagwati, J.N. (1994), 'Free-trade: Old and New Challenges', *Economic Journal*.
Braga, L. and Willmore, L. (1991), 'Technological Imports and Technological Effort: An Analysis of Their Determinants in Brazilian Firms', *Journal of Industrial Economics*.

Caves, R.E. et al. (1983), 'The Imperfect Market for Technology Licences', *Oxford Bulletin of Economics and Statistics.*

Chudnovsky, D. (1981), 'Regulating Technology Imports in Some Developing Countries', *Trade and Development.*

Cohen, W.M. and Levinthal, D.A. (1989), 'Innovation and Learning: The Two Faces of R&D', *Economic Journal.*

Contractor, F.J. (1981), *International Technology Licensing* (Lexington, MA: D.C. Heath and Company).

Devarajan, S. and Rodrik, D. (1991) 'Pro-competitive Effects of Trade Reform: Results from a CGE Model of Cameroon', *European Economic Review.*

Enos, J.L. (1991), *The Creation of Technological Capability in Developing Countries* (London: Frances Pinter).

Forsyth, D.J.C. (1989), *Appropriate National Technology Policies: A Manual for their Assessment* (Geneva: ILO).

Gunasekara, H. and Tyers, R. (1991), 'Imperfect Competition and Returns to Scale in a Newly Industrialising Economy: A General Equilibrium Analysis of Korean Trade Policy', *Journal of Development Economics.*

Helleiner, G.K. (1990), 'Trade Strategy in Medium-term Adjustment', *World Development.*

Katrak, H. (1988), 'Payments for Imported Technologies, Market-rivalry and Adaptive Activity in the Newly Industrialising Countries', *Journal of Development Studies.*

———— (1989), 'Imported Technologies and R&D in a Newly Industrialising Country: the Experience of Indian Enterprises', *Journal of Development Economics.*

———— (1994), 'Imports of Technology, Enterprise Size and R&D Based Production in a Newly Industrialising Country: The Evidence from Indian Enterprises', *World Development.*

Katz, J.M., ed. (1987), *Technology Generation in Latin American Manufacturing Industries* (London: Macmillan).

Lall, S. (1987), *Learning to Industrialise: The Acquisition of Technological Capability by India* (London: Macmillan).

Pack, H. (1988), 'Industrialisation and Trade', in H.B. Chenery and T.N. Srinivasan, eds, *Handbook of Development Economics* (Amsterdam: North-Holland).

Patibandla, M. (1992), 'Industrial Decontrol and Competition Policy: A Few Conceptual Issues', *Economic and Political Weekly.*

Rodrik, D. (1991), 'Closing the Productivity Gap: Does Trade Liberalisation Really Help?', in G.K. Helleiner, ed., *Trade Policy, Industrialisation and Development* (Oxford: Oxford University Press).

UNCTAD (1981), *Planning the Technological Transformation of Developing Countries* (New York: United Nations).

UNIDO (1981), *Technological Self-Reliance of the Developing Countries: Towards Operational Strategies* (Vienna: United Nations).

APPENDIX

This appendix shows how the operating profits of each type of technology are influenced by the production costs, product quality, consumers' income and the price, quality and income elasticities.

Let the demand function for the product made with an imported technology be:

$$Q_m = A_m(P_m)^\rho (Z_m)^\beta Y^\psi \qquad (A1)$$

where subscript m pertains to the imported technology, Q and P are respectively quantity demanded and price, Z is an indicator of product quality, A is a constant reflecting consumers' tastes, Y is consumers' income, ρ is the own-price elasticity, β and ψ are respectively the elasticities with respect to quality and income and we expect $\rho < -1$, $\beta > 0$ and $\psi > 0$.

The operating profits are defined as:

$$\pi_m = (P_m - C_m)Q_m \qquad (A2)$$

where C denotes the constant marginal costs of production.

The first-order condition for profit-maximisation is:

$$d(P_m Q_m)/dQ_m = C_m \qquad (A3)$$

and so the equilibrium price (denoted by P_{em}) is:

$$P_{cm} = [\rho/(1+\rho)]C_m \qquad (A4)$$

and equilibrium quantity (denoted by Q_{em}) is:

$$Q_{em} = [\rho/(1+\rho)]^\rho (C_m)^\rho A_m (Z_m)^\beta Y^\psi \qquad (A5)$$

Substituting (A4) and (A5) into (A2) gives the equilibrium profits (denoted by π_{em}):

$$\pi_{em} = C_m\{[\rho/(1+\rho)] - 1\}\{[\rho/(1+\rho)]^\rho (C_m)^\rho A_m (Z_m)^\beta Y^\psi\} \qquad (A6)$$

A similar procedure can be used to derive the equilibrium profits for the in-house technology. The two profit levels will differ because of differences in the production costs, product quality and the elasticities. The relative profits are shown in equation (2) of the text, where subscript e has been dropped and the own-price and quality elasticities are assumed to be the same for the two types of technologies' products.

Part Two
Trade Policy

5 Neutrality and Export Promotion: Issues, Evidence and Policy Implications

Chris Milner and Andrew McKay

Selected LDC's

I INTRODUCTION

In one of Bhagwati's many important contributions on trade and development, he posed the following question:

> What exactly is meant by an export-promoting trade strategy? Unless we are clear on that critical question, we cannot properly debate the merits of the strategy and its alternatives. Clarification of the question is therefore important, especially as the everyday usage of this phrase evokes many different notions that are wholly unrelated. (Bhagwati, 1990, p. 17)

He answered the question in a clear and unambiguous manner, using an incentive-related definition based on relative (average) effective exchange rates for exports (EER_X) and for imports (EER_M); a 'bias against exports' occurring when $EER_X < EER_M$. The idea that an import substitution (IS) strategy involves a net incentive on average to import-substitutes relative to what international prices dictate can be found in the author's earlier work (Bhagwati, 1968). Given that the typical sequence of trade reforms has involved the movement of countries from an IS strategy closer towards neutrality (i.e. $EER_X \cong EER_M$), the convention among many researchers and policy-makers has been to use export promotion (EP) to encompass both neutrality and pro-export (i.e. $EER_X > EER_M$), or what Bhagwati (1988) had labelled as an 'ultra-EP' strategy.

Since Bhagwati's powerful defence of the case for export-promotion policies, the process of trade liberalisation in developing countries has spread and deepened. There has been fairly widespread acceptance in policy circles that developing countries should pursue more outward-oriented trade strategies. There has been a general lowering of non-tariff barriers and a greater willingness to adjust exchange rates so as to avoid currency overvaluation. This has reduced the extreme 'anti-export bias' that typified many trade regimes in the pre-liberalisation era. There has however been rather less consensus in academic circles about what constitutes an 'export promoting' trade strategy. The model of success that many countries wish to emulate is that of the Asian NICs, which are viewed as having successfully pursued outward-oriented strategies. Some commentators (Bhagwati, 1990; and Greenaway and Nam, 1988), for example, group countries like Hong Kong, Singapore, South Korea and Taiwan together as pursuing export promotion (EP) strategies. But outward orientation has been achieved in these NICs with quite different policy stances. There are the 'free trade' (or approximately so) regimes of Hong Kong and Singapore on the one hand, and the more (selectively) interventionist regimes of South Korea and Taiwan on the other. The difference need not necessarily be fundamental, however, within the context of the liberal tradition, because trade regime bias is concerned with the *average* balance of relative incentives within the tradeables sector. Indeed, Bhagwati (1990) recognised that the mixed interventions of EP and IS may offer benefits over a free trade policy if they help to demonstrate the commitment of government to private sector investors, and thereby increase the credibility of the reforms.

Critiques (e.g. Singer, 1988) of the above representation of trade strategies, none the less, point to a number of possible limitations of relying upon the average biases in the incentive regime as a means of classifying trade strategy where interventions are selective and at variable rates. The possibility that there is substantial variation in incentives among different activities, or that there is the possibility of firm- or industry-level (external) economies of scale that can be induced by mixed interventions does not however render meaningless the distinction between average trade strategies investigated at the broad, sectoral level. Thus we do not investigate these issues further, but concentrate rather on the implications for the concepts of EP and neutrality of introducing non-tradeables into the analysis of trade policy interventions. When a non-tradeables sector is added to the traditional two-sector trade model, Liang (1992) suggests the possibility of using a mixed strategy of promoting tradeables as a whole relative to non-tradeables. Evidence of simultaneously positive rates of subsidisation in exportables and protection in import-substitute sectors is used to represent South Korea's experience of mixed IS–EP policies (what Liang calls 'protected export promotion') and to distinguish it from the neutrality concepts of export promotion referred to above.

The aim of this paper is therefore to investigate both the theoretical and empirical robustness of this interpretation of mixed strategies in the presence of non-tradeables. The nature of these conflicting interpretations is illustrated first (section II) with information on the structure of incentives in some developing countries. Section III sets up a general theoretical structure with which to investigate the general equilibrium responses of relative prices of tradeables and non-tradeables. The empirical evidence presented in section II is then reinterpreted in section IV in the light of this theoretical framework. Finally, the summary conclusions and implications of the analysis are set out in section V.

II ALTERNATIVE INTERPRETATIONS OF MIXED TRADE STRATEGIES

The analytical tool most commonly employed to investigate the impact of trade policy interventions on the structure of incentives is the effective rate of protection or subsidisation. The effective rate of protection (e) captures the net effect of (implicit and explicit) taxes and subsidies on inputs and outputs arising from trade taxes and non-tariff barriers. It can distinguish between the differential sources of taxation and subsidisation which apply in domestic and export sales. In Table 5.1 we report average rates of effective protection for manufacturing activities from a selection of developing countries which applied during their industrialising stage of development. Separate rates are recorded for import-substituting sales to the domestic market (e_M) and for sales to the export market (e_X). The values for e_M are generally positive and for e_X are generally negative, but there are exceptions. There is also considerable variation in the absolute values of the rates and some variation in the combination of rates. The most common pattern of relative incentives is $e_M > 0$ and $e_X < 0$, but in three cases (Barbados, South Korea (1978) and Colombia) both e_M and e_X are positive and in one (South Korea, 1968) both rates are negative. It is, in fact, these non-typical cases that give rise to alternative interpretations of the same evidence.

In line with the balance of incentives tradition advocated by Bhagwati, we might classify the trade strategy of each of the countries at these points in time according to the bias (B) in the trade regime defined as: $B = \frac{1+e_M}{1+e_X}$. In Table 5.2 we report a possible classification based on the trade regime bias indices (reported in Table 5.1). This is fundamentally a three-way classification depending on whether $B \gtrless 1$, though in the case of the pro-importables production bias ($B > 1$) a distinction is drawn between a strongly IS strategy ($B > 2$) and a more moderate degree of import substitution. It is a type of classification that liberal economists have tended to adopt in their assessments of the trade strategy–performance relationship. It has been challenged recently, however, by Liang (1992), who proposes an alternative classification of trade strategies based on the pattern of absolute rates of subsidisation/protection. This classification is applied in Table 5.3 to the same information used in Table 5.2. In the case of most of the countries classified as IS in Table 5.2 there is no change of classification (where $e_X < 0$ and $e_M > 0$ the trade regime index (B) will be greater than 1). Barbados shifts out of the IS category in Table 5.2 into a new category (protected export promotion, PEP) in Table 5.3, because it has positive rates for both e_X and e_M (albeit at absolutely different rates). The other important change in classification applies to Korea (1978), which shifts from neutrality/EP to PEP.[1]

The difference between these two classifications centres on the dimensions of the theoretical framework that we are assuming, and on the role of non-

Table 5.1   Average[1] Effective[2] Rates of Protection for Importables[3] and Exportables[4] and Trade Regime Bias Indices for a Selection of Countries

	Effective Rates of Protection %		Trade Regime Bias
	e_M	e_X	(B)
Barbados (1988/9)	221	10	2.92
Trinidad (1991)	154	−21	3.22
Mauritius (1990)	79	−3	1.85
Uganda (1992)	62	−15	1.91
South Korea (1968)	−12	−9	0.97
South Korea (1978)	33	14	1.17
Israel (1968)	14	−18	1.39
Argentina (1969)	41	−60	3.53
Singapore (1967)	2	−6	1.09
Taiwan (1969)	18	−13	1.36
Colombia (1969)	5	26	0.83

Notes:
1. Unweighted for Barbados, Trinidad, Mauritius and Uganda, otherwise weighted by shares in value-added.
2. Net rates adjusted for currency overvaluation.
3. Strictly protection in domestic sales and exports.
4. Manufacturing sectors but for consumer goods industries only for Trinidad and for non–traditional for Israel.
5. $B = (1 + e_M)/(1 + e_X)$.

Sources: Milner (1994b) for Barbados and Trinidad; Dabee and Milner (1995) for Mauritius; Maxwell Stamp (1993) for Uganda; Balassa et al. (1982) for South Korea (1968), Israel, Argentina, Singapore, Taiwan and Colombia; and Liang (1992) for Korea (1978).

tradeables. In a two-sector model of tradeables only, i.e. importables (*M*) and exportables (*X*), there is no justification for Liang's alternative classification; we can be interested in only one relative price. If we allow for the possibility of non-tradeables, then there will be more than one relative price, and it is

Table 5.2 Classification of Trade Strategies Based on Intra-tradeables Bias

Intra-tradeables Bias (*B*)	Classification[1]	Country
B < 1	Ultra EP	Colombia
B ≅ 1	Neutrality/EP	S. Korea (1968, 1978) Singapore
1 < *B* < 2	Mild–moderate IS	Taiwan, Israel, Mauritius, Uganda
B > 2	Strong IS	Argentina, Trinidad, Barbados

Note:
1. EP = Export promotion. IS = Import substitution.

Table 5.3 Alternative Classification of Trade Strategies-based Pattern of Absolute Incentives

Pattern of Incentives	Classification[1]	Country
$e_X > 0$, $e_M > 0$	PEP	South Korea (1978), Colombia, Barbados
$e_X > 0$, $e_M < 0$	EP	
e_X, $e_M \cong 0$	Free trade	South Korea (1968) Singapore
$e_X < 0$, $e_M < 0$	DIP	
$e_X < 0$, $e_M > 0$	IS	Trinidad, Mauritius, Uganda, Argentina, Taiwan

Note:
1. PEP = Protected export promotion.
   EP = Export promotion.
   DIP = *De facto* import promotion.
   IS = Import substitution.

feasible that the relative prices of *each* tradeable can be differentially or uniformally affected by uniform trade policy interventions. Thus, for example, if we assume that there is a single non-tradeable (*N*) good/sector and that the price of non-tradeables (P_N) is exogenously fixed, then mixed policies of EP and IS can raise the incentive to produce both exportables and importables relative non-tradeables. It is not, however, very satisfactory to assume that the price of non-tradeables will be invariant with respect to trade policy interventions and changes in the domestic prices of tradeables. In order to investigate the robustness of the alternative classifications of trade strategy we need to be able to model P_N endogenously. The existence of non-tradeables is not by itself a sufficient condition for adopting the alternative classification proposed by Liang.

III MODELLING TRADE POLICY AND THE PRICE OF NON-TRADEABLES

Consider a small, open economy producing one non-tradeable good (*N*) and two composite tradeable goods, an exportable *X* and an importable *M*. Consumption preferences are represented by an aggregate utility function defined over the consumption levels of the three goods. The trade expenditure function *E*(.) can be used to represent the equilibrium of the economy.

$$E(P_N, P_X, P_M, U, v) = C(P_N, P_X, P_M, U) - R(P_N, P_X, P_M, v) \qquad (1)$$

where P_N, P_X, P_M represent the prices of the three goods, *U* represents utility and *v* represents the supply of factors of production, assumed fixed. The trade expenditure function represents the excess of home consumption represented by the conventional expenditure function *C*(.), over revenue of the home country from production, represented by the revenue function *R*(.) (Dixit and Norman, 1980).

As the country is a small, open economy, we assume that the world prices of the exportable and importable, represented by P_X^* and P_M^* respectively, are given. However trade policy measures pursued by the home country will influence the domestic price of tradeable goods. We consider the case in which imports are subject to a tariff at an *ad valorem* rate *t*, while exports are subsidised at an *ad valorem* rate *s*.[2] In this case, following standard practice (Edwards and van Wijnbergen, 1987; Connolly and Devereux, 1992), the equilibrium conditions are as follows:

$$E_N(P_N, P_X, P_M, U, v) = 0 \tag{2}$$

$$E(P_N, P_X, P_M, U, v) - tP_M^*E_M - sP_X^*E_X = 0 \tag{3}$$

$$P_X = P_X^*(1 + s) \tag{4}$$

$$P_M = P_M^*(1 + t) \tag{5}$$

where E_i = partial derivative of the trade-expenditure function with respect to P_i. The first condition is the market-clearing condition for non-tradeables, whereas the second condition is the balance of payments constraint at world prices or, equivalently, the requirement that aggregate income equals aggregate expenditure. The third and fourth conditions simply state the relationship between the domestic and world (border) prices of tradeable goods.

Totally differentiating the equilibrium conditions, we obtain:

$$E_{NN}dP_N + E_{NX}dP_X + E_{NM}dP_M + E_{NU}dU + E_V dv = 0 \tag{6}$$

$$\alpha_N dP_N + \alpha_X dP_X + \alpha_M dP_M + (\alpha_U - E_U)dU + (\alpha_v - E_v)dv \\ + E_X dP_X^* + E_M dP_M^* = 0 \tag{7}$$

$$dP_X = (1 + s)dP_X^* + P_X^* ds \tag{8}$$

$$dP_M = (1 + t)dP_M^* + P_M^* dt \tag{9}$$

where $\alpha_i = sP_X^*E_{Xi} + tP_M^*E_{Mi}$ and $i = N, X, M, U, V$ (α_i is the response of revenue from trade taxes to a change in the variable i and E_{ij} is the second derivative of the trade expenditure function with respect to i and j).

In line with the assumption of a small, open economy we consider henceforth that world prices are fixed: $dP_M^* = dP_X^* = 0$. This is a system of four equations for the responses of four endogenous variables (the three domestic prices, and income (as $E_U dU = dy$)) in terms of changes in exogenous variables. In line with our assumption of fixed factor supplies, we henceforth assume that $dv = 0$.

Equations (8) and (9) directly give the change in the domestic price of the exportable and importable respectively in terms of purely exogenous variables. The changes in the price of the non-tradeable good and in income may be obtained by simultaneously solving (6) and (7), which given the above assumptions may be represented as:

$$\begin{pmatrix} dP_N \\ dy \end{pmatrix} = A^{-1} \begin{pmatrix} -E_{NM} \\ -\alpha_M \end{pmatrix} dP_M + A^{-1} \begin{pmatrix} -E_{NX} \\ -\alpha_X \end{pmatrix} dP_X \tag{10}$$

$$\text{where } A = \begin{pmatrix} E_{NN} & \frac{E_{NU}}{E_U} \\ \alpha_N & \frac{\alpha_U - E_U}{E_U} \end{pmatrix}$$

Given (10) the proportionate change in the price of the non-tradeable good can be written as:

$$\frac{dP_N}{P_N} = \frac{1}{P_N \det(A)} \left\{ \left[-\left(\frac{\alpha_U - E_U}{E_U} \right) E_{NM} + \alpha_M \frac{E_{NU}}{E_U} \right] dP_M \right.$$
$$\left. + \left[-\left(\frac{\alpha_U - E_U}{E_U} \right) E_{NX} + \alpha_X \frac{E_{NU}}{E_U} \right] dP_X \right\} \tag{11}$$

Or alternatively normalising by setting $P_M^* = P_X^* = 1$ in the initial equilibrium and rearranging:[3]

$$\frac{dP_N}{P_N} = \left[\left(\frac{-(\alpha_U - E_U)P_M E_{NM}}{\lambda} \right) + \left(\frac{\alpha_M P_M E_{NU}}{\lambda} \right) \right] \frac{dP_M}{P_M}$$
$$+ \left[\left(\frac{-(\alpha_U - E_U)P_X E_{NX}}{\lambda} \right) + \left(\frac{\alpha_X P_X E_{NU}}{\lambda} \right) \right] \frac{dP_X}{P_X} \tag{12}$$

$$\text{where}: \lambda = P_N E_U \det(A) = (\alpha_U - E_U) P_N E_{NN} - P_N \alpha_N E_{NU} \tag{13}$$

(A corresponding expression can be obtained from (10) for dy.)

Equation (12) may alternatively be written in terms of dt and ds by using the facts that

$$\frac{dP_M}{P_M} = \frac{P_M^*}{P_M} dt = \frac{dt}{1+t} \text{ and that } \frac{dP_X}{P_X} = \frac{P_X^*}{P_X} ds = \frac{ds}{1+s}$$

When analysing about an initial undistorted equilibrium ($t = s = 0$), the change in the prices of the importable and exportable goods will be simply the *ad valorem* tariff and subsidy rates respectively but in general this will not be the case.

The signs of the bracketed terms on the right-hand side of (12) cannot be determined in the general case; they depend among other things on whether the goods are substitutes or complements in net demand, on whether the goods are normal or inferior goods in consumption and on the degree of initial distortion (which is a major factor influencing the sign of $(\alpha_U - E_U)$). In the ensuing discussion we assume normal goods, substitutability rather than complementarity, and that the stability condition ($\lambda > 0$) is satisfied. The impact of trade policy interventions on the price of non-tradeables will depend, therefore, on the degree of uniformity of the policy interventions and the degree of initial distortion. If the initial policy distortion is not too large (i.e. $\alpha_U - E_U < 0$), then given the above assumptions we can attach unambiguous signs to each of the bracketed terms in (12). Specifically:

$$\frac{dP_N}{P_N} = (a_M + b_M) \frac{dP_M}{P_M} + (a_X + b_X) \frac{dP_X}{P_X} \tag{14}$$

where $a_i = -(\alpha_U - E_U) P_i E_{Ni}/\lambda$ and $b_i = \alpha_i P_i E_{NU}/\lambda$, $\quad i = M, X$

Given the above assumptions a_i will be unambiguously positive. The sign of b_i is indeterminate in general, but is likely to be negative if intervention is approximately uniform and own-price effects dominate cross-price effects. The a_i terms capture the substitution effect of changes in the prices of tradeables on non-tradeables prices; a higher tariff and/or subsidy draws resources out of the non-tradeables sector, diverts consumption towards non-tradeables and drives P_N up. The b_i terms capture the income effect. An increase in the distortionary cost of the trade policy interventions (i.e. a reduction in welfare or income) is likely to reduce expenditure on non-tradeables and tends, *ceteris paribus*, to exert a downward pressure on P_N.

Deviations from Undistorted General Equilibrium

If the economy is initially at balanced trade with free trade, then there are no income effects associated with the introduction of tariffs or subsidies (i.e. $b_i = 0$ in equation 14). Indeed the a_i terms reduce to indices of pure substitutability between tradeables ($i = X, M$) and non-tradeables, i.e.:

$$\frac{dP_N}{P_N} = a'_M \frac{dP_M}{P_M} + a'_X \frac{dP_X}{P_X} = a'_M dt + a'_M ds \qquad (15)$$

where $a'_i = -E_{Ni} / E_{NN}$, $i = X, M$. Since $E_{Ni} > 0$ (given substitutability) and $E_{NN} < 0$ then each $a'_i > 0$. As both traded goods are assumed to be substitutes for the non-tradeable good, then $a'_i < 1$. Further, the homogeneity characteristics of the trade expenditure function mean that $a'_M + a'_X = 1$.[4] Thus:

$$dt \gtrless \frac{dP_N}{P_N} \gtrless ds \text{ as } dt \gtrless ds$$

In other words, it is not possible in this pure substitution case to use uniform or non-uniform mixed intervention of tariffs and export subsidies to raise (or lower) the price of both tradeables relative to non-tradeables; the pro-tradeables or protected export promotion (PEP) strategy can not be achieved *ex post*.

Deviations from Distorted Equilibrium

When t and/or s are already different from zero, changes in P_X and P_M will give rise to income effects on P_N. If the initial distortion is not too large, then income will fall as a result of further intervention (i.e. $\alpha_U - E_U < 0$). The effect on the size of the coefficients on dt and ds in equation 13 is ambiguous. On the one hand, $a_i > a'_i$ (i.e. the substitution effect in the general case will be greater than the substitution effect in the undistorted equilibrium), but on the other hand, it is likely that $b_i < 0$, in which case $a_i + b_i \gtreqless a'_i$. This, as we shall see shortly will, however, only allow for pro-tradeable or protected export promotion in the specific case where b_i is sufficiently negative that $a_i + b_i < 0$ for $i = X$ or $i = M$. Otherwise, only IS or EP trade regime strategies are possible. To see this, note that the homogeneity properties of net demand function require that:

$$\sum P_i E_{Ni} = 0 \text{ and } \sum P_i \alpha_i = 0 \qquad (16)$$

$[i = X, M, N]$.

In which case $(a_M + b_M) + (a_X + b_X)$ equals unity, and the proportionate change in P_N is again a weighted average of the proportionate changes in P_M and P_X in the uniform or non-uniform case of mixed intervention. It is only possible to raise or lower the price of both exportables and importables relative to non-tradeables when either $(a_M + b_M) < 0$, or when $(a_X + b_X) < 0$, conditions which may only apply in a highly distorted economy.[5]

However, it should be noted that in the case of a highly distorted economy the income effect may be positive rather than negative, and the possibility of increasing the pro-tradeables bias through the use of a pure strategy disappears. Thus, while theoretically a pro-tradeables trade strategy may be possible in particular circumstances, in practice such an outcome may be considered highly unlikely.

IV 'TRUE' MEASURES OF TRADE STRATEGY

The preceding theoretical analysis has implications for the formulation of commercial policies and trade strategy in an *ex-ante* sense. For instance, the analysis has demonstrated that the equilibrium pattern of relative prices or incentives post-commercial policy intervention will depend on the nature or pattern (i.e. uniformity or not) of the policy interventions, on the extent of the policy-induced changes in non-tradeable goods prices and on the endogenous characteristics of the economic system. Apparent mixed policies of import-substitution and export promotion (uniform or otherwise) that raise the absolute price of tradeables do not necessarily alter the relative price of tradeables in general, or of specific types of tradeables in particular. By contrast, however, uniform intervention in the substitution-only case means that all prices rise uniformly and relative prices remain unaltered. A trade strategy may be described therefore as mixed in so far as instruments of import substitution and export promotion are employed, and a mixed outcome of promotion or protection for all tradeables may be intended. The actual or 'true' outcome may diverge however from what is intended, the outcome depending in part on factors outside the policy-maker's control.

Given that the effects of commercial policy interventions depend crucially on how the price of non-tradeables responds to these interventions, the measurement of the post-intervention structure of relative incentives (and *ex post* or 'true' classification of trade strategies) depends crucially therefore on being able to measure changes in relative not absolute (net or gross) prices. Net (effective) rates of protection are typically absolute measures of protection or subsidisation, adjusted for currency overvaluation which is measured on some purchasing power parity (PPP) basis. But it is the measurement of domestic relative prices, not relative international prices that is crucial to the measurement of trade strategy. As Connolly and Devereux (1992) show, non-uniform tariffs and export subsidies will increase the domestic price level relative to external prices, causing an appreciation of the purchasing power parity real exchange rate. Adjustment of the (gross effective) rates of subsidisation for this overvaluation reduces the measured rates of (net) protection for all tradeables, but does not necessarily make the net rate negative in absolute terms for either importables or exportables. But this is also consistent with a situation where $s < \hat{P}_N < t$. In which case the strategy would be better classified as import substitution.

Some Evidence on True Protection

The measurement of (*ex post*) trade strategy has been shown to require relative, not absolute, measures of incentives or protection. We can define the relative or true rates of protection (t^* and s^*) for each tradeable as follows:

$$t^* = \Delta\left(\frac{P_M}{P_N}\right) \tag{17a}$$

$$s^* = \Delta\left(\frac{P_X}{P_N}\right) \tag{17b}$$

The effects of commercial policy interventions depend upon the structure of (nominal) protection and the value of $w = a_M{}'$ (substitution only case) or $w = (a_M + b_M)$ (substitution and income effects case). We can see this formally from equations (18a) and (18b), which we obtained by substituting equation (15) into equations (17a) and (17b) and rearranging (assuming prices initially set to unity). Thus:

$$dt^* = \frac{(1 - w)(dt - ds)}{1 + wdt + (1 - w)ds} \tag{18a}$$

$$ds^* = \frac{w(ds - dt)}{1 + wdt + (1 - w)ds} \tag{18b}$$

With uniform intervention ($dt = ds$), $dP_N = dt = ds$ and dt^* and ds^* are zero. With non-uniform, mixed intervention ($dt > ds$ or $ds > dt$) true protection is always less than nominal protection if $0 < w < 1$. Indeed with non-uniform intervention dt^* and ds^* will have opposite signs for any positive value of w. In other words, the *ex post* or true strategy is always an IS or EP outcome.

Note also that true protection rates of both importables and exportables will tend to diverge from nominal protection rates if a pure nominal strategy is pursued. Where $dt > 0$ and $ds = 0$ for instance, then $0 < dt^* \gtreqless ds^*$ as $w \gtreqless 0$. In the substitution only case or where substitution effects dominate income effects (i.e. $w > 0$), the change in true protection rates for importables and exportables again are always in opposite directions. Thus, a true mixed strategy (pro- or anti-tradeables) can only be achieved by a pure nominal strategy where the income effect dominates the substitution effect. Thus, if $w < 0$ and $dt > 0$ and $ds = 0$ (i.e. an *ex ante* IS strategy), then we can show from equations (18a) and (18b) that it is *possible* for both dt^* and ds^* to be positive. The value of the parameter w is crucial, therefore, to the scope for achieving true mixed strategies.

Some Evidence on 'True' Strategies

Estimates of w are, in fact, to be found in the empirical literature on the incidence or shifting of protection. Researchers have used regression and cointegration techniques to estimate equation (14), using time-series data of price indices of importables, exportables and non-tradeables from domestic sources (see Greenaway and Milner (1993) for a discussion of the methodology). In Table 5.4 the estimated w coefficients for 21 countries are reported. Despite the variety of time-periods, data frequencies and types of economies involved, all the coefficients are positive and fall in the range that is consistent with the substitution-only or dominant substitution effects cases. Note also that in all but two cases the estimated coefficient is greater than 0.5 (with 75 per cent of reported estimates falling in the range 0.5–0.75). This implies, given the homogeneity requirement, that the responsiveness of P_N to trade policy interventions is greater in the case of IS measures than EP measures (i.e. $w > 1-w$ in equation 14). This is consistent with the likelihood that for the time-periods in question exports in many of the developing countries were natural resource-intensive and less likely to be substitutable in production or consumption.

Table 5.4 Estimated Incidence Parameters for a Sample of Countries

Country	Data Analysed	$\hat{w}$	Source
Argentina	1935–79 (A)	0.57	Sjaastad (1980b)
Australia	1950–80 (M)	0.71	Sjaastad and Clements (1981)
Barbados	1980–88 (M)	0.91	Milner (1994a)
Brazil	1950–78 (A)	0.70	Fendt (1981)
Cameroon	1976–87 (Q)	0.81	Milner (1990)
Chile	1959–71 (M)	0.55	Sjaastad and Clements (1981)
Colombia	1970–78 (M)	0.95	Garcia (1981)
El Salvador	1962–77 (Q)	0.69	Diaz (1980)
Ivory Coast	1960–84 (A)	0.68	Greenaway (1989)
S. Korea	1971–89 (Q)	0.44	Kim (1990)
Mauritius	1976–82 (M)	0.71	Greenaway and Milner (1986)
Madagascar	1974–84 (M)	0.69	Milner (1992)
New Zealand	1977–88 (M)	0.78	Wang and Brooks (1989)
Nigeria	1960–82 (A)	0.55	Oyejide (1986)
Panama	1966–81 (A)	0.45	Sjaastad (1984)
Peru	1966–83 (M)	0.74	Valdes and Leon (1987)
Philippines	1950–79 (A)	0.86	Bautista (1987)
Trinidad	1987–91 (M)	0.51	Milner (1993)
Uganda	1989–93 (M)	0.66	Maxwell Stamp (1993)
Uruguay	1966–79 (M)	0.53	Sjaastad (1980c)
Zaire	1970–82 (A)	0.52	Tshibaka (1986)

A = Annual   Q = Quarterly   M = Monthly

Given this evidence on the pattern of substitutability found in developing countries and the earlier arguments about the difficulty of producing a 'true' or *ex post* pro- or anti-tradeables bias in the trade regime through pure or mixed (*ex-ante*) strategies, we are in a position to return to the alternative interpretation of the evidence in Table 5.1 on patterns of effective protection in a number of selected countries. Clearly (gross or net) effective rates of protection estimated in the traditional partial equilibrium manner are potentially misleading, since they suggest the possibility of simultaneous promotion of importables and exportables (i.e. $\bar{e}_M > 0$ and $\bar{e}_X > 0$) and abstract from general equilibrium considerations. In the absence of more sophisticated general equilibrium estimation procedures (derived, for example, from a CGE model), it is possible to employ a relative measure of effective protection – namely, a true effective rate of protection.

We define the true effective rate of protection as:

$$e_i^* = \Delta \left(\frac{P_i'}{P_N} \right) \qquad (19)$$

where P_i' = net price of tradeable $i(i = M$ or $X)$.

If we set prices initially equal to unity, then (19) can be rewritten as:

$$e_i^* = \frac{e_i - dP_N}{1 + dP_N} \qquad (20)$$

where e_i = effective rate of protection of $i(i = M$ or $X)$.

Using equation (20), the estimates of w from Table 5.4 and the nominal rates of protection (t and s) used to estimate the effective rates of protection reported in Table 5.1, we can recalculate true effective rates of protection for importables and exportables for our sample of countries. We also report true nominal rates of protection based on (gross) nominal rates of protection. These are reported in Table 5.5.

Table 5.5   Average True Rates of Protection for Importables and Exportables for a Selection of Countries[1]

| | True Rates of Protection | | | |
| | Nominal[2] | | Effective[3] | |
	t^*	s^*	e_M^*	s_x^*
Barbados	3	−32	119	−25
Trinidad	17	−18	145	−24
Mauritius	7	−17	49	−19
Uganda	7	−14	39	−27
South Korea (1968)	5	−4	−13	−10
Israel	8	−17	14	−16
Argentina	21	−28	30	−57
Singapore	2	−5	52	−2
Taiwan	5	−11	5	−18
Colombia	0	−5	−1	19

Notes:
1. Same as Table 5.1, except South Korea (1978) is excluded because information on nominal protection is not available.
2. Gross rates without adjustment for currency overvaluation.
3. Net rates with adjustment for currency overvaluation.

The true nominal rates give a consistent picture of positive true tariffs and negative true export subsidies across the sample of countries. Interestingly, the levels of true protection of importables are quite low in absolute terms, while the disprotection of exportables tends to be larger in absolute terms. This is consistent with the theoretical expectation in general of opposite signs of the true protection of importables and exportables. On this evidence, none of these countries can be represented as pursuing a 'true' PEP strategy or ultra-EP strategy. There are some countries with approximate neutrality (South Korea, Singapore and Colombia), with the remainder pursuing an IS strategy in true terms. Of particular interest is the 'true' position of Barbados. Rather than viewing Barbados as pursuing a PEP strategy, its exporters are subject to the largest true tax in this set of countries as a result of its IS policies.

A similar, general pattern emerges from the evidence on true effective rates of protection, though there are some important differences in the case of South Korea (1978) and Colombia. In the latter case the signs on the true nominal and effective rates are reversed. The change appears to be due to the adjustment for exchange rate realignment, since both net nominal rates are positive and $s > t$. The same argument applies also to South Korea. The true nominal protection rates are qualitatively similar for Korea, however, irrespective of whether gross or net rates of nominal protection are employed. The problem arises in the use of effective protection or net price evidence, combined with evidence on gross prices. This argues for attaching greater weight on true (nominal) evidence when classifying trade strategies.

V   CONCLUSIONS

Unlike the standard two-sector trade model, a three-sector model which includes non-tradeables appears to offer the possibility of pursuing mixed strategies of import-substitution and export promotion which result in an unambiguous pro-tradeables bias ('protected export promotion'). Partial equilibrium estimates of positive net effective protection in both import-substitution and export activities may also be interpreted as giving support for this classification of trade strategy. This paper has argued that both the theoretical and empirical basis of this interpretation are subject to important deficiencies. In classifying trade strategies in principle we need to distinguish clearly between the *ex ante* motivation of policy (i.e. the desire to simultaneously pursue EP and IS policies) and the *ex post* outcome in terms of changes in the structure of domestic relative prices. In models of endogenously determined prices of non-tradeables mixed IS/EP policies cannot lead to the outcome of 'protected export promotion' for a standard model for a wide range of substitution and income effects. Crucial, therefore, to the measurement of the revealed trade strategy is the measurement of the trade policy response of non-tradeable goods prices and of relative or 'true', not absolute, measures of protection. In this regard the use of partial equilibrium measures of effective protection (gross or net) may produce misleading evidence. Such measures suggest that countries like Barbados are achieving overall 'protected export promotion' with positive net rates of protection in both import-substitution and export activities. Re-estimation of true protection measures reveals very different patterns of relative incentives. This forcibly demonstrates that the outcome of trade policy interventions is influenced by characteristics of the economy that are not controllable by policy-makers. It also demonstrates that simple representations may be extremely robust.

ACKNOWLEDGEMENT

This is a revised version of a paper presented at a conference on Trade and Development in honour of Professor Jagdish Bhagwati, at the University of Lancaster, December 1994. The authors are grateful for the comments of the conference participants on the earlier draft, and in particular for helpful suggestions from Jagdish Bhagwati, David Greenaway, Sajal Lahari and John Whalley.

NOTES

1. South Korea (1968) might be included as an example of a DIP strategy, with $e_X < 0$ and $e_M < 0$. We follow Liang's interpretation however, given the small absolute rates involved.
2. The case of quantitative import restrictions is considered in the Appendix (pp. 78–80).
3. Note that there is no loss of generality in setting the world prices to unity. The analysis which follows applies irrespective of the initial world prices.
4. Note that this result does not depend upon the assumptions relating to substitutability, but is a general feature of the model as set out in equation (14).
5. Note that in the present static model intervention is viewed as permanent. In a dynamic setting temporary, mixed interventions might bring about a pro-tradeables bias (see Chen and Devereux, 1994).

REFERENCES

Balassa, B. et al. (1982), *Development Strategies in Semi-Industrialised Countries* (Washington: World Bank).

Bautista, R.M. (1987), *Production Incentives in Philippine Agriculture: Effects of Trade and Exchange Rate Policies*, Research Report 59 (Washington, DC: International Food Policy Research Institute).

Bhagwati, J.N. (1968), *The Theory and Practice of Commercial Policy*, Princeton University, Frank D. Graham Memorial Lecture.

————— (1988), 'Export Promoting Trade Strategy: Issues and Evidence', *World Bank Research Observer*, vol. 3, pp. 22–58.

————— (1990), 'Export-promoting Trade Strategy: Issues and Evidence', in C.R. Milner, ed., *Export Promotion Strategies: Theory and Evidence from Developing Countries* (New York: New York University Press).

Chen, L.L. and Devereux, J. (1994), 'Protection, Export Promotion and Development', *Journal of Development Economics*, vol. 43, pp. 387–95.

Clague, C. and Greenaway, D. (1994), 'Incidence Theory, Specific Factors and the Augmented Heckscher–Ohlin Model', *Economic Record*, vol. 70, pp. 36–43.

Connolly, M. and Devereux, J. (1992), 'Commercial Policy, the Terms of Trade and Real Exchange Rates', *Oxford Economic Papers*, vol. 44, pp. 507–12.

Dabee, B. and Milner, C.R. (1995), 'Evaluating Trade Liberalisation in Mauritius', mimeo, University of Nottingham.

Diaz, D.B. (1980), *The Effects of Commercial Policy in El Salvador: An Estimate of The True Tariff and True Subsidy*, PhD thesis (Geneva: Institute Universitaire des Hautes Etudes Internationales).

Dixit, A.K. and Norman, V. (1980), *Theory of International Trade* (Cambridge: Cambridge University Press).

Dornbusch, R. (1974), 'Tariffs and Nontraded Goods', *Journal of International Economics*, vol. 4, pp. 177–85.

Edwards, S. and van Wijnbergen, S. (1987), Tariffs, the Real Exchange Rate and the Terms of Trade: On Two Popular Propositions in International Trade, *Oxford Economic Papers*, vol. 39, pp. 458–64.

Fendt, R. (1981), 'Brazilian Trade Liberalization: A Reassessment', in L.A. Sjaastad, ed., *The Free Trade Movement in Latin America* (London: Macmillan Press for the Trade Policy Research Centre).

Garcia, J.G. (1981), *The Effects of Exchange Rates and Commercial Policy on Agricultural Incentives in Colombia: 1953–1978*, Research Report 24 (Washington DC: International Food Policy Research Institute).

Greenaway, D. (1989), 'Commercial Policy and Policy Conflict: An Evaluation of the Incidence of Protection in a Non-industrialised Economy', *Manchester School*, vol. 57, pp. 125–41.

Greenaway, D. and Milner, C.R. (1986), 'Estimating the Shifting of Protection across Sectors: An Application to Mauritius', *Industry and Development*, vol. 16, pp. 1–23.

————— (1987), 'True Protection Concepts and their Use in Evaluating Commercial Policy in Developing Countries', *Journal of Development Studies*, vol. 23, pp. 200–19.

————— (1988), 'Intra-industry Trade and the Shifting of Protection across Sectors', *European Economic Review*, vol. 32, pp. 927–45.

78   *Trade and Development*

Greenaway, D. and Nam, C.H. (1988), 'Industrialisation and Macroeconomic Performance in Developing Countries, under Alternative Liberalisation Scenarios', *Kyklos*, vol. 41, pp. 419–45.

Kim, J.D. (1991), *The Incidence of Protection: The Case of Korea*, mimeo (The University of Chicago).

Liang, N. (1992), 'Beyond Import Substitution and Export Promotion: A New Typology of Trade Strategies', *Journal of Development Studies*, vol. 28, pp. 447–72.

Maxwell Stamp (1993), *Study of the Effectiveness of Policies, Facilities and Incentives for Investment Promotion in Uganda* (London: Maxwell Stamp).

Milner, C.R. (1990), 'Identifying and Quantifying Anti-Export Bias: The Case of Cameroon', *Weltwirtschaftliches Archiv*, vol. 126, no. 1, pp. 142–55.

————— (1994a), 'Trade Strategy and Revealed Trade Bias: An Evaluation for a Small Industrializing Economy', *World Development*, vol. 22, pp. 587–99.

————— (1994b), 'The Impact of Southern Regional Trading Arrangements on Trade Regime Bias: Some Evidence for CARICOM', *Journal of Economic Integration*, vol. 9, pp. 327–45.

Oyejide, T.A. (1986), *The Effects of Trade and Exchange Rate Policies on Agriculture in Nigeria*, Research Report 55 (Washington DC: International Food Policy Research Institute).

Singer, H.W. (1988), 'The World Development Report 1987 on the Blessings of Outward Orientation: A Necessary Correction', *Journal of Development Studies*, vol. 24, pp. 232–6.

Sjaastad, L. (1980a), 'Commercial Policy, "True" Tariffs and Relative Prices', in J. Black and B. Hindley, eds, *Current Issues in Commercial Policy and Diplomacy* (London: Macmillan).

————— (1980b), *Commercial Policy Reform in Argentina: Implications and Consequences*, mimeo (CEMA).

————— (1980c), *The Incidence of a Uniform Tariff in Uruguay*, mimeo (The University of Chicago).

————— (1984), 'Commercial Policy for Panama in the 1980s', in M.J. Boskin, ed., *Modern Developments in Public Finance: Essays in Honor of Arnold Harberger* (Oxford: Basil Blackwell).

Sjaastad, L. and Clements, K. (1981), 'The Incidence of Protection: Theory and Measurement', mimeo, University of Chicago.

Tshibaka, T.B. (1986), *The Effects of Trade and Exchange Rate Policies on Agriculture in Zaire*, Research Report 56 (Washington DC: International Food Policy Research Institute).

World Bank (1987), *World Development Report, 1987* (Washington, DC).

APPENDIX

QUANTITATIVE RESTRICTIONS ON IMPORTS AND THE PRICE OF NON-TRADEABLES

Here we assume that there are no trade taxes, but that the quantity of imports of the importable good is controlled by quantitative restrictions at the level $\overline{M}$. In this case the equilibrium can be represented as follows:

$$E_N(P_N, P_X, P_M, U, v) = 0 \qquad \text{(A1)}$$

$$E(P_N, P_X, P_M, U, v) = 0 \qquad \text{(A2)}$$

$$E_M(P_N, P_X, P_M, U, v) = \overline{M} \qquad \text{(A3)}$$

$$P_X = P_X{}^* \qquad \text{(A4)}$$

As before, equation (A1) represents the market clearing condition for non-tradeable goods and equation (A2) the balance of payments constraint. Equation (A3) states that imports of the importable good are subject to a binding quantitative restriction set at level $\overline{M}$. Equation (A4) simply states that as there are no export subsidies the domestic price of the exportable good must equal the world price (in local currency).

Totally differentiating the equilibrium conditions, we obtain:

$$E_{NN}dP_N + E_{NX}dP_X + E_{NM}dP_M + E_{NU}dU + E_{NV}dv = 0 \qquad \text{(A5)}$$

$$E_{NN}dP_N + E_{NX}dP_x + E_{NM}dP_M + E_{NU}dU + E_{NV}dv = 0 \qquad \text{(A6)}$$

$$E_{MN}dP_N + E_{Mx}dP_X + E_{MM}dP_M + E_{MU}dU + E_{MV}dv = d\overline{M} \qquad \text{(A7)}$$

$$dP_X = dP_X{}^* \qquad \text{(A8)}$$

Again, this system of equations solves for the four endogenous variables, the three prices and income/welfare, in terms of the changes in the exogenous variables. The domestic price of the exportable good is trivially determined by (A8) and will remain constant when the world price remains constant, as assumed here. Equations (A5)–(A7) solve simultaneously for the changes in income, the price of the non-tradeable and the price of importables.

Again assuming factors to be in fixed supply and world prices fixed, the solution may be represented as follows:

$$\begin{pmatrix} dP_N \\ dP_M \\ dy \end{pmatrix} = B^{-1} \begin{pmatrix} 0 \\ 0 \\ 1 \end{pmatrix} d\overline{M} \qquad \text{(A9)}$$

$$\text{where } B = \begin{pmatrix} E_{NN} & E_{NM} & \dfrac{E_{NU}}{E_U} \\ E_N & E_M & 1 \\ E_{MN} & E_{MM} & \dfrac{E_{MU}}{E_U} \end{pmatrix}$$

From which it follows that:

$$\begin{pmatrix} dP_N \\ dP_M \\ dy \end{pmatrix} = \frac{1}{\det(B)} \begin{pmatrix} E_{NM} - \dfrac{E_M E_{NU}}{E_U} \\ -E_{NU} \\ E_{NN} E_M \end{pmatrix} d\overline{M} \qquad \text{(A10)}$$

where $\quad \det(B) = \dfrac{E_M}{E_U}(E_{NN}E_{MU} - E_{MN}E_{NU}) - (E_{NN}E_{MM} - E_{MN}E_{MN})$

Making the assumptions that:

1. the importable and non-tradeable goods are normal goods in consumption; and
2. the importable and non-tradeable goods are substitutes in net demand;

then, given the concavity of the expenditure function $E(.)$, it follows that $\det(B) < 0$. From this it follows that a relaxation of the quantitative restriction necessarily has the following effects. Income/welfare unambiguously rises ($dy > 0$), the price of the importable good unambiguously falls, whereas the price of the non-tradeable good may rise or fall depending on whether $E_{NM} < E_M E_{NU} / E_U$ or $E_{NM} > E_M E_{NU} / E_U$, respectively. The ambiguity in the direction of change in the price of the non-tradeable good arises from the fact that there are substitution and income effects operating in opposite directions. The increase in income associated with the relaxation of the ratio tends to drive up the price of the non-tradeable good, whereas the fall in the price of the importable good will exert downward pressure on the price of the non-tradeable, given that these are substitutes. The overall outcome obviously depends on the balance of these two effects. A tightening of the quantitative restrictions, which represents a move to increased protection, will have the reverse effects.

In general, it is not possible to determine unambiguously the direction of change in the price of the non-tradeable good relative to the importable good. It is conceivable, however, that in this case tightening protection ($d\overline{M} < 0$) can increase the price of *both* tradeable goods relative to the non-tradeable good, but this will only happen if the income effect on the price of the non-tradeable good exceeds the substitution effect. This is analogous to the case considered in section III where the change in the price of only one of the tradeable goods can drive down the price of the non-tradeable good if the relevant coefficient $a_i + b_i$ in equation 14 is negative. Similarly a relaxation of the ratio can bring about a situation in which the price of the non-tradeable good rises relative to the prices of both tradeable goods.

If one or other of the assumptions 1 and 2 above do not hold then in many cases it is not possible to determine unambiguously the sign of $\det(B)$ and so determine the direction of response of endogenous variables to a change in $\overline{M}$.

Finally, notice that in this case, where the export subsidy is zero, the characteristics of the exportable good do not affect the direction and magnitude of change in the endogenous variables.

6 Trade Liberalisation and Economic Development: The Asian Experience – Turkey, Malaysia and India

Subrata Ghatak and Utku Utkulu

I INTRODUCTION

This paper examines, theoretically and empirically, the impact of trade policy on the long-run output growth rate in the context of the new endogenous growth model. In section II, we describe the old and the new views of the relationships between trade and economic growth. Section III reviews the different ways to measure trade liberalisation. Section IV provides the trade liberalisation experiences of Turkey, Malaysia and India since the 1950s which largely followed different strategies (e.g. inward-looking import-substitution industrialisation (ISI) policies via exchange rate distortions and other protectionist measures in the case of India and Turkey,[1] and an open, export-led growth (ELG) strategy as in the case of Malaysia[2]) to promote physical and human capital accumulation and economic growth. Section IV sets out the cointegration and error-correction techniques to analyse the long-run relationship between an index of exchange rate distortions/trade liberalisation and economic growth of Turkey, Malaysia and India. The data and empirical results are described in section V. The final section draws some conclusions.

The Old View of Trade and Economic Growth

In the traditional analysis, exports (x) are usually determined by domestic price at time t (P_{dt}), foreign price (P_{ft}), or some other measure of competitiveness like the purchasing power parity (PPP) times the nominal exchange rates and foreign demand (usually proxied by foreign income (Y_f). Thus we can write:

$$X_t = P_{dt}^n P_{f_1}^\delta Y_f^\varepsilon \qquad (1)$$

81

If we take the proportional growth rates of variables in equation (1), we have equation (2), where lower case letters stand for the growth rates:

$$x_t = \eta(p_{dt}) + \delta(p_{ft}) + \varepsilon(y_{ft}) \tag{2}$$

Assume now that P_{dt} is endogenous we have:

$$P_{dt} = \left(\frac{W}{R}\right)_t (M_t) \tag{3}$$

where M_t is 1+ percentage markup on costs, R_t is the average productivity of labour and W_t is money wages. Once again, allowing lower case letters to stand for the rates of change of the variables and assuming the labour productivity growth a function of output growth (the so-called Verdoorn's law) from (3) we have equations (4) and (5):

$$p_{dt} = w_t - r_t + m_t \tag{4}$$
$$r_t = r_{at} + \mu(g_t) \tag{5}$$

where $\mu > 0$

r_{at} = rate of autonomous productivity growth and

g_t = output growth rate

In equation (5), μ captures the Verdoorn's law. Note that this equation also displays the link between exports and growth via productivity growth and prices. A rapid expansion of exports entails a fast growth rate of output, and a quick growth rate of output also implies a rapid growth rate of exports as goods are sold at more competitive prices due to productivity growth. Collecting terms from (5), (4), (2) and (1) and postulating:

$$g_t = \gamma(x_t) \text{ we have :} \tag{6}$$
$$g_t = \frac{\gamma[n(w_t - r_{at} + m_t) + \delta(P_{f_t}) + \varepsilon(y_{f_t})]}{1 + \gamma\eta\mu} \tag{7}$$

Now as relative prices remain unchanged, equation (7) reduces to:

$$g_t = \gamma\varepsilon(y_{ft}) \tag{8}$$

For equilibrium in the balance of trade $(m = x)$, i.e. where m = growth rate of imports, and assuming $\gamma = 1$, we have:

$$g_t\pi = \varepsilon(y_{ft}) \tag{9}$$

where π = the income elasticity of the demand for imports.

Trade Liberalisation and Development 83

Hence:

$$\frac{g_t}{y_{ft}} = \frac{\varepsilon}{\pi} \ . \tag{10}$$

Thus the relative growth rates depend on the ratio of income elasticities of demand of a country's exports and imports (see, e.g. Thirlwall, 1994).

The New View of Trade and Economic Growth

We assume that consumers maximise utility as infinitely lived households, i.e.:

$$U = \int_0^\alpha u(c_t)L_t e^{-pt}dt \tag{11}$$

where c = consumption per head
p = constant rate of time preference $p > 0$
L = labour which grows at n rate
In steady state $p > n$

The instantaneous utility function is:

$$U(c_t) = \frac{c^{1-\theta}}{1-\theta} \qquad \text{for } \theta > 0 \tag{12}$$

where $-\theta$ = constant marginal utility.
There are no foreign assets and the real rate of return on assets (a) r. The budget constraint of the household is given by:

$$\dot{a} = ra + w - c - na \tag{13}$$

$$w = \text{real wage}$$

maximising (12) subject to (13) and to a given initial assets $a(0)$, the first order condition (FOC) for maximising the consumption growth rate is:

$$\frac{\dot{c}}{c} = (1/\theta)(r-p) \tag{14}$$

(See (18) below where r is substituted to obtain growth rate c).
Following Lee (1993), let the production function be given by the CES function:

$$Q = [\gamma_1(K^\alpha \cdot \hat{H}^{1-\alpha})^\mu + \gamma_2 M^\mu]^{1/\mu} \tag{15}$$
$$\mu < 1, \gamma_1 > 0, \gamma_2 > 0, 0 < \alpha < 1$$

where Q = total output
M = imported input

H = human capital
K = physical capital

$$\text{Let } \hat{H}_t = H_t e^{(x+n)t} x > 0 \tag{16}$$

x = rate of technological progress

Assume

$$\hat{q} = Q/\hat{H}, \ \hat{m} = M/\hat{H}; \ \hat{k} = K/\hat{H} \ \text{ and } \ Z = \hat{m}/\hat{k}^\alpha$$

The production function (5) simplifies to

$$\hat{q} = \hat{k}^\alpha h(Z), \quad h_Z > 0 \text{ and } h_{ZZ} < 0 \tag{17}$$

The FOC for profit-maximisation in a competitive economy is:

$$r_t = V - \delta = \alpha \hat{k}^{\alpha-1} / [(1-\varphi)h(Z)]^{1/\sigma} - \delta \tag{18}$$

$$P_t = (\varphi h(Z)Z^{-1})^{1/\sigma} \tag{19}$$

$$W_t = (q_t - \hat{k}_t V - P_t \hat{m}_t) e^{xt} \tag{20}$$

where $V = MP$ of capital
δ = rate of depreciation
P = relative price of foreign goods in terms of domestic goods
σ = elasticity of substitution
φ = imported input in total output under free trade, i.e $\varphi = r_2^\sigma$ and
$(1-\varphi) = \gamma_1^\sigma$

In equilibrium:

$$\bar{Z} = \bar{Z}(P) = (1-\varphi)^{1/(\sigma-1)} \varphi [P^{\sigma-1} - \varphi]^{\sigma/(1-\sigma)} \tag{21}$$

$$h(\bar{Z}) = (1-\varphi)^{1/(\sigma-1)} [1 - P^{1-\sigma} \varphi]^{\sigma/1-\sigma} \tag{22}$$

The resource constraint is given after substituting (18)–(22) into (13):

$$\dot{\hat{k}} = \hat{k}^\alpha (1 - P^{1-\sigma} \varphi) h(\bar{Z}) - \hat{c} - (x + n + \delta)\hat{k} \tag{23}$$

where $\dot{\hat{c}} = ce^{-et}$ and $k(0)$ is given.
Substituting (18) into (14) we get:

$$\dot{\hat{c}}/\hat{c} = (1+\theta)\{\alpha \hat{k}^{\alpha-1} [(1-\varphi)h(\bar{Z})]^{1/\sigma} - \delta - P - \theta x\} \tag{24}$$

Equations (23) and (24) are the transversality conditions governing the growth path of effective capital stock and consumption per head. In the steady state, consumption, investment capital, output, etc. grow at an exogenously given rate of growth of technical progress, x.

With free trade $P_t = 1$ and

$$\bar{Z} = (1 - \varphi)^{-1}\varphi$$

$h(\bar{Z}) = (1 - \varphi)^{-1}$ and rewriting (23) and (24) as

$$\dot{k} = \hat{k}^\alpha - c - (x + n + \delta)k \qquad (23')$$

$$\dot{c}/\hat{c} = 1/\theta(\alpha k^{\alpha-1} - \delta - P - \theta x) \qquad (24')$$

In free trade steady state:

$$\hat{k}^* = [\alpha(\delta + p + \theta x)^{-1}]^{1/(1-\alpha)}$$

$$\hat{y}^* = \hat{k}^{*\alpha} = [\alpha(\delta + p + \theta x)^{-1}]^{\alpha/(1-\alpha)}$$

What really matters is free trade policy and not the import share itself (Lee, 1993).

However, if trade is distorted, the size of the import share matters and it has an effect on income.

If $M = 0$ under autarky

$$\hat{q}^* = 0 \qquad \sigma < 1$$

$$\hat{q}^* = (1 - \varphi)^{1/(\sigma-1)}\hat{k}^{\alpha*}, \text{ if } \qquad \sigma > 1$$

III   MEASURING TRADE LIBERALISATION[3]

The empirical definition of the concept of 'trade liberalisation' – a topic very dear to the heart of Jagdish Bhagwati – is difficult for both conceptual and practical reasons. Trade liberalisation may embody a number of different aspects of policy reform. Different aspects of trade liberalisation are likely to impinge on the interventionism, neutrality or openness of a reforming economy. Many countries may employ a wide array of interventions in the traded goods sector and non-tariff controls in the importables sector.

Openness Measures

Some simple trade/*GDP(Y)* ratios ($M/Y, X/Y$ or $X + M/Y$ where $X =$ exports and $M =$ imports) have often been employed as crude indicators of openness. Comparisons across countries can, of course, be particularly misleading. This has led authors such as Leamer (1988) and Edwards (1922) to take differences between 'predicted' and actual trade intensity ratios to proxy the extent of trade barriers. The predicted trade flows are derived from Leamer's Heckscher–Ohlin model (Leamer, 1984), estimated from cross-country data on factor endowments. The unavailability of time-series data on endowments for individual countries prevents the use of this type of approach in the present study. We fall back by necessity on crude trade intensity ratios,[4] export and import volumes, and assume that such openness measures are directly related over time to the degree of trade liberalisation initiated.

Trade and Other Distortion Measures[5]

The above problems and the desire to capture a wide range of price distortions have encouraged attempts at the constructing of composite indices of distortion (Agarwala, 1983). Subjectivity is required to rank the distortions from different sources. Agarwala's results are cross-country in nature and inappropriate for the present work. We therefore prefer to use here information on the black market exchange rate premium to capture the extent of distortions. The difference between the black market rate and official exchange rate, expressed as a proportion of the black market rate, seeks to capture the effects of trade interventions; the greater the difference the more distorted the economy, with a reducing difference being interpreted as increased liberalisation.

Measures of Bias or Trade Orientation

Early works on trade regimes (see Bhagwati, 1978; see also, Krueger, 1978; Bhagwati and Srinivasan, 1983) emphasise overall trade orientation, i.e. the degree to which the protective/incentives structure in a country is biased against exports. This is the tradition followed also by the recent World Bank comparative study on trade liberalisation (Michaely et al., 1991), in which trade liberalisation is viewed as a move towards neutrality. In that study the country authors were required to assess each liberalisation on a subjective scale of the degree of liberalisation. (The scale ranges from 1 to 20; 1 = the most restricted trade regime and 20 = free trade.) This subjectivity has been strongly criticised as a tool for comparing episodes of liberalisation across countries (for a critical review, see e.g. Edwards, 1993; Greenaway, 1993). Thus, we compare the subjective data and measures of the intensity of liberalisation by the country authors of the Turkish study (Baysan and Blitzer, 1991) with that indicated by the indices used in the present work.

Strictly, we require some measure of the ratio of the exchange rate facing importers to that effectively faced by exporters (as effected by official exchange rates and any taxes and subsidies on traded goods). There is also some cross-country information on the bias between non-tradeables and tradeables as a whole (Dollar, 1992; Milner, 1994). The present analysis focuses on openness and distortion indices.[6]

IV COUNTRY EXPERIENCES[7]

Turkey 1955–90

Baysan and Blitzer (1991) focus on development in Turkish foreign trade between 1950 and 1984. They identify four dates over this period when attempts to reduce trade and other distortions were initiated, namely the years 1950, 1958, 1970 and 1980. In the first three cases the authors conclude that the liberalisation was not sustained, and the reforms were not part of a planned programme to establish a liberal trade regime. Indeed, in none of these brief liberalising episodes do Baysan and Blitzer assess the reforms to have been sufficient to merit the status of an outward-oriented regime.[8] However, the 1980 liberalisation is regarded as the start of a more fundamental liberalisation: the index is set at 6 (within the restrictionist trade regime range) in 1980 and rises steadily to 14 (well into the 'outward-oriented' range) by 1985 (see Figure 6.1). The reforms started a near 50 per cent devaluation,

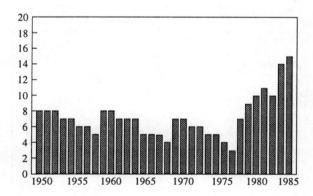

Figure 6.1   Trade Liberalisation Index for Turkey (1950–85)
Source: T. Baysan and C. Blitzer (1991), 'Turkey', in *Liberalizing Foreign Trade: New Zealand, Spain and Turkey: Vol. 6*, D. Papageorgiou, M. Michaely and A.M. Choksi (eds.), A Research Project of the World Bank (Cambridge, MA: Basil Blackwell), p. 289.

an increase in direct export incentives, a demand for stabilisation measures and a declared intention gradually to liberalise the economy (dismantling the quantity restriction (QR) system, capital account liberalisation, etc.). Besides the introduction of direct export incentives at the start of the episode, the Bank's view was that relatively little was achieved in terms of import policy until 1984. Some commodities were shifted from the more restrictive to the less restrictive list, and in 1981 some licensed imports were liberalised and the explicit import quota system was abolished. The system remained dominated by licensing, QRs and a protective tariff structure until the beginning of 1984, when about 60 per cent of previously licensed imports were liberalised. There were also changes in the administrative system; only goods explicitly listed as prohibited could not now be imported, where previously imports were banned if not explicitly listed as liberalised (see Aricanli and Rodrik, 1990; Togan, 1994; Uygur, 1993).

Ghatak et al. (1994a) show how the Baysan-Blitzer (BB) index of liberalisation for Turkey compares well with the indices of openness and distortion used in their work. There is a fairly close correlation (+0.7) between the two indices (compare Figures 6.1 and Figure 6.2). The liberalisations of 1950, 1958 and 1970, and the subsequent reversals, are captured. The timing and scale of the liberalisation episode starting in 1980 is also dramatically captured by their openness index. Besides, the exchange rate distortion index, i.e. ERDI (see Figure 6.3), does also seem to pick up these two steps in the post-1980 liberalisation; the black market

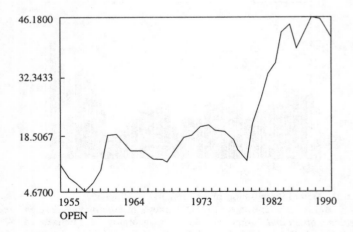

Figure 6.2   Openness Measure [(exports + imports)/RGDP per capita]: Turkey

premium falls sharply between 1979 and 1980 and falls further and sharply again between 1983 and 1984. Note also the re-emergence of the premium in the 1985–8 period, a reversal which is not as evident from the openness index. For the period as a whole (1955–90), however, their two indices correlate closely (–0.69); the distortion index also captures the 1958 and 1970 temporary liberalisations well. Other alternative measures for trade liberalisation such as real exports (see Figure 6.4) and real

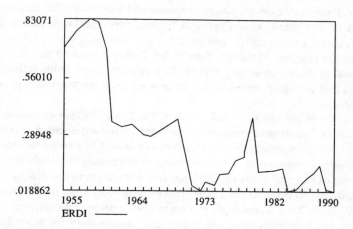

Figure 6.3   Exchange Rate Distortion Index [ERDI = (BM–OF)/BM]: Turkey

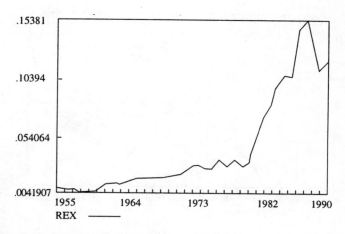

Figure 6.4   Real Exports (in US$): Turkey

imports (see Figure 6.5) also capture the transitory nature of the earlier liberalisation, but record a continuous liberalisation after 1980. Taken together, the consistency between various measures for trade liberalisation and between these and the subjective index provided by Baysan and Blitzer is reassuring. Since Ghatak et al. (1994a) also show that trade liberalisation in Turkey does affect economic growth, the indices appear to be sufficiently adequate measures of liberalisation to capture these growth effects. They examine the impact of trade liberalisation on the long-run economic development as measured by the real GDP in Turkey. Based on the 'endogenous' growth theory, they employ bivariate and multivariate cointegration analyses to test the long-run relationship among the relevant variables. Results for Turkey suggest a stable, joint, long-run relationship among real GDP, a measure of trade liberalisation, human and physical capital in accordance with the 'endogenous' growth theory.

With GNP per capita at US$1640 in 1990, the Turkish economy has achieved an impressive transformation from an inward-oriented economy based on import-substitution to an outward-oriented one based on export-promotion. Turkey is one of the few countries that managed to maintain high GNP growth in real terms (about 5 per cent per annum in the 1980s), after rescheduling its debts in the 1980s. Turkey's recovery from its debt during the 1980s has been increasingly subject to investigation in recent years. The country has frequently been referred to as a success story for other debtor

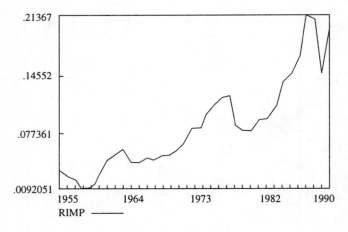

Figure 6.5   Real Imports (in US$): Turkey

Table 6.1   Basic Macroeconomic Indicators of Turkey, 1978–90

	Real GDP growth (%)	Exports of goods and services earnings* (US$ billion)	Rate of inflation (%)	Fiscal deficit as percentage of GNP
1978	−2.9	3.0	45.3	−3.0
1979	−2.6	3.5	58.7	−5.4
1980	−1.0	3.7	110.2	−3.5
1981	4.1	6.0	36.6	−1.7
1982	4.5	7.8	30.8	n.a.
1983	3.4	8.0	31.4	−4.2
1984	6.0	9.8	48.7	−10.0
1985	5.1	11.0	45.0	−7.4
1986	8.1	10.4	34.6	−3.2
1987	7.4	14.1	38.8	−4.0
1988	3.4	17.4	75.4	−3.9
1989	1.6	18.1	69.6	−4.4
1990	9.0	21.4	63.5	−4.0

Notes: *Excluding workers' remittances.
n.a. = not available.
Sources: State Planning Organisation (various years); OECD (various years); IMF (various years).

countries (see, e.g., Arslan and van Wijnbergen, 1993; Aricanli and Rodrik, 1990). Riedel (1991) in particular, citing the Turkish stabilisation programme implemented in the 1980s, argues that the outward-orientation of trade can boost export growth rates of LDCs. The most successful aspect of the Turkish experience has most probably been the considerable growth in exports during the 1980s (see Table 6.1 and Figure 6.4). Exports (FOB) rose from US$2.9 billion in 1980 to US$21.4 billion in 1990. The export composition changed in favour of manufactured goods and the export/import ratio improved (i.e. the share of manufactured goods in total export rose from 36 per cent in 1980 to 77 per cent in 1988). The export boom was mainly in manufactured goods. In addition to the leading subsectors like textiles and clothing, iron and steel, several other subsectors also enjoyed remarkable expansion. Along with the manufactured sectors, many service export industries such as tourism, transportation and contracting also increased their shares.

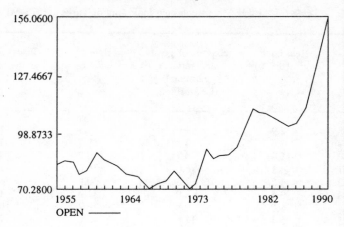

Figure 6.6   Openness Measure: Malaysia

Malaysia, 1957–90

Since Independence in 1957, Malaysia has followed a relatively open economy, generally driven by market forces (see Figure 6.6) During the colonial period, the Malaysian economy was mainly supported by the tin and rubber industries. Between 1964 and 1984, along with increasing

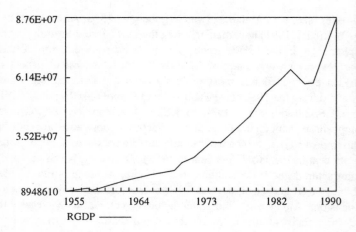

Figure 6.7   Real GDP (in US$): Malaysia

diversification, real GDP grew by an impressive 6–8 per cent p.a. (see Figure 6.7). Malaysia went into recession during 1985–6 as commodity prices collapsed. Since 1987, manufactured exports have registered strong growth. In 1991, real GDP grew by 8.6 per cent (see World Bank, 1992).

Although the Malaysian economy mainly relies on market forces, the government plays an important role in the economy, both as a producer and a regulator. Malaysia also encourages foreign investment in the export sector. To create a favourable macroeconomic environment, the government has so far followed a prudent fiscal policy, with a surplus in the operating account and a small deficit in the capital budget, funded mainly by bond sales. Recently, the government is also pre-paying foreign debt. National savings as a percentage of GDP reached 30 per cent in 1991. Similarly, the use of monetary policy has so far been targeted to achieve price stability by controlling monetary aggregates, the rate of interest, reserve requirements and sometimes, open market operations. Tight control of the public sector deficit as a proportion of GDP helped the creation of a macroeconomic environment within which commerce and industry flourished considerably (see World Bank, 1991).

As regards exchange rate policy, Malaysia has so far followed an open foreign exchange regime as reflected in low rates of distortion between the black market and the official exchange rate (see Figure 6.8).[9] The Central Bank intervenes in the market from time to time to smooth the fluctuations of the Malaysia Ringgit against, say, the US dollar. The long-run stability of the

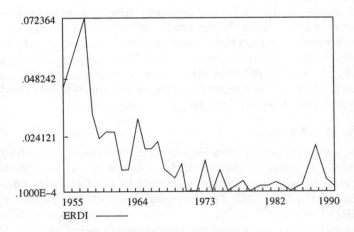

Figure 6.8   Exchange Rate Distortion Index: Malaysia

Ringgit in the international currency market reflects its real underlying value rather than direct interventions to stimulate exports. Foreign payments (remittances) are freely permitted. Most prices (except those for fuel, rice, sugar, flour, public utility goods and tobacco) are market-determined. In comparison with most LDCs Malaysia experienced a fairly stable rate of inflation. Between 1980–1991, manufacturing exports registered strong growth among all the export categories. Both the short- and long-term debt/ GDP ratio declined substantially between 1987 and 1991. Average tariffs account for only 15 per cent of prices on a trade-weighted basis. However, in the agricultural sector, there are important tariff and non-tariff barriers to encourage domestic production.

With a GNP per capita in 1990 of US$2320, Malaysia is on the verge of becoming an upper middle-income country. Three factors have been the main determinants in Malaysia's economic development: remarkable attention and priority have been given to agriculture, resulting in high productivity gains; manufacturing growth has been rapid, at about 12 per cent a year over the last two decades, initially led by domestically oriented subsectors, but more recently led by export-oriented industries; and the economy has been kept very open[10] (World Bank, 1992, p. 327). Exports reached 74 per cent of GNP in 1989, while imports, stimulated by high growth, have risen to 70 per cent of GNP. Besides, the increasing export orientation of the economy has been accompanied by a transition from an initial dependence on rubber and tin to a broadly diversified range of products, including palm oil, logs, petroleum and gas, cocoa and manufactured goods (see Table 6.2).

Ghatak et al. (1994b) comprehensively tested the export-led growth hypothesis for Malaysia for the period 1955–90, using cointegration and causality testing based on Hsiao's synthesis of the Granger test and Akaike's minimum final prediction error criterion. Their results provide a robust support for the export-led growth hypothesis; aggregate exports Granger-cause real GDP and *non-export* GDP. This relationship is found to be driven by manufactured exports rather than by traditional exports.

India 1950–90

India has a population of 850 million and one of the lowest per capita GNP in the world. In 1990 per capita was US$360. Nearly 70 per cent of the labour force is employed in agriculture, accounting for one-third of the GDP (US Department of State, 1992). From Independence in 1947 until the late 1970s, India's economic policies focused on self-sufficiency, import-substitution and state control of basic infrastructure and manufacturing industries. While this approach led to rapid expansion of India's industrial base, productivity

Table 6.2   Key Economic Indicators: Malaysia

	Growth Rate (% per year) (from constant price data)				
	1965–73	1973–80	1980–91	1990	1991
Gross domestic product	6.7	7.5	5.6	9.8	8.6
Agriculture	–	–	3.7	0.4	0.1
Industry	–	–	7.7	14.5	12.6
of which manufacturing	–	–	9.6	17.9	15.5
Services	–	–	4.6	9.9	8.3
Resource balance					
Exports of goods & NFS	6.4	8.7	11.5	18.3	16.2
Imports of goods & NFS	4.4	11.3	9.2	27.0	22.2
Total expenditure	5.8	8.6	4.5	15.5	13.3
Total consumption	4.9	8.3	4.6	12.1	10.6
Private consumption	4.4	8.1	5.0	13.6	10.1
General government	6.9	8.8	3.3	6.5	12.8
Gross domestic investment	9.1	9.7	4.3	23.6	18.9
Fixed investment	11.3	10.2	4.2	22.0	17.2

	Share of Gross Domestic Product (GDP) (from current price data)					
	1965	1973	1980	1989	1990	1991
Gross domestic product	100.0	100.0	100.0	100.0	100.0	100.0
Resource balance	4.3	5.5	2.5	5.0	–0.1	–5.5
Exports of goods & NFS	42.5	39.8	57.5	73.9	78.0	83.7
Imports of goods & NFS	38.2	34.3	55.0	68.9	78.1	89.1
Total expenditures	95.7	94.5	97.5	95.0	100.1	105.5
Total consumption	76.0	69.9	67.1	66.1	67.7	69.8
Gross domestic investment	19.7	25.5	30.4	28.8	32.3	35.7
Gross domestic saving	24.0	31.0	32.9	3.9	32.3	30.2

	Inflation Rate (% per year)				
	1965–73	1973–80	1980–91	1990	1991
Consumer prices	2.1	5.4	2.6	2.6	4.4
Implicit GDP deflator	1.2	7.2	1.7	2.9	3.2
Implicit expenditures deflator	2.3	5.7	2.1	3.0	4.2

Table 6.2 cont.

Growth Rate (% per year)	1965–73	1973–80	1980–91
Population	2.6	2.4	2.6
Labour force	3.2	3.7	2.8
Gross national income p.c.	2.8	6.5	2.4
Private consumption p.c.	1.8	5.6	2.3

Note that mid-1990 population and 1990 per capita GNP in Malaysia are 17.9 millions and 2320 US$ respectively.

Merchandise Exports	Volume Index (1987=100)					
	1980	1987	1988	1989	1990	1991
Fuel	62.4	100.0	110.4	118.4	122.8	128.1
Rubber	94.1	100.0	99.4	91.8	81.6	78.3
Timber	65.9	100.0	89.6	92.1	88.8	84.0
Food	52.4	100.0	101.8	121.4	138.7	134.7
Manufactures	34.3	100.0	127.0	161.1	194.8	–
Residual	91.4	100.0	106.1	118.7	148.4	–
TOTAL EXPORTS F.O.B.	56.5	100.0	113.2	135.9	157.8	180.3
Merchandise Imports						
Food	71.4	100.0	112.2	120.8	130.9	–
Fuel and energy	426.2	100.0	83.9	53.6	58.4	–
Other consumer goods	117.8	100.0	133.7	160.2	193.7	–
Other intermediate goods	83.7	100.0	117.3	143.8	161.8	–
Capital goods	99.6	100.0	131.2	195.0	235.2	–
TOTAL IMPORTS C.I.F.	95.9	100.0	122.8	158.0	184.1	230.7

Merchandise Exports	Value at Current Prices (US$ millions)					
	1980	1987	1988	1989	1990	1991
Fuel	3,082	2,496	2,335	2,910	3,932	3,706
Rubber	2,121	1,554	2,007	1,458	1,119	1,079
Timber	1,202	1,696	1,530	1,608	1,494	1,435
Food	1,155	1,301	1,729	1,728	1,626	1,797
Manufactures	3,601	8,110	10,253	13,510	17,429	20,576
Residual	1,780	2,792	3,247	3,824	3,356	5,672
TOTAL EXPORTS F.O.B.	12,941	17,949	21,101	25,038	28,956	34,264
Merchandise Imports						
Food	1,225	1,253	1,545	1,702	1,694	1,867
Fuel and energy	2,116	1,455	1,579	1,995	2,366	2,561
Other consumer goods	552	983	1,381	1,103	1,666	1,958
Capital goods	4,183	5,715	7,392	10,772	14,734	19,595
TOTAL IMPORTS C.I.F.	10,773	12,674	16,532	22,467	29,251	36,680

growth was repressed by lack of foreign and domestic competition. During this period, GNP growth rates seldom exceeded 3.5 per cent.

A consensus began to build in the late 1970s, and especially after 1984, that India would have to liberalise its economy to reduce poverty rapidly, create adequate resources for social programmes and modernise its infrastructure and manufacturing sector (World Bank, 1992, p. 262). In the late 1980s, especially, successive governments relaxed some restrictions on trade and investment, while at the same time boosting domestic demand through debt-financed deficit spending. India's private sector reacted well to the opportunities opened up under the new policies. GDP growth accelerated to over 5 per cent during the 1980s and there was a marked increase in exports of manufactures (see World Bank, 1991). Various measures of trade liberalisation confirm the increasing openness of the Indian economy, especially, in the second half of the 1980s (see Figures 6.9–6.12).

Nevertheless, macroeconomic imbalances became a serious problem. The budget deficit of the government rose steadily from 6.4 per cent of GDP in fiscal 1981 to over 9 per cent in fiscal 1991, while the current account deficit rose from 1.7 per cent to 3 per cent of GDP. In 1991, the government's domestic debt had risen to 56 per cent of GDP. Besides, India's external debt rose from US$20 billion in 1981 to US$70 billion in 1991, while the debt service ratio increased from 10 per cent to 29 per cent. The government that came to power in June 1991 inherited an economy in crisis. However, in less than a year, the new government had overcome the immediate balance of

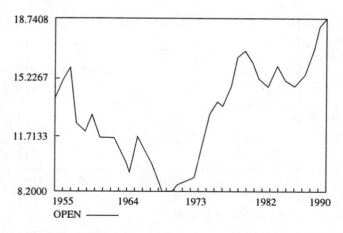

Figure 6.9   Openness Measure [(exports + imports)/RGDP percap.]: India

payments problems, had reduced macroeconomic imbalances and had initiated a major transformation of India's development strategy. Radical industrial, trade and financial policy changes beginning in 1991 have made remarkable progress in starting to liberalise what was one of the most closed and regulated economies in the world (Ghatak, 1993).

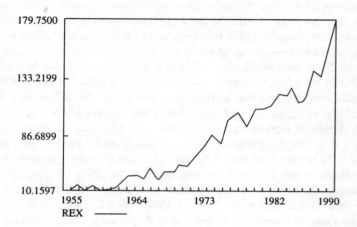

Figure 6.10   Real Exports (in US$): India

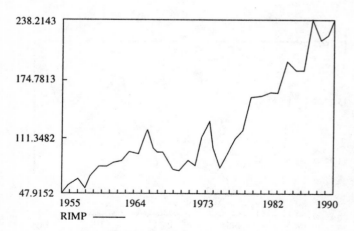

Figure 6.11   Real imports (in US$): India

V   METHODOLOGY

Since our main aim in this paper is to examine the robustness of the long-run relationship between various trade liberalisation measures set out in section III and the real GDP for Turkey, Malaysia and India, we first estimate the correlation matrix of the variables over the sample period 1955–90 to see the correlation level between various liberalisation measures of trade and the corresponding real GDP using the formula:

ρ_{ij} = correlation coefficient of x_i and x_j

$$\rho_{ij} = \sum_{t=1}^{n}(x_{it} - x_i)(x_{jt} - x_j)/(n - 1)S_i S_j, \quad i, j = 1, 2, \dots k$$

where x_i and S_i are the means and the standard deviations of x_{it}, respectively (see, e.g., Pesaran and Pesaran, 1991). However, results regarding 'simple correlation coefficient' should be assessed as 'preliminary' and thus 'indicative' rather than 'conclusive'. That is, a possible high correlation does not necessarily imply that there exists a causal and/or 'genuine' relationship between the long-run development of trade liberalisation and output (either GDP or GNP), as they may arise from a purely short-run 'spurious' relationship.

Thus, in the light of the new growth theory outlined in section II, we examine the multivariate cointegration and causality issues among the

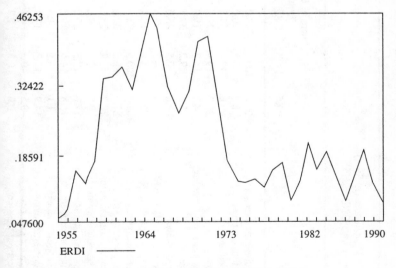

Figure 6.12   Exchange Rate Distortion Index (ERDI): India.

Table 6.3 The Indian Economy, 1965–91: Key economic indicators

| | | Mid-1990 population (million) | 849.5 |
| | | 1990 per capita GNP in US$ | 360 |

	Share of Gross Domestic Product (from current price data)						Growth Rate (% per year) (from constant price data)				
	1965	1973	1980	1989	1990	1991	1965–73	1973–80	1980–91	1990	1991
Gross domestic product	100.0	100.0	100.0	100.0	100.0	100.0	3.7	3.8	5.6	5.5	2.2
Net indirect taxes	8.0	8.1	10.0	10.9	10.8	10.4	–	–	–	–	–
Agriculture	40.6	42.8	34.3	28.2	28.9	28.3	3.3	1.8	3.2	4.2	0.0
Industry	20.2	19.9	23.3	25.2	24.6	23.9	3.9	5.2	6.3	6.7	–0.
of which manufacturing	14.3	14.3	15.9	16.4	16.2	15.6	4.3	4.9	6.7	7.3	–1.5
Services	31.3	29.2	32.4	35.7	35.8	37.4	4.1	4.9	6.8	5.9	7.0
Resource balance	–2.0	–0.5	–3.6	–2.5	–2.4	–0.8	–	–	–	–	–
Export of goods & NFS	3.6	4.3	6.5	7.7	7.7	8.9	2.8	6.7	6.0	3.8	–0.4
Imports of goods & NFS	5.6	4.8	10.1	10.3	10.1	9.8	1.8	7.9	5.0	1.8	–9.3
Total expenditures	102.0	100.5	103.6	102.5	102.4	100.8	3.6	3.9	5.5	5.3	1.4
Total consumption	87.0	83.5	82.6	76.7	53.4	79.8	3.6	3.8	5.8	5.7	3.8
Private consumption	78.2	75.2	73.0	65.0	41.3	68.0	3.4	3.6	5.5	5.3	4.5
General government	8.8	8.3	9.6	11.8	12.1	11.8	5.7	5.7	7.7	8.4	–0.4
Gross domestic investment	17.0	18.3	20.9	23.2	22.8	21.0	3.6	4.2	4.7	3.9	–6.8
Fixed investment	15.8	14.6	19.3	21.0	20.1	18.9	2.5	5.7	4.9	2.8	–4.7
Changes in stocks	1.1	3.6	1.6	2.1	2.8	2.1	–	–	–	–	–
Gross domestic saving	14.9	17.7	17.4	20.6	20.4	20.2	5.2	3.0	5.2	4.4	–0.8
Net factor income	–0.5	–0.3	0.2	–1.2	–1.3	–1.5	–	–	–	–	–
Net current transfers	0.0	0.2	1.7	0.8	0.7	1.0	–	–	–	–	–

	In billions of LCUs (at constant 1987 prices)						Inflation rate (% per year)				
	1965	1973	1980	1989	1990	1991	1965–73	1973–80	1980–91	1990	1991
Gross domestic product	1,391	1,814	2,337	3,877	4,091	4,182	3.7	3.8	5.6	5.5	2.2
Capacity to import	67	119	137	256	263	287	6.8	4.1	7.0	2.8	9.1
Terms of trade adjustment	–10	19	–19	–6	–9	16	–	–	–	–	–
Gross domestic income	1,381	1,833	2,318	3,871	4,082	4,198	4.0	3.7	5.7	5.5	2.8
Gross national product	1,378	1,805	2,344	3,836	4,046	4,132	3.8	3.9	5.5	5.5	2.1
Gross national income	1,369	1,824	2,325	3,830	4,037	4,149	4.0	3.8	5.5	5.4	2.8

	Index (1987 = 100)						Growth rate (% per year)				
	1980	1986	1988	1989	1990	1991	1965–73	1973–80	1980–91	1990	1991
Price indices											
Consumer prices (IFS 64)	54.2	91.9	109.4	116.1	126.5	145.2	5.9	5.3	8.6	9.0	–
Wholesale prices (IFS 63)	62.9	94.3	108.6	–	128.1	146.1	6.6	7.0	6.7	–	13.4
Implicit GDP deflator	58.2	92.1	108.2	116.2	129.4	146.1	6.2	6.8	8.2	11.4	12.8
Implicit expenditures defl.	58.9	91.5	108.2	116.8	130.2	145.8	6.1	7.1	8.2	11.5	11.9

	1965–73	1973–80	1980–91
Other indicators			
Population	2.3	2.3	2.1
Labour force	1.6	1.7	2.0
Gross national income p.c.	1.6	1.4	3.3
Private consumption p.c.	1.0	1.3	3.3
Import elasticity			
Imports (goods & NFS)/GDP	0.5	2.1	0.9
Marginal savings rates			
Gross national saving	27.7	24.9	20.6
Gross domestic saving	26.6	15.9	23.6
ICOR (period averages)	–	6.1	4.1

Table 6.3   cont.

Share of labour force (%)

	1965	1973	1980	1990
Labour force	100.0	100.0	100.0	100.0
Agriculture	72.9	71.1	69.7	–
Industry	11.9	12.8	13.2	–
Services	15.1	16.1	17.0	–

Volume index (1987 = 100)

	1980	1987	1988	1989	1990	1991
Merchandise exports		–		–	–	–
BEV.TEA	116.2	100.0	98.1	106.0	113.7	119.4
MET.FE	79.2	100.0	116.5	126.0	118.9	126.1
BEV.COFFEE	101.5	100.0	92.9	129.6	103.7	76.7
Manufactures	60.4	100.0	117.3	136.6	135.2	131.4
Residual	91.3	100.0	93.7	104.6	146.5	157.5
Total exports fob	70.2	100.0	111.5	128.7	135.1	134.4
Merchandise imports						
Food	78.8	100.0	115.1	50.6	52.1	22.4
Fuel and energy	111.9	100.0	113.2	122.2	139.0	157.3
Other consumer goods	11.5	100.0	145.3	118.8	114.6	80.9
Other intermediate goods	81.9	100.0	136.4	147.6	145.9	132.8
Capital goods	58.7	100.0	71.7	83.3	79.4	37.4
Total imports cif	75.1	100.0	117.5	116.3	119.3	105.2

Value at current prices (US$ million)

	1980	1987	1988	1989	1990	1991
Merchandise exports				–	–	
BEV.TEA	539	457	414	543	599	537
MET.FE	384	419	464	557	585	645
BEV.COFFEE	271	203	193	206	141	101
Manufactures	5,067	9,013	11,105	13,185	14,383	13,795
Residual	2,071	2,552	2,087	2,360	2,777	2,923
Total exports fob	8,332	12,644	14,262	16,850	18,485	18,002
Merchandise imports						
Food	1,348	1,292	1,203	714	713	303
Fuel and energy	6,669	3,148	2,938	3,766	5,967	5,158
Other consumer goods	371	3,139	4,575	3,962	4,015	2,590
Other intermediate goods	5,197	7,502	10,967	11,783	11,440	10,558
Capital goods	2,307	4,732	3,657	4,189	4,292	2,058
Total imports cif	15,892	19,812	23,339	24,414	26,427	20,667

Index (1987 = 100)

	1980	1987	1988	1989	1990	1991
Merchandise terms of trade	93.9	100.0	101.2	103.6	108.2	105.9
Export price index	106.9	100.0	100.2	106.0	111.8	99.2
Import price index	87.9	100.0	100.9	97.7	96.7	106.8
Terms of trade						

Value at current prices (US$ million)

	1980	1987	1988	1989	1990	1991
Balance of payments						
Export of goods & NFS	11,281	16,215	18,218	20,913	22,685	21,950
Merchandise (fob)	8,332	12,644	14,262	16,850	18,485	18,000
Non-factor services	2,949	3,571	3,956	4,063	4,200	3,950
Imports of goods & NFS	17,408	22,839	26,564	27,752	29,807	23,990
Merchandise (fob)	15,892	19,812	23,339	24,414	26,430	20,670
Non-factor services	1,516	3,027	3,225	3,338	3,377	3,320
Resource balance	-6,127	-6,624	-8,346	-6,839	-7,122	-2,040
Net factor income	356	-2,471	-2,985	-3,305	-3,741	-3,650
(interest per DRS)	642	2,728	3,148	3,504	3,936	4,379
Net current transfers	2,860	2,698	2,654	2,256	2,000	2,685
(workers' remittances)	2,786	2,724	2,225	2,186	1,947	2,020
Curr. a/c bal. before off. transfers	-2,911	-6,397	-8,677	-7,888	-8,863	-3,005
Net official transfers	643	410	406	500	480	450
Curr. a/c bal. after off. transfers	-2,268	-5,987	-8,271	-7,388	-8,383	-2,555

variables considered. Accordingly, we now set out a model to test rigorously the long-run relationships and 'causality' issues. A necessary precondition to causality testing is to check the cointegrating properties of the variables under consideration since standard tests for causality (i.e. Granger/Sims tests) are not valid if 'cointegration' exists (see especially Granger, 1988; Bahmani–Oskooee and Alse, 1993). Thus, cointegration analysis and error-correction modelling are recommended as an effective remedy. Error-correction models establish causality between two variables after reintroducing long-run information (through the error-correction term) into the analysis. Note that if two variables are cointegrated, then the Granger causality would run in at least one direction. In other words, cointegration implies causal effects (Engle and Granger, 1987).

We are mainly interested in analysing the following multivariate long-run relationship:

$$Y = f(\text{TRADE}, K, H) \tag{25}$$

where Y, TRADE, K, and H represent real GDP, a measure of trade liberalisation, and proxies for physical and human capital, respectively. Let us now express this long-run relationship as a regression in natural logarithms (prefixed with the letter L) since their first differences reflect the rate of change of each variable:

$$LY_t = \alpha_0 + \alpha_1 LTRADE_t + \alpha_2 LK_t + \alpha_3 LH_t + u_t \tag{26}$$

As regards cointegration, error-correction mechanism (ECM) and causality, our methodology consists of two steps. Since it is essential to check for the cointegrating properties of the original series before applying the standard Granger test, *in the first step*, considering the cointegration analysis in the Engle–Granger sense (see Engle and Granger, 1987), we estimate the cointegrating regression (26) by ordinary least squares (OLS).

Let us now apply integration and cointegration analyses in the Engle–Granger sense. Accordingly, a time-series, say, X_t is said to be integrated of the order d if, after differencing d times, it becomes stationary, denoted as $X \sim (d)$. Moreover, two time-series, X_t and Y_t are said to be cointegrated of order d, b where d > b > 0), denoted as:

$$X_t, Y_t \sim CI(d, b),$$

if:
(a) both are I(d), and
(b) their linear combination $a_1.X_t + a_2. Y_t$ is I(d − b);
that is, the residuals of the long-run regression should be stationary (i.e. integrated of order zero). The vector $[a_1, a_2]$ is referred to as the

'cointegrating vector' (see Engle and Granger, 1987). Thus, we employ the Augmented Dickey–Fuller (ADF) test and the residual-based ADF test to determine the integration level and the possible cointegration among the variables, respectively.[11] To see if any (exogenous) outlier changes the integration level of the series under consideration, we apply Perron's additive outlier integration level test with structural break (see Perron, 1990; Perron and Vogelsang, 1992).[12]

The *next step* is to see if the error-correction term is statistically significant or not, using ECMODs. Note that the relevant error-correction term is included in the standard Granger causality procedure if the variables are found to be cointegrated. Otherwise, the standard Granger test is carried out without the error-correction term.[13] The ECMOD is formulated as follows:

$$
\begin{aligned}
\text{DLY}_t = \beta_0 - \beta_1\, u_{t-1} &+ \sum_{i=1}^{m} c_i\, \text{DLY}_{t-i} + \sum_{j=1}^{n} d_i\, \text{DLTRADE}_{t-j} \\
&+ \sum_{k=1}^{q} f_i\, \text{DLK}_{t-k} + \sum_{l=1}^{r} g_i\, \text{DLH}_{t-1} + e_t
\end{aligned}
\tag{27}
$$

where u_{t-1} is the lagged residuals (i.e. error-correction term) obtained from the cointegrating regression (26). The latter D represents the first-differences. Statistically significant β_1 suggests that trade liberalisation, physical and human capital *jointly* Granger-cause real GDP. The ECMODs introduce an additional channel through which Granger causality could be detected. This is because if the variables are cointegrated, there should be a causal relationship between them. This causal relationship among the variables provides the short-run dynamics necessary to obtain long-run equilibrium (Granger, 1988). For instance, focusing on regression (27), trade liberalisation is said to Granger-cause output not only if the d_i's are jointly significant, but also if β_1 is significant. Thus, unlike the standard Granger test for causality, the ECMODs allow for the finding that trade liberalisation Granger-cause output as long as the error-correction term, u_{t-1}, carries a significant coefficient with negative sign.[14] Jones and Joulfaian (1991) suggest the interpretation that the changes of the lagged independent variable describes the short-run causal impact, while the error-correction term captures the long-run effect. To determine the optimal lag lengths in the Granger causality tests (see equations (2a) and (2b)), we use the approach of Hsiao (1979, 1981), which combines the Granger test with the Akaike's minimum Final Prediction Error (FPE) criterion to avoid the ambiguity in the arbitrary choice of lags.

One drawback of the Engle–Granger cointegration analysis is that it assumes uniqueness of the cointegrating vector. However, in a multivariate context, such as regression (26), the number of cointegrating vectors could be more than one.[15] The Johansen Full Information Maximum Likelihood (ML) method can be used to check for the number of cointegrating vectors (if there is any!) (see Johansen, 1988; Johansen and Juselius, 1990).[16] Once a joint cointegration among variables is confirmed, the next step would be to model the short run with the use of ECMOD. The existence of joint cointegration among the variables in (26) and statistically significant error-correction terms with negative signs in ECMODs, would be regarded as robust evidence in favour of the new growth theory.

VI DATA AND EMPIRICAL RESULTS

'Indicative' Evidence from Estimated Correlation Matrix

Table 6.4 reports the results of the estimated correlation matrix on the correlation between various trade liberalisation measures and the real GDP for Turkey, Malaysia and India.[17] The results refer to a 'strong' positive correlation between the real GDP (RGDP) and various measures of trade liberalisation such as openness measure (OPEN), real exports (REX), real imports (RIM) and real exchange rate (RER). A negative (expectedly) correlation is observed as regards real GDP (RGDP) and exchange rate distortion index (ERDI). Overall, we have 'preliminary' and 'indicative' evidence for all three countries that the underlying relationship between trade liberalisation and real GDP is rather strong as shown by high correlation coefficients estimated. However, these results are only indicative and do *not necessarily* imply a causal and/or genuine long-run relationship between trade liberalisation and output. To be more conclusive and to make sure that we do not deal with a spurious relationship, we need to apply cointegration analysis.

Searching for a Genuine Long-run Relationship: Cointegration Analysis[18]

In the light of the econometric methodology presented in the previous section, we now check for the cointegrating properties of the variables involved in regression (26). Accordingly, we apply integration and cointegration analyses in the EG sense. The data used in this study are annual for the period 1955–90.

Table 6.4 Estimated Correlation Matrix of Variables: Correlation between the Real GDP and the Measures of 'Trade Liberalisation' for Turkey, Malaysia and India

	RGDP	OPEN	REX	RIM	ERDI	RER
Turkey						
RGDP	1.00	0.87	0.88	0.95	−0.72	0.75
Malaysia						
RGDP	1.00	0.90	0.98	0.95	−0.55	0.68
India						
RGDP	1.00	0.70	0.97	0.95	0.41	0.80

The visual inspection of the variables in hand (i.e. LY, LTRADE, LK, LH) for Turkey, Malaysia and India suggests that they are all non-stationary in levels, but stationary in first differences (graphs available on request). The relevant sample autocorrelation functions (i.e. correlograms) are also supportive in the same direction (graphs available on request). We then apply the Augmented Dickey–Fuller test for unit roots as a formal test. The ADF test results for unit roots (see Table 6.5) confirm that all variables are integrated of order 1 in levels but integrated of order 0 (i.e. stationary) in first differences (denoted as $LY \sim I(1)$, $LTRADE \sim I(1)$, $LK \sim I(1)$ and $LH \sim I(1)$)[19]

These results are validated despite some structural changes which occurred within the sample period by applying the Perron Additive Outlier test; that is, switching regimes are taken into account (results available on request). To make sure that our hypothesised break years are correctly chosen, we also calculate the split-sample ADF statistics. Our split-sample ADF test results confirm the validity of the choice for break years. As a whole, our Perron test results suggest that there is no spurious unit root resulting from changing means as far as the variables under search are concerned. (Note that we use the appropriate critical values for the Perron test recently tabulated for small samples by Rybinski (1994).)

Table 6.6 reports the residual-based ADF test results for cointegration for the long-run regression (26). Results appear to support stable, genuine long-run relationships, i.e. cointegration exists among the variables involved. That is, we are able to reject the null hypothesis of *'no cointegration'* at the 5 or 10 per cent significance levels. However, as far as the EG cointegrating

Trade and Development

regression results are concerned, we still face the following problems: (a) the number of cointegrating vectors may be more than one, since we have more than two variables involved in each cointegrating regression. Because the EG approach assumes the uniqueness of the cointegrating vector, we need to employ the system-based Johansen method to check for the number of

Table 6.5 The ADF Test for Unit Roots: Turkey, Malaysia and India

| Variable | Test Statistic | | Critical Value | | | |
| | Levels | 1st differences | Lower values | | Upper values | |
			%5	%10	%5	%10
Turkey						
LRGDP	−1.05	−4.22	−2.22	−1.77	−2.01	−1.61
LOPEN	−1.57	−4.12				
LERDI	−1.65	−4.09				
LREX	−0.50	−4.51				
LK	−1.87	−4.68				
LH	−1.81	−3.90				
Malaysia						
LRGDP	0.43	−3.88	−2.22	−1.77	−2.01	−1.61
LNRGDP	−2.20	−3.25				
LREX	−0.02	−6.33				
LREXm	−0.31	−4.91				
LREXf	−0.53	−3.14				
LREXp	1.06	−2.45				
LK	−1.50	−3.99				
LH	−2.21	−3.29				
India						
LRGDP	1.08	−5.01	−2.22	−1.77	−2.01	−1.61
LRIM	−0.71	−5.28				
LRER	−0.85	−4.93				
LK	−2.16	−5.44				
LH	−1.67	−3.69				

Note:
The reported critical values are obtained from Charemza and Deadman (1992). Approximately, they correspond to 35 number of observations. It is worth noting that the intercept terms are included in the ADF equations. An augmentation of 1 or 2 appeared to be sufficient to secure lack of autocorrelation of the error terms. All variables are expressed in natural logarithms, prefixed with the letter *L*. For definitions and data sources, see the Appendix.

Table 6.6 The Residual-based ADF Test for Cointegration: Turkey, Malaysia and India

Cointegrating Regression	Adjusted R^2	CRDW Residuals	Estimated ADF	Critical Value			
				Lower value		Upper value	
				5%	10%	5%	10%
Turkey							
$LRGDP=f_1(LREX, LK,LH)$	0.96	1.03	−3.54	−3.73	−3.37	−3.53	−3.20
Malaysia							
$LRGDP=f_2(LREXm, LREXf, LREXp, LK,LH)$	0.99	1.64	−4.10	−4.22	−3.83	−4.05	−3.65
$LNRGDP=f_3(LREXm, LREXf,LREXp, LK,LH)$	0.96	1.84	−5.08	−4.22	−3.83	−4.05	−3.65
India							
$LRGDP=f_4(LRIM, LRER,LK)$	0.92	1.23	−3.94	−3.72	−3.35	−3.52	−3.18

Note:
The reported critical values are obtained from Charemza and Deadman (1992). They correspond to (annual) number of observations of 41 (1950–90) for Turkey; 25 (1966–90) for Malaysia; and 36 (1955–90) for India. Note that the intercept term is not included in the residual-based ADF equations. An augmentation of 1 appeared to be sufficient to secure lack of autocorrelation of the error terms. CRDW represents the Cointegrating Durbin–Watson statistic. For definitions and data sources, see the Appendix. All variables are expressed in natural logarithms, prefixed with the letter *L*.

cointegrating vectors; (b) OLS long-run estimates may be remarkably biased;[20] and (c) resulting *t*-statistics have only a descriptive role due to the non-stationary nature of the variables under search (Banerjee et al., 1986). Thus, we applied the Johansen system-based approach (Johansen, 1988; Johansen and Juselius, 1990). Our Johansen results confirm not only the existence of a unique cointegrating vector but also the robustness[21] of the long-run coefficient estimates for the three countries considered, Turkey, Malaysia and India (the Johansen estimation results available on request).[22]

The existence of joint cointegration among the variables in long-run regressions (26) is confirmed (see Table 6.6) for Turkey, Malaysia and India.[23] The next step would be to model the short run with the use of ECM. It is important to note that both short-run models with the use of ECM produce statistically significant coefficient estimates with negative signs for the corresponding error-correction terms (results available on request). Overall, the findings imply that right-hand side variables in the ECMODs jointly Granger-cause real GDP growth. Following Jones and Joulfaian (1991) we can suggest an interpretation that the changes of the lagged independent variables describe the short-run causal impact, while the statistically significant error-correction term introduces the long-run effect.

It is important to note that in reporting the multivariate long-run estimation results with alternative measures of 'trade liberalisation' in Table 6.6, we concentrate on the most statistically robust results; that is, the positive effects of the growth rates of real exports (REX) for Turkey and Malaysia, and the real imports (RIM) and the real exchange rates (RER) for India on the real output growth rate. Satisfactory results in a multivariate cointegration framework were also obtained for both the openness measure (OPEN) and the real exchange rates (RER) for both Turkey and Malaysia. Besides, in the multivariate analysis, the exchange rate distortion index (ERDI) appears to be working satisfactorily. The ERDI, however, does not produce satisfactory results for Turkey and Malaysia (results and detailed information available on request).

The empirical evidence favours the long-run complementary effects of the physical and human capital accumulation on the output growth for Turkey and Malaysia. However, for India we have a wrong signed coefficient if both physical and human capital proxies are included in the cointegrating regression which implies *no* long-run complementary effects of physical and human capital accumulation on the output for India. We believe this is due to a 'multicollinearity' problem. Thus, for India, we exclude the human capital variable in the final cointegrating estimation.

VII CONCLUSIONS

The following conclusions can be drawn on the basis of our case studies for Turkey, Malaysia and India:

1. For all three countries under investigation, our multivariate cointegration analyses and the ECMODs accord well with the hypothesised role of trade policy in the new growth theory; that is, trade policy can affect both the short- and the long-run output growth rate. In the long run, the effect on output growth rate is jointly determined with increasing physical and human capital accumulation.

2. Our analyses indicate that real export growth also Granger-causes *non-export* real GDP growth for Malaysia. The Malaysian evidence highlights the relative importance of non-traditional exports in total exports.

3. The Indian evidence particularly supports the positive joint effect of *imports*, physical capital accumulation and real exchange rates on the long-run output growth. However, the trade liberalisation in India in the conventional sense, i.e. export promotion via elimination of exchange rate distortions, reduction of tariffs and quotas and many other bureaucratic interventions, has begun fairly recently. Hence, further research is necessary to draw firm conclusions.

ACKNOWLEDGEMENT

We are grateful to Professors Jagdish Bhagwati, V. Balasubramanyam, Chris Milner, David Sapsford and other participants of the Conference at Lancaster University for helpful comments. The usual disclaimer applies.

NOTES

1. Note that India and Turkey opted for more open economic and trade policies with export promotion in the mid-1980s and the early 1980s, respectively.
2. Malaysia has followed a relatively open economy, generally driven by the market forces since Independence (1957).
3. This section draws on Ghatak et al. (1994a).
4. Exports plus imports relative to real GDP per head and taken from the Penn–World data set.
5. For influential early work on the theory of distortions in trade and welfare, see Bhagwati (1971), and Bhagwati and Srinivasan (1983, Part III, esp. chapter 16).
6. There is, in any case, some overlap between the alternative indices, and the indices used here may also capture the effects of trade regime bias.
7. For various measures of trade liberalisation used in the present work, and also for their definitions and data sources, see the Appendix (p. 115).
8. The range 10–20 of their trade liberalisation index is reserved for 'outward-oriented' trade regimes. The highest value given by the authors in these periods is 8.
9. For the definition of our exchange rate distortion index (ERDI), see the Appendix (p. 115).
10. This point is strongly confirmed by various measures of the trade lliberalisation for Malaysia. See relevant figures.
11. Haug (1993) compares seven different residual-based tests for cointegration with the Monte Carlo method. Among the tests considered, Engle-Granger's residual-based ADF test shows the least size distortion.
12. Perron (1990) suggests two types of model to test for unit roots with structural break, namely, the Additive Outlier Model (AOM) and the Innovational Outlier Model (IOM). The AOM is recommended for 'sudden' structural changes while

the IOM is said to be more appropriate for 'gradual' structural changes. We believe that structural changes in the economy are generally 'sudden' in nature. This is also thought to be the case for the economies under consideration, i.e. the economies of Turkey, Malaysia and India. Thus, the AOM is preferred in this study.

13. If two time-series are cointegrated, then there would exist and error-correction representation (i.e. error-correction mechanism is well determined), and vice versa. This is known as the Granger Representation Theorem (GRT). Empirically, in small samples, statistically significant error-correction terms provide further evidence in favour of the presence of a 'genuine' long-run relationship. It is also true that, by definition, cointegration implies causal effects.

14. To avoid an explosive process, the coefficient should take a value between −1 and 0.

15. In this case, there is no longer a unique long-run relationship towards which the error-correction model (ECMOD) is adjusting. Then, a single equation cointegrating regression will estimate the linear combination of existent vectors. Many researchers in applied econometrics overcome this problem by choosing the cointegrating vector which makes 'economic sense'. This implies choosing the cointegrating vector where the estimated long-run elasticities correspond closely (in both magnitude and sign) to those predicted by economic theory.

16. It should be noted that the Engle–Granger and Johansen methods are grounded within different econometric methodologies and thus cannot be directly compared. The Engle–Granger method is a single equation-based modelling while the Johansen method is a system approach based on VAR modelling. Charemza and Deadman (1992, p. 201) suggest that the Johansen method can be used for single equation modelling as a supplementary tool. Assume, for instance, that the Johansen method indicates the existence of a unique cointegrating vector. In this case, as pointed out by Charemza and Deadman, if the estimated cointegrated coefficients have, after normalisation, economically sensible signs and are approximately similar in size to those estimated by the Engle–Granger method, this could be regarded as some confirmation of the single equation model to which the Engle–Granger method was employed.

17. For definitions and data sources of the variables used, see the Appendix, p. 115.

18. Since our multivariate cointegration results for Turkey and Malaysia draw on Ghatak et al. (1994a, 1994b), the readers are referred to these sources for more information and details.

19. Econometric computations in this study have been carried out by Microfit 3.0 version (see Pesaran and Pesaran, 1991).

20. Note that, as a rule, the higher the R^2 statistic in a cointegrating regression, the less biased the estimated static long-run estimates are (Banerjee et al., 1986).

21. Following Banerjee et al. (1986), our reasonably high R^2 values in the relevant cointegrating regressions should be regarded as additional evidence to suggest that our long-run OLS estimators are *not* remarkably biased.

22. At this point, as a reminder of the complementary relationship between the EG and the Johansen approaches, see esp. notes 15 and 16.

23. Since the cointegrating Durbin–Watson (CRDW) test value is higher than the R^2 (i.e. CRDW > R^2) in the relevant cointegrating regressions, the joint cointegration among the variables is ensured (Banerjee et al., 1986).

REFERENCES

Agarwala, R. (1983), 'Price Distortions and Growth in Developing Countries', *World Bank Staff Working Paper*, No. 515 (Washington DC: World Bank).

Aricanli, T. and Rodrik, D. eds., (1990), *The Political Economy of Turkey: Debt Adjustment and Sustainability* (London: Macmillan).

Arslan, I. and van Wijnbergen, S. (1993), 'Export Incentives, Exchange Rate Policy and Export Growth in Turkey', *Review of Economics and Statistics*, vol. 75, no. 1, pp. 128–33.

Bahmani-Oskooee, M. and Alse, J. (1993), 'Export Growth and Economic Growth: An Application of Cointegration and Error-Correction Modelling', *The Journal of Developing Areas*, vol. 27, July, pp. 535–42.

Banerjee, A., Dolado, J., Hendry, D.F. and Smith, G. (1986), 'Exploring Equilibrium Relationships in Econometrics through Static Models: Some Monte Carlo Evidence', *Oxford Bulletin of Economics and Statistics*, vol. 48, pp. 253–77.

Baysan, T. and Blitzer, C. (1991), 'Turkey', in *Liberalising Foreign Trade: New Zealand, Spain and Turkey*, vol. 6, D. Papageorgiou, M. Michaely and A.M. Choksi, eds., A Research Project of the World Bank (Cambridge, MA: Basil Blackwell).

Bhagwati, J. (1971), 'The Generalized Theory of Distortions and Welfare', in *Trade, Balance of Payments, and Growth: Papers in International Economics in Honor of C.P. Kindleberger*, Chapter 12 (Chicago: University of Chicago Press).

———— (1978), *Anatomy and Consequences of Exchanges Control Regimes* (Cambridge, MA: Ballinger Publishing Co. for NBER).

———— and Srinivasan, T.N. (1983), *Lectures on International Trade* (Cambridge, MA: The MIT Press).

Charemza, W.W. and Deadman, D.F. (1992), *New Directions in Econometric Practice* (Aldershot: Edward Elgar).

Dollar, D. (1992), 'Outward-oriented Developing Economies Really Do Grow More Rapidly: Evidence from 95 LDCs, 1976–1985', *Economic Development and Cultural Change*, vol. 40, pp. 523–44.

Edwards, S. (1992), 'Trade Orientation, Distortions and Growth in Developing Countries', *Journal of Development Economics*, vol. 39, pp. 31–57.

———— (1993), 'Openness, Trade Liberalization, and Growth in Developing Countries', *Journal of Economic Literature*, vol. 31, September, pp. 1358–93.

Engle, R.F. and Granger, C.W.J. (1987), 'Cointegration and Error-Correction: Representation, Estimation, and Testing', *Econometrica*, vol. 55, March, pp. 251–76.

Fishelson, G. (1988), 'The Black Market for Foreign Exchange', *Economics Letters*, vol. 27, pp. 67–71.

Ghatak, S. (1993), 'Exchange Rate Liberalisation and Recent Trade Performance', *Oxford Analytica*, May, pp. 23–8.

———— Milner, C. and Utkulu, U. (1995), *Trade Liberalisation and Endogenous Growth: Some Evidence for Turkey, Economics of Planning*, October.

———— (1996), *Exports, Export Composition and Growth: Cointegration and Causality Evidence for Malaysia, Applied Economics* (forthcoming).

————— and Utkulu, U. (1993), *Trade Orientation and Economic Growth: The Turkish Evidence, 1955–1990: A Cointegration Analysis*, Discussion Papers in Economics, No. 93/11 (Department of Economics, University of Leicester).

————— (1994), *Exchange Rate Distortions and Real Exports in Turkey: A Cointegration and Error-correction Analysis: 1955–1990*, mimeo (Department of Economics, University of Leicester).

Granger, C.W.J. (1988), 'Some Recent Developments in a Concept of Causality, *Journal of Econometrics*, vol. 39, September–October, pp. 199–211.

Greenway, D. (1993), 'Liberalising Foreign Trade through Rose Tinted Glasses', *Economic Journal*, vol. 103, pp. 208–22.

Haug, A.A. (1993), 'Residual-based Tests for Cointegration: A Monte Carlo Study of Size Distortions', *Economics Letters*, vol. 41, pp. 345–51.

Hsiao, C. (1979), 'Autoregressive Modelling of Canadian Money and Income Data', *Journal of the American Statistical Association*, vol. 74, pp. 553–60.

————— (1981), 'Autoregressive Modelling and Money-Income Causality Detection', *Journal of Monetary Economics*, vol. 7, pp. 85–106.

Johansen, S. (1988), 'Statistical Analysis of Cointegrating Vectors', *Journal of Economic Dynamics and Control*, vol. 12, pp. 231–54.

————— and Juselius, K. (1990), 'Maximum Likelihood Estimation and Inference on Cointegration: With Application to the Demand for Money', *Oxford Bulletin of Economics and Statistics*, vol. 52, pp. 169–210.

Jones, J.D. and Joulfaian, D. (1991), 'Federal Government Expenditures and Revenues in the Early Years of the American Republic: Evidence from 1792 and 1860', *Journal of Macroeconomics*, vol. 13, no. 1, pp. 133–55.

Kamin, S.B. (1993), 'Devaluation, Exchange Controls, and Black Markets for Exchange Rates in Developing Countries', *Journal of Development Economics*, vol. 40, pp. 151–69.

Krueger, A. (1978), *Liberalization Attempts and Consequences* (New York: Ballinger).

Leamer, E. (1984), *Sources of International Comparative Advantage* (Cambridge, MA: MIT Press).

————— (1988), 'Measures of Openness', in *Trade Policy and Empirical Analysis*, ed. R. Baldwin (Chicago: University of Chicago Press).

Lee, Jong-Wha (1993), 'International Trade, Distortions, and Long-Run Economic Growth', *IMF Staff Papers*, vol. 40, no. 2, pp. 299–328.

Michaely, M., Papageorgiou, D. and Choksi, A.M., eds. (1991), *Liberalising Foreign Trade: Lessons of Experience in the Developing World*, vol. 7, A Research Project of the World Bank (Cambridge, MA: Basil Blackwell).

Milner, C. (1994), *Real Exchange Rate Concepts and the Measurement of Trade Liberalisation: Some Evidence for Mauritius*, Paper presented to Workshop on Trade Liberalisation in Africa (University of Nottingham).

Perron, P. (1990), 'Testing for a Unit Root in a Time Series with a Changing Mean', *Journal of Business and Economic Statistics*, vol. 8, no. 2, pp. 153–62.

————— and Vogelsang, T.J. (1992), 'Testing for a Unit Root in a Time Series with a Changing Mean: Corrections and Extensions', *Journal of Business and Economic Statistics*, vol. 10, no. 4, pp. 467–70.

Pesaran, M.H. and Pesaran, B. (1991), *Microfit: An Interactive Econometric Software Package (User Manual)* (Oxford: Oxford University Press).

Riedel, J. (1991), 'Strategy Wars: The State of Debate on Trade and Industrialisation in Developing Countries', in *International Trade and Global Development: Essays in Honour of Jagdish Bhagwati*, ed. A. Koekkoek and L.B.M. Mennes (London: Routledge).

Rybinski, K. (1994), *Extended Tabulations for Perron Additive Outlier Test*, mimeo (University of Gdansk).

Summers, R. and Heston, A. (1991), 'The Penn World Table (Mark5): An Expanded Set of International Comparisons, 1950–1988', *Quarterly Journal of Economics*, vol. 106, no. 2, May, pp. 327–68.

Thirlwall, A.P. (1994), *Growth and Development*, 4th edn (Basingstoke: Macmillan).

Togan, S. (ed.) (1994), *Foreign Trade Regime and Trade Liberalisation in Turkey During the 1980s* (UK: Avebury).

US Department of State (1992), *Country Reports on Economic Policy and Trade Practices* (St. Louis).

Uygur, E. (1993), 'Trade Policies and Economic Performance in Turkey in the 1980s', in *Trade and Growth: New Dilemmas in Trade Policy*, ed. M.R. Agosin and D. Tussie (New York: St Martin's Press).

World Bank (1991), *Trends in Developing Countries* (Washington, DC).

————— (1992), *Trends in Developing Economies*, Yearbook (New York: World Bank).

APPENDIX

Data Sources

The data used in this study are annual for the period 1955–90 and are taken from the following sources:

1. International Monetary Fund (IMF), *International Financial Statistics*, Yearbooks (various issues).
2. World Bank, *World Tables*, Yearbook (various issues).
3. State Planning Organisation (SPO), Turkey.
4. State Institute of Statistics (SIS), Turkey.
5. Cowitt, P.P., *World Currency Yearbook* (previously known as *Pick's Currency Yearbook*), various issues (International Currency Analysis, Brooklyn).
6. Penn-World data developed by Summers and Heston (1991).

Definitions of the Variables

RGDP: Real GDP expressed in US dollars (source 6).
RNGDP: Non-export real GDP (sources 1 and 2).
REX: Real exports expressed in US dollars (sources 1, 2 and 3).
REXm, REXf and REXp: Refer to the real exports for manufactured, fuel and primary products respectively (sources 1 and 2).
ERDI: Exchange rate distortion index of Turkey constructed on the basis of the formula ERDI = (BM\$–OF\$)/BM\$ where BM\$ (source 5) and OF\$ (source 1)

represent annual average black market and official exchange rates both expressed in domestic currency per US dollar. The same definition of ERDI is used by Ghatak and Utkulu (1993, 1995).

The ERDI here is like the black market premium used by others as it measures the difference between the BM$ and OF$ as a proportion of BM$ (see Fishelson, 1988; Kamin, 1993; Edwards, 1992). Note that, in LDCs, BM$-OF$ is generally observed to be positive.

RIM: Real imports expressed in US dollars (sources 1, 2 and 3).

OPEN: Openness index (source 6) defined as OPEN = [(exports + imports)/real GDP per capita] expressed in US dollars.

RER: Real exchange rates defined as RER = (OF*WPIUS)/CPI where OF,WPIUS and CPI represent official nominal exchange rate expressed in domestic currency per US dollar (source 1), wholesale price index of the USA (source 1) and consumer price index of the country under consideration (source 1).

TOT: Terms of trade defined as TOT = export prices/import prices both expressed in US dollars (source 1).

H: Measure of human capital (source 4) proxied by secondary school enrolment rates: (number of students enroled at secondary schools/total population (000)).

K: Measure of physical capital (source 6) proxied by real gross domestic investment (private and public) as percentage of real GDP per capita.

7 People Who Live in Greenhouses

Martin Wolf

Since trade is important to linking the world together, it seems appropriate for the WTO to undertake formal co-ordination with other international institutions and to establish serious work groups on the environment, labour standards, culture, community or any other issue with systemic implications.
(Steve Charnowitz, Policy Director, Competitiveness Policy Council, Washington, DC)

Jagdish Bhagwati has not only been the finest international trade theoretician of our era, he has also been the most influential analyst of trade policy issues. This involves three main talents: first, identifying the important issues; second, analysing these logically and rigorously, without accepting for a moment that 'political reality' justifies falling short of the highest intellectual standards; and third, putting forward that analysis in lucid and widely comprehensible language.

One of the areas in which Bhagwati has shown particular interest in recent years has been the question of the international harmonisation of standards, particularly on the environment and labour. This paper represents a journalist's attempt to repeat much of what Bhagwati has already said.[1] Its justification can only be that imitation is the sincerest form of flattery. But it has another: repetition is the price of entry into the policy arena. So here is Bhagwati, according to Wolf.

The discussion below starts with some general remarks on the issue of harmonisation, trade and diversity. It then considers the two most contentious areas: labour standards and environmental standards. These matter, partly because of what has happened within the European Union and the North American Free Trade Arrangement, but still more because the ink was not even dry on the agreement closing the Uruguay Round of multilateral trade negotiations before the Clinton administration insisted on inserting minimum labour standards into the World Trade Organisation and making it more environmentally friendly as well. But these two demands could, over time, halt the entire liberalising thrust of the Uruguay Round. Neither is defensible.

Indeed both are open to the charge of egregious hypocrisy.

Hostile reaction to the new demands has, in fact, been strong. Mrs Rafidah Aziz, for example, Malaysia's redoubtable trade minister, argued at the ministerial meeting in Marrakesh in April 1994 that the linkage of trade with labour standards 'would, in effect, provide a convenient cover for trade protectionism'. Such reactions are not that surprising when the arguments of those who believe that labour and environmental standards must be a central element in the new trade agenda are examined more closely.

THE CASE AGAINST HARMONISATION

While practical men and women, both in business and politics, have largely come to accept the arguments for the broad economic benefits of liberal trade, they balk when there is trade between countries with different standards. Arguments for liberal trade are all very well, they say, but where are the gains from trade when countries compete unfairly, by exploiting their workers or destroying their environments? Is it not a necessary condition for trade to be beneficial that it be fair? Yet how can it be fair when there is 'social' and 'environmental dumping'? As Bhagwati has remarked, 'Central to American thinking on the question of the Social Clause is the notion that competitive advantage can sometimes be "illegitimate". In particular, it is argued that if labour standards elsewhere are different and unacceptable morally, then the resulting competition is illegitimate and "unfair".'[2]

However persuasive they may appear, these arguments are largely mistaken. In certain cases, it is true, the elimination of dangerous products or fraudulent services from the market being obvious examples, the attempt to impose regulations may be justified, provided they apply equally to domestic production and imports. Where there are to be no border controls, as in the Single European Market, minimum safety standards may also need to be agreed amongst participating countries.

More generally, however, gains from trade exist even when there are diverse standards. Indeed diverse standards are one of the sources for gains from trade.

Trade and the State

In the first place, free trade – including mobility of capital, labour and ideas – makes resources less captive. It provides those who own them with greater freedom to evade exactions imposed on behalf of those who lack them. The extent of the increased freedom – and the consequent threat to taxation and regulation – must not be exaggerated. But trade will tend to even out the extremes, as jurisdictions compete with one another for mobile resources and buyers move to places that offer the cheapest purchases. The monopoly power of the state will be eroded by trade.

Consider, for example, minimum wages, a regulation with a purely redistributive intent. High minimum wages transfer income from capital to certain workers. They also tend to increase unemployment, as capital is substituted for labour. The relative size of these effects depends on the responsiveness of employment to the cost of labour. If responsiveness is low, income redistribution will dominate increased unemployment.

Imports make that outcome substantially less likely. Under autarky, minimum wages raise the relative cost of labour-intensive products. Under liberal trade, however, the relative prices of those products are prevented from rising. Instead, imports replace part or all of domestic production, thereby creating more unemployment than under autarky. Under liberal trade it is far more difficult to tax capital in favour of labour. Such taxes must then be overt, instead of covert.

Value of Diversity

In the second place, regulatory diversity is a natural and proper reflection of differences in incomes, natural resources and values. Inhabitants of wealthy countries will have different preferences for work and leisure, as well as for the environment, from inhabitants of poor ones.[3] Similarly, peoples with access to vast open spaces will value the environment differently from inhabitants of more densely populated countries. Again, peasants whose crops are threatened by elephants may value elephants differently from the children of Surrey stockbrokers.

Trade and Transparency

In the third place, liberal trade under regulatory diversity makes the effects of domestic regulatory interventions more powerful and transparent. By making intervention more transparent, inappropriate interventions, like minimum wages, should be rendered more difficult to impose. In addition, trade makes the regulation of 'bads' even more effective than it would otherwise be, by forcing production away from the most disliked activities.

Suppose, for example, that two countries, similar in other ways, have different preferences for, and consequently different regulations on, the emission of pollutants whose effects are felt locally. Provided barriers to trade are small, polluting processes will move to the country with the more liberal regulations. In this case, the country that has imposed the tighter regulation loses the processes its people dislike, while still enjoying, through trade, the products they desire.

Liberal trade works like a turbo-charger on a car: it makes the effects of regulations more dramatic than they would be without it. The aim of such regulations are secured at lower economic cost. To attempt to regulate emissions, while adopting protection to prevent the resultant flight of the polluting industry, is absurd.

Why, then, is this apparently benign process denigrated as environmental dumping? The reason is that loss of jobs to imports makes the implications of the regulation more powerful. Such transparency is precisely what politicians wish to avoid.

Harmonisation and Protection

Finally, harmonisation of regulatory regimes may lead to outright protection. International harmonisation must, in any case, be limited to what can be agreed and enforced. The alternative to consent is coercion. But not only are there limits to its feasibility, there is also a risk that coercion would undermine the legitimacy of an international regime.

LABOUR AND WAGES

With these general remarks in mind, let us turn our attention to the question of labour standards and the related question of the effects of trade with developing counties on wages in industrial countries.

International Enforcement of Labour Standards

Mr Robert Reich, US Secretary of Labour, justified US demands for the international enforcement of labour standards in an article in the *Washington Post* of 22 May 1994, itself a response to an article in *The Economist* on 9 April 1994. In his article he argues that 'some labour practices simply place countries outside the community of civilised nations. A consensus list of "core" labour standards will certainly proscribe goods produced by prison or slave labour and by very young children.' To this is added the right to form trade unions and bargain collectively. Action against countries that violate such standards is, he insists, justified on humanitarian grounds.

But is it? Slavery is a red herring in this debate. Nobody has seriously argued that many exports are produced by slaves. Prison labour sounds equally dreadful, but what of the argument that prisoners need to learn useful skills to help support their families? What better way can there be than for them to produce goods for export? Provided wages and conditions are in line with those in the market, this seems better than for inmates to rot in useless idleness.

Should the small children of a destitute Bangladeshi widow be forced to beg or starve, rather than work? Parents want what is best for their children. But if the children of the poor are to be educated, resources must be found to support them and their parents. So one test of US sincerity is the scale of its aid effort. At one fifth of 1 per cent of GNP, it is, in fact, the worst among all industrial countries, except for little Ireland.

This leaves by far the most significant 'right', that to bargain collectively. Stripped of its progressive gloss, however, collective bargaining is merely cartelisation of the labour market. Why is this a fundamental right, to be placed alongside free speech, the vote or habeas corpus?

Mr Reich accuses critics of the sin of 'laissez-faire dogmatism'. On the contrary, they base themselves on experience. There has been an astounding rise in real wages in the export-oriented economies of East Asia. Does this perhaps reflect the ability of trade unions to push up wages, thereby producing what Mr Reich desires, 'the emergence of middle-class economies'?

The answer is no. As the World Bank says in its study of the East Asian economic miracle, 'Korea, Singapore, and Taiwan, China, suppressed independent unions. Malaysia has independent unions but highly restrictive labour laws. Hong Kong and Japan do not intervene in labour relations. However, in Japan most unions are company based.' Mr Reich talks of the expectation that labour standards should improve as economies develop. So they did, not because of unions, but because of rapid growth, full employment and specialisation on the basis of comparative advantage.

In the early stage of development, when massive migration of workers from the countryside to modern industry is required, strong trade unions virtually ensure, instead, the emergence of narrow labour aristocracies. Which country did better in raising labour standards in the 1970s, Korea, which repressed trade unions, but had export-oriented industrial growth at 15 per cent a year, or India, where a highly unionised, but stunted, advanced industrial sector grew at only 4.5 per cent?

Raising the wages of a chosen few engaged in visible formal sector production will slow economic development and reduce the rate at which labour is absorbed into modern production. It is for this perfectly moral reason that virtually every country in the world, including the advanced industrial countries of today, suppressed or restricted trade union activities when large quantities of low productivity labour still had to be shifted into industry from agriculture – or, in the case of countries of immigration, from abroad. Again, industrial countries barred child labour only when most parents had become rich enough to afford to keep their children economically unproductive throughout childhood.

Mr Reich does more than call for basic rights. He suggests, as a further test of a country's probity, that 'low-wage workers should become better off, not worse off, as trade and investment boost national income'. This is a peculiarly ill-judged suggestion, since the US is one of the few countries to fail this test over the past two decades. Indeed, by continental European standards it falls short on many criteria of how an advanced economy should treat workers. This demonstrates how intellectually fragile labour standards are, not that the US should sink in the European quagmire.

If the supposed rights are debatable, action against alleged abuses will be more questionable still. Most of these abuses will, after all, occur in areas that have little to do with trade. Action might be taken against Sri Lanka, but we know it will not be taken against China. Furthermore, before action there must be international agreement on the content of labour standards. Otherwise, it is no more than bullying.

Is there anyone so naive as to suppose this issue has come to the fore because of concern for the poor? It is, instead, a response to the adjustments imposed by the rapid growth of developing country exports, itself among the most effective ways to reduce destitution. If people doubt that this is the origin of the demand for imposition of minimum labour standards, they need only know that it is being pushed jointly by the US, where real wages have stagnated for two decades, and France, the most outspokenly protectionist of major industrial countries.

It is a demand that lacks justification, will not be honestly enforced and would not significantly improve the lot of developing country workers if it were to be. Under the pretence of helping the poor, the industrial countries propose either to undermine their competitiveness or impose protection against their exports. From the point of view of developing countries, this appears, inevitably and rightly, to be pure hypocrisy.

Trade with Pauper Labour

Some protectionists hope that the mere act of imposing minimum labour standards on a country like China will eliminate its comparative advantage in labour-intensive products. They are wrong. Under any justifiable regulations, the price of labour in China will still be kept down, as it should be, by the negligible opportunity cost of surplus farm labour. Any minimum standards that might drive a substantial wedge between labour costs in advanced factories and the opportunity cost of labour would be both economically inefficient and certain to generate unemployment.

This then raises a worry deeper even than that about standards. It is about the effects of a flood of cheap labour-intensive exports from countries with infinite supplies of low-wage labour. Two question arise: first, how significant an effect might such imports have on wages and employment in industrial countries? Second, is protection the right alternative?

The extent to which exports of manufactures have already driven down demand for, and relative wages of, unskilled labour in rich countries is controversial. Adrian Wood of the Institute of Development Studies at Sussex University, for example, argues that the cumulative effect, to 1990, of North–South trade in manufactures was to lower demand for unskilled labour in Northern economies, as a proportion of 1985 employment, by 6 per cent and demand for manufacturing labour by 12 per cent.[4] These are not negligible figures.

Simultaneously, however, Bhagwati has called into question the conclusion reached in such studies, including those of influential labour economists working in the US, that imports of commodities that use unskilled labour intensively had been responsible for the decline in the real wages of unskilled labour in the US in the 1980s.[5] He has argued that, if this were indeed so, the relative prices of such labour-intensive imports should have fallen. But this they did not seem to have done.

Subsequently, two other American academics, Robert Lawrence of Harvard University and Matthew Slaughter of the Massachusetts Institute of Technology, investigated this objection, to find that the relative prices of labour-intensive goods had not fallen and that the factor proportions within these industries had also gone in a direction opposite to what would be predicted by the hypothesis that trade with poor countries was producing paupers in the US, They concluded that trade 'has not been the major contributor to the performance of US average and relative wages in the 1980s'.[6]

Whatever the truth about the past, continued rapid expansion of exports of manufactures from developing countries may have a significant effect on future demand for unskilled labour. Protection is the idiot's answer. But piecemeal protection would be irrelevant. High and sustained protection against imports of labour-intensive manufactures would be needed.

Such a policy would be open to powerful objections: it would fail to preserve lost export markets, unless rich countries were to combine to create a discriminatory free trade area against poorer ones. It would shift resources from efficient export industry to inefficient import-competing industry. It would lower aggregate economic welfare, by forgoing the gains from trade, and impose a large tax on consumers of labour-intensive products in rich countries, many of them poor. It would also create growing friction between old economic powers and new ones.

A far better response would be a mixture of increased investment in education with subsidies to unskilled employment. This would require redirection of welfare state spending, with the relatively better off bearing more of the cost of their own pensions and health spending. But pressures to retreat behind a protectionist wall against Asian exporters of manufactures are bound to grow. Defeating those pressures will need courage and imagination. Morally, it would be wrong to block the peaceful commercial road to economic progress. To avoid redistributing income openly amongst ourselves, the hopes of hundreds of millions of people would be blighted. Practically, the enticing economic opportunities created by the global spread of industrialisation would also be forgone.

GREENING TRADE

If anything, the introduction of environmentalism into the trading system is a greater worry even than that of labour standards. This is so for four reasons: first, trade measures – however convenient to powerful economies, such as the US and the European Union – are never the first-best instrument for achieving environmental objectives; second, the environmental lobby is probably stronger and more self-righteous than the one calling for labour standards; third, its concerns are still more ideally suited to capture by protectionist interests; and, finally, an escalation of trade disputes over the environment could undermine the entire multilateral trading system.

Whatever the dangers, the topic is already securely on the world trade agenda, following the ministerial meeting in Marrakesh. This established a committee on trade and the environment to report to the first WTO ministerial meeting in 1996. It has already decided to start by looking at the compatibility with trade rules of environmental taxes and charges, such as carbon taxes, and of environmental product requirements, such as those for packaging, labelling and recycling.

What is the environmentalist agenda for trade? As explained by Daniel Esty of the Institute for International Economics in Washington, it is based on four concerns:

1. trade liberalisation causes economic growth, which harms the environment;

2. countries with lax environmental standards enjoy an unfair competitive advantage;

3. trade rules and trade liberalisation may undermine or override domestic environmental regulations;

4. and, finally, GATT limits the use of trade restrictions as a form of leverage upon the environmentally recalcitrant.[7]

None of these four propositions stands up to careful scrutiny.

Trade and Economic Growth

Where the production of goods, such as clear air, or of bads, such as the extinction of a species, carries no price, then growth may indeed be harmful to overall welfare. Yet this has nothing exclusively to do with that portion of economic growth directly connected to trade. It applies to any and all growth. The answer is, of course, internalisation of environmental costs.

Economic growth is, however, not necessarily bad for the environment. As the World Bank pointed out in its World Development Report of 1992, the most important cause of deforestation is felling for firewood, something that occurs when people cannot afford commercial energy.[8] Higher incomes will reduce this cause of deforestation. Similarly, the quality of water, sanitation and the urban atmosphere improves sharply with wealth, as anyone who has visited New Delhi in winter knows. No less relevant, even casual examination of the history of environmentalism shows how closely its rise has coincided with that of a large, well-educated and prosperous middle class.

To the extent that it is true that higher incomes are environmentally damaging, as it certainly tends to be for the emission of greenhouse gases, it follows *a fortiori* that the advanced industrial countries pose the biggest problem. So indeed they do. US residents emitted 16 times as much carbon dioxide per person as their counterparts in low income countries in 1991. Almost a quarter of global CO_2 output from fossil fuel consumption and cement manufacture came from the US that year, more than twice as much as from any other single country. When people in rich countries tell poor countries that economic growth is bad for the environment, what they mean is that it is bad for poor countries to emulate the standard of living they themselves have no intention of giving up.

So much for charges against economic growth *per se*, but what of complaints against the alleged evils of trade liberalisation? It is, in fact, wrong to assume that trade liberalisation, even in the absence of environmental pricing, necessarily damages the environment. On the contrary, by economising on scarce commercialised resources, it often helps. The closed economies of the former communist countries, for example, generated phenomenal pollution. By pricing energy at well below world prices, the rate at which China emits CO_2 per unit of its gross domestic product is twice as high as India's and, incredibly, 16 times as high as Japan's, the most efficient of the major economies.

In a similar vein, a well-known Australian international economist, Kym Anderson, argues that in the case of agriculture 'countries with relatively low producer prices, such as Argentina, Australia and Thailand use less than one twentieth the amounts of chemical fertiliser per cropped hectare that high price countries such as Switzerland use.'[9] Liberalising agricultural trade should improve the environment, by reducing the use of such additives.

Environmental Dumping

The second main concern, that about so-called 'eco-dumping', is equally misplaced. In the first place, there is no obvious difference between the competitive implications of divergent environmental standards and the consequences of many other policy differences between countries. Some countries subsidise education more than others. Does this justify protection against imports of skill-intensive goods?

In the second place, there is little evidence that high environmental standards do impose a substantial handicap even on the most obviously affected industries. A paper by Ms Piritta Sorsa of the World Bank argues, from a study of seven advanced economies, that industries that spent most on pollution control generally maintained their international competitiveness between 1970 and 1990.[10] This is not surprising, since advanced countries have a strong comparative advantage in precisely the most environmentally-sensitive, capital-intensive process industries, such as chemicals. For this reason, global trade liberalisation is also likely to shift the production of the most polluting industries towards countries with the strictest pollution controls.

In the third place, as has been pointed out above, there is no reason to suppose that optimal environmental regulations would be the same everywhere. Optimal regulations must depend on resources, geography, wealth and tastes, all of which will quite properly diverge amongst countries. The cost even of toxic waste inevitably seems higher to rich, secure people than to those whose main concern is finding a clean water supply.

Finally, a country as a whole cannot be put at a competitive disadvantage by having higher environmental standards than its neighbours, only those specific industries on which the costs of high standards fall relatively more heavily. But these are also the most polluting industries. The fact that they are put at a disadvantage in trade and are, therefore, more likely to migrate to less politically unfriendly climes, other things being equal, should surely be welcomed by consistent environmentalists, who presumably want to see polluting domestic industry shrink. Trade is on their side. It is not an enemy.

Trade and Domestic Regulation

The third concern on Mr Esty's list – that trade rules and trade liberalisation may undermine or override domestic environmental regulations – is almost equally misplaced. Environmentalists argue, for example, that industrial opposition to high environmental standards is a political obstacle to their achieving and sustaining the domestic regulations they desire. The natural answer to this complaint is 'tough'. It is cheeky to argue that Mexico should be forced to adopt an environmental standard it does not want or need merely to make it easier for US environmentalists to purchase the acquiescence of US industrialists in the regulations they desire.

The more valid argument here concerns the regulatory 'race to the bottom'. It is obviously possible that if each country imposed what seems an optimal regulation in the absence of any influence over the regulations imposed elsewhere, the outcome may be less than optimal regulation overall. Here two points arise. The first is that, in practice, it is far from clear that either economic or political pressures have, in practice, created such a race to the bottom. An interesting example is trade between the US and the EU, which is liberal in most areas, even though EU labour standards are much higher than in the US. Nor is it at all obvious that relocation to take advantage of differences in environmental standards is at all common. The second is the issue of transparency. Perhaps what trade does is merely offset the distortion created by the intrinsic over-representation of single-issue zealots within democratic political systems.

Trade Rules and Environmental Regulation

What is to be made of the fourth of Mr Esty's concerns, that GATT prevents use of trade restrictions as a lever? So indeed it does. A distinction needs to be made here between cases where one country's policies impose direct environmental harm on others and those where they do not.

Where there is no such direct overspill, the main questions are those of dumping (discussed above) and the closely related issue of process regulation (another area where environmentalists argue that the policies of others undermine those they seek for their own countries). It is highly questionable, however, whether countries should be allowed to restrict imports merely because they are produced in ways deemed unacceptable. As the GATT Secretariat noted, in its own lucid discussion of these questions, 'it is difficult to think of a way to contain the cross-border assertion of divergent environmental priorities.'[11]

The risks of unilateral application of a particular country's standards were excellently revealed in the tuna/dolphin case, brought by the US against Mexico, in which the former banned imports of tuna caught in dolphin-unsafe nets. Mexican fishermen, it was argued, caught tuna in ways that also killed dolphins. Eating such tuna supposedly causes great moral anguish to American consumers.

A panel subsequently ruled that this embargo was GATT-inconsistent, its reasoning being based on the view that if the US argument were accepted, then any country could ban imports of a product merely because the exporting country pursues environmental or health policies different from its own. This form of environmental imperialism is evidently threatening to any international regime. How threatening it might be can be seen from the fact that the dolphin issue is not even about the environment, but about the still more contentious area of animal rights. Dolphins are sacred in the US. But how would the US feel if India were to argue the case for equivalent respect for cows? Or is the US right because it is powerful and India wrong because it is not?

Furthermore, there are many solutions to this dilemma, other than banning imports or simply forcing Mexico to adopt US regulations. The way the fish are caught might be put on labels, so allowing consumers to choose whether or not to buy 'dolphin-unsafe' tuna. Alternatively, the US might pay Mexican fishermen to cease using nets thought likely to entrap dolphins.

Where there is international overspill, the question is whether trade policy is the best instrument to change another country's policies. The absence of a regulation or control may indeed create a direct physical externality outside the jurisdiction in question. Failure to control emissions of airborne particles in the UK contaminates air breathed in Western Europe. There is a case for international standards in such cases; and this is also true for emission of greenhouse gases.

If what is desired is something that demands international co-operation – such as preservation of the ozone layer, or of some endangered species – the best course, often the only one, is international agreements that govern domestic policies. If such agreements are reached, trade restrictions may perhaps play a subsidiary role as a means of enforcement. Yet it is clear that such global objectives cannot be achieved by measures directed at trade alone. Elephants will not be conserved merely because their ivory cannot be exported. Nor will the ozone layer be preserved merely by preventing China from exporting the wrong kinds of refrigerators. In such cases, a gamut of essentially domestic policies must also be changed.

Furthermore, trade restrictions will certainly not be effective in changing the domestic policies of the big and powerful, who often do the most damage. Does anyone suppose the US would introduce, say, a $1 a gallon gasolene tax as a result of sanctions on its exports, or even that anyone would dare try? Just how restricted is the effectiveness of trade sanctions against big countries has been discovered by the US in the case of the human rights violations of China. The approach is ineffective partly because it imposes large costs on those who use it. It may also lead to damaging cycles of retaliation. Not least, it is a way for the powerful to coerce weaker countries to change what they do.

The best policy is to create a global system of property rights, which compensates countries for the things they do in the global interest. Those adversely affected could pay polluters to cease to pollute, instead. Under a different allocation of the implicit property rights in air, the polluter could be required to pay compensation to those adversely affected. The higher the compensation, the greater the incentive to reduce pollution. Either way, procedures to monitor emissions would also have to be agreed.

At present, countries with large forests, for example, are exporting carbon dioxide elimination to countries that emit it. Because they are not recompensed for doing so, there is inadequate incentive for them to continue. The obvious answer is for them to be paid for this beneficial service. Proceeds of a carbon tax regime could be used for that purpose. This would be an imaginative application of the polluter pays principle which Mr Esty endorses, along with global co-operation, as the right solution for global environmental problems. Cost internalisation is indeed the only feasible solution, though it should also be stressed how difficult it will be to agree on what, for example, elephants are worth.

If arguments for higher labour standards in the interests of citizens of poor exporting countries carry a mild stench of hypocrisy, demands for the imposition of environmental standards simply reek of it. Citizens of European countries that have eliminated all large wild animals insist that Indians must protect their tigers and Africans their elephants. Similarly, citizens of countries that have destroyed their forests demand that developing countries keep theirs standing, on pain of trade sanctions. And why should they do that? To reduce global warming comes the answer.

Yet whose emission of greenhouse gases is it that is creating this danger? In 1989 some 60 per cent of global emissions of greenhouse gases came from the 15 per cent of the global population who live in the advanced industrial countries.[12] Furthermore, their emissions per capita were almost $3\frac{1}{2}$ times greater than those of people living in middle-income developing countries and 10 times greater than those of people living in low-income countries, among whom fall China and India. If the rich wish the poor to behave in ways different from themselves, they should have the decency to pay them. Otherwise, both here and in the case of labour standards, the rich countries are merely proposing to punish the poor for their poverty. Before much further progress towards effective global agreements on environmental protection will be achieved, the environmental lobby of advanced countries must acknowledge that their countries do not occupy the moral high ground.

ASSESSING THE NEW AGENDA

The two new items on the agenda have much in common. In both cases, the US administration is advancing proposals that have very little substantive merit. In both cases, protectionism can be readily concealed under a cloak of hypocritical concern for workers in developing countries or for the global environment. In both cases, interests hostile to liberal trade lie behind the new demands. In both cases, poorer countries believe they are being asked to pay a price for the sins of the rich, who not only do most of the environmental damage but who have failed to equip their own labour forces with the means to meet the new global competition. There is, in fact, no responsible case for introducing labour standards into trade and very little for introducing the environment into it either. People who live in greenhouses should, in short, stop emitting so much moralistic gas.

NOTES

1. See, for example, J.N. Bhagwati. 'The Demands to Reduce Diversity among Trading Nations', mimeo; J.N. Bhagwati, 'The Case for Free Trade', *Scientific American*, November 1993; J.N. Bhagwati, 'Labour Standards, Social Clause and WTO', House Banking Committee Testimony, 28 June 1994; J.N. Bhagwati and T.N. Srinivasan, 'Trade and the Environment: Does Environmental Diversity Detract from the Case for Free Trade?' mimeo, July 1994; J.N. Bhagwati. 'The WTO: What Next?', 1994 Harold Wincott Memorial Lecture (London: Institute for Economic Affairs, 1994).
2. See Bhagwati, 'Labour Standards, Social Clause and WTO'.
3. It is often forgotten how big international income differences are: even measured at common international prices, the incomes per head of the Swiss are 20 times higher than those of Indians. See World Bank, *World Development Report 1993, Investing in Health* (Washington, DC: Oxford University Press, for the World Bank) World Development Indicators, Table 30.

4. Adrian Wood, 'The Factor Content of North–South Trade in Manufactures Reconsidered', *Weltwirtschaftliches Archiv*, vol. 127, no. 4, 1991, pp. 719–43. See also his *North–South Trade, Employment and Inequality* (Oxford: Clarendon Press, 1994).

5. See Bhagwati, *Free Traders and Free Immigrationists: Strangers or Friends?*, Working Paper 20 (New York: Russell Sage Foundation, April 1991).

6. Robert Z. Lawrence and Matthew J. Slaughter, 'Trade and US Wages: Great Sucking Sound or Small Hiccup?' *Brookings Papers on Economic Activity, Microeconomics*, 1993, no. 2, p. 208. This conclusion is also supported in a review article by Jagdish Bhagwati and Vivek Dehejia. See 'Free Trade and Wages of the Unskilled: Is Marx Striking Again?', presented at a conference on the Influence of International Trade on US Wages organised by the American Enterprise Institute, 10 September 1993.

7. Daniel C. Esty, *Greening the Gatt: Trade, Environment and the Future* (Washington, DC: Institute for International Economics, 1994).

8. *World Development Report 1992: Development and the Environment* (Oxford: Oxford University Press, for the World Bank).

9. Kym Anderson, *Economic Growth, Environmental Issues and Trade*, Discussion Paper No. 830 (London: Centre for Economic Policy Research, 1993).

10. Piritta Sorsa, 'Competitiveness and Environmental Standards', Working Paper 1249 (International Economics Department, World Bank).

11. *International Trade 90–91*, vol. 1 (Geneva: GATT, 1992).

12. See World Bank, *World Development Report 1992: Development and the Environment* (Washington, DC: Oxford University Press, for the World Bank), Figure 6.

Part Three
International Institutions

8 Multilateral Institutions and Unilateral Trade Liberalisation in Developing Countries

Selected LDCs

Titla
019
F13,
F33

David Greenaway and Oliver Morrissey

Jagdish Bhagwati has been a major figure in the fields of international trade and economic development for almost 40 years now. Two generations of scholars and policy-makers have been influenced to a significant degree by his thinking and writing. So too have the major multilateral agencies, in particular the World Bank and the GATT. In 1986–7 he held a senior advisory post in the World Bank; from 1992–4 he was Economic Adviser to the Director-General of GATT. He has vigorously defended the role of these international agencies, in particular the Bank's role in promoting more open trade regimes in developing countries and the GATT's role in providing a stable set of rules within which international commerce is conducted. In our tribute to Bhagwati we evaluate the role of the World Bank and GATT in recent liberalisation efforts in developing countries and speculate on how these roles might evolve in the post-Uruguay Round setting.

I INTRODUCTION

Whether independently or as part of a World Bank Structural Adjustment Loan (SAL), virtually all developing countries have attempted some degree of trade liberalisation since 1980, and there are numerous episodes of trade liberalisation attempts in previous decades. There is a strong consensus among economists that trade liberalisation is desirable, but the success of many liberalisation episodes has been very mixed, whether evaluated according to the amount of trade liberalisation actually undertaken or the ultimate effect on economic growth (for recent reviews, see Greenaway and Morrissey, 1994, on the former; and Greenaway and Sapsford, 1994, on the latter). Our concern here is not with evaluating the success of trade liberalisation episodes *per se* but with examining the role of global institutions, notably the World Bank and GATT, in promoting trade liberalisation in developing countries (hereafter LDCs) since 1980. We also consider how these roles may evolve in the future, especially as the post-Uruguay Round GATT evolves into the World Trade Organisation (WTO).

In the post-war period, among the multilateral institutions, GATT has had the clearest responsibility for trade liberalisation. (GATT's role has been evaluated by Bhagwati on numerous occasions: see for example Bhagwati, 1990.) Its principal successes have, however, been in reducing and binding tariffs between developed countries, through periodic Rounds of multilateral trade negotiations. Initially, the World Bank was primarily concerned with financing investment, but introduced trade liberalisation as a fundamental component of SAL conditionality from 1980. The IMF has mainly had responsibility for monetary management and stabilisation. However, through its structural adjustment facility it has taken an interest in trade reform. Moreover, through cross-conditionality it has began to co-ordinate more closely with the Bank over SAL programmes, and its conditions on exchange rates have had trade implications. These institutions have few, if any, formal mechanisms for co-ordination among themselves. However, since the mid-1980s they have shown the semblance of a common front, at least with respect to trade liberalisation in LDCs. When, together but independently, they appear to be pushing in the same direction the argument for trade liberalisation may be more convincing to LDCs. This is especially true because their institutional facets, how they interact with LDCs, vary significantly.[1]

The GATT, as the central facilitator of multilateral trade liberalisation, has proceeded by multilateral negotiation. The guiding principles have been most favoured nation status (a concession or barrier to one contracting party should be extended to all), reciprocity (concessions from a given partner be matched with comparable reciprocal concessions) and national treatment (foreign goods should be treated in the same way as domestic goods). However, much of the content of the GATT texts detail circumstances when GATT principles need *not* be adhered to. There are important exemption clauses for LDCs, notably that they may retain protection for infant industries or in the face of balance of payments crises, as a consequence of which GATT has made little direct progress in encouraging trade liberalisation in LDCs (see Bhagwati, 1991). By contrast, the Bank and IMF operate through bilateral negotiations and, perhaps because they are providing finance, are usually the more powerful bargaining party. The fact that the Bank and IMF had begun to co-ordinate on economic policy reform in LDCs, especially trade liberalisation, during the Uruguay Round negotiations, which introduced many new areas of trade to GATT discipline, is coincidental. It is none the less important.

The strategic organisational approach, proposed by Yarbrough and Yarbrough (1992) and discussed in section III, is a useful framework for examining the role of multilateral institutions. The essence of this approach is that institutions are developed to mediate international relations which take place within an imperfect information environment, and in particular that the institutional forms of trade liberalisation reflects the nature of these imperfections. Agents (whether firms or governments) are constrained to act according to bounded rationality in an environment subject to uncertainty over time. Consequently, long-term contracts are infeasible and periodic renegotiation is necessary. Recourse to legal enforcement of any (implicit) contract is, at best, problematic. In the absence of effective third party enforcement, parties have to rely on self-help, negotiation and reputation. This precarious environment gives reason for opportunism: there are inherent incentives for one party to try to cheat on (or renegotiate to their own advantage) an agreement. In such an environment institutions evolve to provide norms and dispute settlement procedures, which lead to a modicum of third party enforcement, so that opportunism is discouraged, if not pre-empted, and mutually beneficial co-operation is feasible.

This strategic organisational approach offers an explanation for why trade liberalisation takes a particular institutional form, notably depending on costs of withdrawal and third party enforcement. We examine a separate but related issue: namely, how global institutions can expand their powers of enforcement and hence facilitate multilateralism (in trade liberalisation). This is especially important under GATT, where the Trade Policy Review Mechanism (TPRM) has increased transparency hence facilitating enforcement via monitoring, and where new issues have been brought within its remit via the Uruguay Round Agreements. It is also important for the Bank, which has complemented GATT by becoming a powerful proponent of trade liberalisation in LDCs through SAL conditionality.

Section II sets the context in the form of a brief review of the literature on trade liberalisation in LDCs, focusing on the period since 1980. Our intention is to clarify what is meant by trade liberalisation, how it is implemented and how it relates to general economic policy reform. Having clarified our subject matter, we then turn to the institutional aspects of trade liberalisation in section III, which elaborates on the relevance of the strategic organisational approach, outlined above, and then discuss aspects of the roles of the GATT and the Bank in section IV. Some conclusions are drawn in section V.

II DEFINING TRADE LIBERALISATION

There is no concise and generally agreed definition of trade liberalisation in the literature (Bhagwati, 1988; and Greenaway and Morrissey, 1994, discuss the main alternatives). It is, however, helpful to adopt a broad definition of trade liberalisation as *any reform that brings the relative incentives for production of exportables and importables in an economy more closely into line with relative world prices.*[2] This allows us to identify two principal types of liberalisation, noting that in all cases we are moving from a situation of anti-export bias (arising principally but not exclusively from protection which favours the import-competing sector). Import liberalisation encompasses those reforms which reduce protection, making it possible to import at world prices. This includes the removal of quantitative restrictions (QRs) and the reduction of traiffs. Export promotion reforms involve the use of compensatory export incentives to encourage domestic resources to be redirected to the exportables sector. Such reforms frequently take the form of export subsidies, and it may seem strange to argue that the introduction of distortions can amount to liberalisation. The rationale is that removing protection will reduce the return to importables, but this alone may not guarantee that resources are redirected to exportables. Hence, *temporary* export promotion may ensure that resources do not go to non-tradeables.[3] We can note that Bank-sponsored trade liberalisation includes both forms, but that liberalisation under GATT would typically refer to import liberalisation; export subsidies to promote exporting activity are now proscribed under GATT, except in the least developed countries (defined in the Uruguay Round Agreements as countries with GDP per capita of under $1000).

It is common to include reforms of the exchange rate regime as an element in a trade liberalisation programme. This can be justified most clearly for devaluation, which increases returns to exports and is intended to bring the exchange rate closer to its equilibrium level. Easing access to foreign exchange makes it easier to import, and thus could be considered an element of import liberalisation. More generally, the 'correct' real exchange rate is required to keep relative domestic incentives in line with relative world prices for importables and exportables. If we include exchange rate 'liberalisation' as an element of trade liberalisation, we should address the role of the IMF in this element of the process. While recognising that role, we will confine attention largely to GATT and the World Bank as these are the most important in respect of trade liberalisation *per se*.

Tables 8.1–8.3 summarise elements of trade liberalisation in a large number of countries, classified according to the components outlined above. As can be seen, reductions in nominal tariffs figure prominently, as does the

Table 8.1   Summary of Pre-1980 Trade Liberalisations[1]

| Country | Policy Reforms Present or Not[2] | | | | Post-reform Growth[3] | |
	QRs	Tariffs	Exports	ER	Exports	GDP
Argentina (2)		✓	✓	✓	+	?
Brazil	✓	✓	✓		+	+
Chile (2)	✓	✓			+	+
Colombia (2)	✓	✓	✓		–ve	+
Indonesia (2)	✓	✓	✓	✓	+	+
Israel (3)	✓	✓		✓	?	+
Korea (2)	✓	✓	✓	✓	+/–ve	+/–ve
New Zealand (3)	✓	✓		✓	+	?
Pakistan (2)			–ve	✓	+	+
Peru	✓	✓			–ve	–ve
Philippines (2)	?	?		✓	+	+
Spain (3)		✓	✓	✓	+	?
Sri Lanka (2)	✓	–ve	–ve	✓	–ve/+	?/+
Turkey (2)	✓	✓	✓	✓	+	?
Uruguay	✓	✓		✓	+	+
Yugoslavia	✓	✓	–ve	✓	–ve	–ve
Singapore	✓	✓	✓		+	+
Totals 17	**13**	**14**	**8**	**12**	**12+**	**10+**

Notes:
These are broad indications of diverse reform packages from a variety of countries and time-periods (numbers in parenthesis refer to number of liberalisation episodes), and are no more than indicative.
1. These are 17 of the 19 liberalisations in the PMC study. Details are not provided for Greece and Portugal.
2. Policy areas: QRs – reduction in the number/extent of quantitative restrictions on imports; tariffs – reduction in average level or range of tariffs; exports – direct measures to promote exports; ER – rationalisation and/or devaluation of the exchange rate. A ✓ indicates the reforms were present; ? indicates that the reforms were ambiguous or very limited; –ve implies opposite reforms (eg. export disincentives or increases in tariffs).
3. Comparison of annual average growth rates for three years prior to reforms and the three years after reforms: + implies growth increased after reform; –ve implies growth slowed; ? implies minimal difference; two keys imply significant differences between reform episodes (e.g. Sri Lanka).
Source: Adapted from Greenaway and Morrissey (1994), Tables 1, 4 and 5.

Trade and Development

Table 8.2   Elements of Recent Trade Liberalisations

Country	Average Pre-Reform	Nominal Current	Tariff[1] Ratio	Tax[2] Dependence	ER[3]
South Asia					
Bangladesh (1989, 1992)	94	50	0.53	0.42	−5.3
India (1990, 1993)	128	71	0.55	0.30	−7.7
Pakistan (1987, 1990)	69	65	0.94	0.38	−11.7
Sri Lanka (1985, 1992)	31	25	0.81	0.22	−0.5
Average	**80**	**53**	**0.71**	**0.40[4]**	
East Asia					
China (1986, 1992)	38	43	1.13		−43.9
Philippines (1985, 1992)	28	24	0.88	0.29	1.8
Indonesia (1985, 1990)	27	22	0.81	0.03	−23.2
Korea (1984, 1992)	24	10	0.42	0.17	13.1
Thailand (1986, 1990)[5]	13	11	0.88	0.22	−0.5
Average	**29**	**25**	**0.82**	**−0.65[4]**	
SSA					
Ivory Coast (1985, 1989)	26	33	1.27	0.31	CFA
Ghana (1983, 1991)	30	17	0.57	0.18	−11.1
Kenya (1987, 1992)	40	34	0.85	0.23	−5.4
Madagascar (1988, 1990)	46	36	0.78	0.32	−11.2
Nigeria (1984, 1990)	35	33	0.93	0.23	−71.2
Senegal (1986, 1991)	98	90	0.92	0.43	CFA
Tanzania (1986, 1992)	30	33	1.10	0.07	−145.2
Zaire (1984, 1990)	24	25	1.04	0.17	−13.1
Average	**41**	**38**	**0.94**	**0.29[4]**	
Latin America					
Colombia (1984, 1992)	61	12	0.20	0.13	−36.1
Peru (1988, 1992)	57	17	0.30	0.22	106.7
Costa Rica (1985, 1992)	53	15	0.28	0.13	−15.8
Brazil (1987, 1992)	51	21	0.41	0.02	9.5
Venezuela (1989, 1991)	37	19	0.51	0.05	0.2
Chile (1984, 1991)	35	11	0.31	0.11	−14.5
Argentina (1988, 1992)	29	12	0.41	0.05	43.7
Mexico (1985, 1987)	29	10	0.34	0.03	3.7
Average	**44**	**15**	**0.35**	**0.74[4]**	

Notes:

Years given in parenthesis are pre-reform and current.

1.   Unweighted average nominal tariff (tends to be biased upwards), rounded; ratio is current/pre-reform – lower ratio implies greater tariff reductions; figures in Average rows are simple averages for each region.

Table 8.2 *Notes (cont.)*
2. Tax dependence is tariff revenue as proportion of tax revenue in 1984.
3. Percentage real exchange rate depreciation between the first year of reform and 1992.
4. Figure is the rank correlation between countries ranked in descending order of tax dependence against descending order of tariff ratio; i.e. a high positive correlation implies that countries most dependent on tariffs are least able to reduce average tariffs.
5. Import-weighted average nominal tariff.
Source: Derived from various tables in Dean et al. (1994).

Table 8.3   Intensity of Trade Policy Reform Proposals

Item	Intensity of Reforms[1]			Presence	
	Strong	Medium	Weak	Yes	No
Overall import policy	14	15	11		
QRs[2]	14	15	11		
Tariff level[2]	7	21	12		
Tariff dispersion	7	24	9		
Schedule of future reduction	6	29	5		
Overall export policy	15	15	10		
Reduction in anti-export bias	17	12	11		
Exchange rate flexibility[3]				38	2
Export promotion measures[4]				33	7
Studies of effects of trade policy reform				28	12

Notes:
Assessments refer to proposals supported by the World Bank in 40 countries receiving adjustment lending in the 1980s; they do not refer to implementation (experience with which is very varied).
1. Totals are 40 in all cases.
2. Reforms which replaced QRs with tariffs are included in both lines.
3. Often these were not explicit conditions, but constituted understandings made under the programme, usually as part of a standby agreement.
4. Includes such schemes as export credits, insurance, guarantees and institutional development.
Source: Thomas and Nash (1991), Table 1.

tariffication of quotas. Both would be widely regarded as acts of import liberalisation. Exchange rate reforms also feature regularly and, less commonly, export promotion; both reduce anti-export bias. Most of the pre-1980 liberalisation programmes listed in Table 8.1 were unilateral and voluntary. The data in Table 8.3 and most of the cases in Table 8.2 refer to the outcome of World Bank SAL programmes; some were tied in to World Bank/IMF cross-conditionality.

Table 8.1 summarises the experience of 17 countries with a combined total of 32 liberalisation episodes in the period 1960–84 (all but the second Turkish episode of 1980–4 commenced before 1980). These are 17 of the 19 countries which are the subject of the Papageorgiou, Michaely and Choksi (1991) study. In 80 per cent of the countries tariffs were reduced, QRs were reduced in almost 70 per cent while direct export promotion was evident in almost half; there was exchange rate adjustment in 80 per cent of the countries. Seventy per cent of the countries experienced improved export performance following liberalisation (but no single class of policy reform appears to have been a necessary and sufficient condition for this), and in just over half of the countries this appeared to promote improved economic growth. This has been used to lend evidence to the claim that trade liberalisation has a beneficial impact on economic performance.[4]

Table 8.2 provides recent evidence on trade liberalisation since 1985 for 25 of the countries covered in Dean et al. (1994). The tariff ratio (the ratio of the post-reform average nominal tariff to its pre-reform level) provides a summary measure of liberalisation: a ratio above unity implies an increase in average nominal tariffs while a ratio of, for example, 0.7 implies a 30 per cent reduction. As a summary measure it has problems: the unweighted average nominal tariff is biased upwards as heavy weight is attached to the highest tariff rates; in not distinguishing between input and output tariffs, the ratio may not be highly correlated with changes in effective protection; and it does not account for non-tariff measures (typically, these too are significantly reduced under trade liberalisation, although there is great variation in experience). Nevertheless, it is one of the easiest measures to obtain and a basic measure employed by multilateral institutions; it is at least indicative of the direction of reform.

It is clear that, of the regions, tariff reductions were least in SSA, which exhibited enormous variability across countries. Only Ghana achieved a significant reduction in tariffs while Kenya and Madagascar also demonstrated considerable liberalisation; The Ivory Coast and Zaire appear to have had no liberalisation, and Tanzania only liberalised import restrictions. (Morrissey (1994) suggests that actual liberalisation in Tanzania, as it included considerable rationalisation of tariff rates, was more impressive than suggested by these figures.) Latin America reduced tariffs the most, and to the lowest regional average level, according to these figures; however, current macroeconomic crises faced by some of these countries may have led to recent reversals of these reductions, Brazil being one example where many tariffs were increased in March 1995. East Asia, if one excludes China, continued its general pattern of tariff reduction. The South Asian sample is small and only Sri Lanka exhibits reductions of tariffs to relatively low levels. On the basis of this evidence, one cannot be overwhelmed by the extent of liberalisation.

A number of factors will influence the extent of tariff reductions, and import liberalisation in general. In particular is the willingness of the government to implement liberalisation which will be related to the expected fiscal impact and the extent of opposition, both of which can be proxied by tax dependence (tariff revenue as a share of total tax revenue). *A priori*, a high dependence on tariff revenue could limit the extent of tariff reductions: the government will not be able to accommodate a potentially large revenue loss, and a high level of protection pre-reform implies high rents and, hence, strong opposition. This implies a negative correlation between tax dependence and tariff reductions, which implies a *positive* rank correlation between the tax ratio and tariff ratio, reported for Regions in 'tax ratio' columns (Table 8.2). This is observed for all regions except East Asia. Before considering the evidence, some factors operating against this hypothesis are worth considering. First, exchange rate devaluation increases the domestic currency value of imports and in such cases, if external finance is available to prevent import compression, tariff reductions can be revenue enhancing; there is evidence for this in Tanzania (Morrissey, 1994). Second, concertina reforms could reduce the unweighted average nominal tariff but increase tariff revenue. Third, tariffication of QRs is a revenue-enhancing form of trade liberalisation. Thus, we should not be at all surprised about the relatively low correlations reported in Table 8.2 (especially given the small samples).

The rank correlation coefficient is greatest for Latin America, which tended to be least dependent on tariffs, reduced tariffs the most and to the lowest average level. South Asia broadly conforms to expectations, but one should note that many of these countries started from relatively high tariff levels. India raises the possibility of a country which begins with prohibitively high tariffs so that reductions can actually increase revenue, as goods previously effectively prohibited become imported. East Asia exhibits a relatively high negative correlation: this reflects the fact that Korea reduced tariffs by far more than the other countries, but its dependence was not lowest; while Indonesia had minimal tariff dependence, but did reduce tariffs by significantly more than other countries. The SSA countries exhibited a far more mixed performance, although there is a general pattern of countries with high tax dependence being disinclined to reduce tariffs significantly. A failure to devalue significantly suggests import liberalisation without general export promotion, and is likely to have been revenue-depleting as lower tariffs applied to a relatively unchanged domestic currency price. The countries that appeared to reduce tariffs the most – Ghana, Kenya and Madagascar – did also devalue. In general, there is evidence that fiscal impact acts as a constraint on liberalisation

Table 8.3 shows that for World Bank programmes in general, exchange rate flexibility (95 per cent) and some export promotion (83 per cent) were present in most cases. It is also clear from Table 8.3 that the Bank takes a broad view of the components of trade liberalisation, encompassing as we do import liberalisation, export promotion (especially reducing anti-export bias) and exchange rate reforms. We can also note that the Bank supported studies of the impact of trade reform in some 70 per cent of cases; this is an important form of technical support which can promote reform and institutional change in adjusting countries, an issue we return to in section IV.

Why have there been so many liberalisation attempts since 1980? Greenaway and Morrissey (1994) offer a partial answer in suggesting why the Bank embraced liberalisation so enthusiastically. By the late 1970s the dominant economic ideology, at least in the US, Britain and among Bank technical staff, advocated free markets and minimal government. This view was perhaps strongest in respect of trade policy, where economic theory provided a rare near-consensus that trade interventions were never the optimal welfare-increasing policy (even when distortions were present).[5] In addition, a persuasive body of empirical evidence demonstrated a significant positive correlation between outward orientation and economic growth. Furthermore, economic techniques for evaluating and monitoring trade policy are relatively well developed and the evidence seemed to point to pervasive and significant distortions in developing countries (see Greenaway and Milner, 1993). Thus, by 1980, the Bank was persuaded of the need for economic liberalisation and the arguments for trade liberalisation, in particular reducing protection, were especially persuasive. The ability of the Bank to imbue LDCs with this commitment depended on the nature of its relationship with LDCs (discussed in section III).

We can offer an explanation for why the Bank adopted economic liberalisation and why trade reforms figured so prominently in SALs, and this helps to explain why so many countries implemented trade liberalisation in the 1980s, if only because this was an intrinsic component of a Bank-sponsored adjustment programme. The burgeoning literature on economic policy reform in LDCs, based on the experiences of numerous countries, demonstrates how varied the extent of actual liberalisation and the effects on economic performance have been in practice (recent reviews are Greenaway and Morrissey, 1993; Haggard and Webb, 1993). Trade liberalisation is not a neatly defined policy package, nor is it a panacea. We have argued for a fairly wide view of the components of trade liberalisation: particular countries will incorporate some of these components, will implement them to a greater or lesser degree, and will enact other economic policies and reforms at the same time (which may or may not be complementary). It is clear that LDCs will commit themselves to reforms in order to receive the external financing associated with SALs. This in itself, however, does not mean that the countries will implement *effective* reforms.

Early evaluations of SALs concentrated on the types of reforms proposed, the extent of implementation and the economic results (Greenaway and Morrissey, 1993, review these evaluations). More recently, emphasis has shifted to the politics of economic policy reform: why is it that some polities are better able to reform than others, and what factors determine the political capacity to implement effective reforms (Haggard and Webb, 1993, provide an extensive review). An emerging literature addresses the role of institutions and administrative capacity, and links this to political commitment to assess the evolution of the policy reform process (Levy, 1993; Morrissey, 1994). In the remainder of this section we consider the implications of this work for promoting trade liberalisation, although the arguments are more general.

Trade reforms generate winners and losers, and political capacity relates to the ability of the government to mobilise support for reform (a coalition of winners) and to manage the opposition and compensate losers.[6] Import liberalisation generates losers among those previously earning rents from protection, usually a politically influential lobby. Export promotion, in contrast, mobilises support by building a lobby of winners. The combination of the two in a programme of trade reform can have important implications for success and sustainability. Turkey, for example, provided extensive export promotion early in the reform process but was very slow in implementing import liberalisation. The effect was to complement support for reforms and an early surge in exports which fuelled economic growth and reinforced the perception that the adjustment programme was successful. However, failure to reform the public sector and borrowing to support budget deficits, both of which are forms of compensation and reflect an unwillingness to create losers, threaten the sustainability of the reforms (Morrissey, 1993). Tanzania, by contrast, liberalised imports but did little to promote exports directly (devaluation and agricultural reforms increased the returns to exporters); losers may have outnumbered winners, which helps to explain the slow pace and limited success of the reforms (Morrissey, 1994). An example where effective import liberalisation combined with effective export promotion resulted in a serious commitment to sustaining liberalisation was in Mauritius.

Many other examples can be found to support our point that political factors must be incorporated into the design of effective trade liberalisation programmes. This has never been an explicit concern of GATT, nor is it likely to be one for the WTO, which may be simply because the operating process of multilateral negotiations implies that a country's political position will be reflected in its negotiating stance – it will contract to those agreements it supports. Furthermore, as we have already stated, GATT did little to enforce trade liberalisation in LDCs. Indeed through its 'special and differential' provisions it endowed them with a right to protect. However, the current situation is that all signatories to the Uruguay Round are contracted to *all* disciplines in GATT 1994, and the WTO is intended to have a broader remit. It is also intended to make it more difficult for developing countries to take unilateral action under one of the exemption clauses and therefore make it more difficult for pro-protectionist lobbies to emerge. Moreover, for the first time, an explicit graduation criterion has been included, which confines special and differential treatment to the least developed. The role of the WTO will have to differ from that of GATT, as elaborated in the following sections of this paper. The Bank, in contrast, has adopted a more active role and clearly recognises the importance of political factors.

III INSTITUTIONS AND TRADE LIBERALISATION

Global institutions play a number of important roles in facilitating trade liberalisation (and reform in general). First, they will have some capacity to encourage or cajole countries into attempting reforms. Second, they can monitor and enforce the implementation. Third, multilateral institutions can give a reform programme credibility thereby enhancing the prospects for sustainability of reforms. Fourth, and more generally, 'policy choices are influenced by international networks and socialisation that result in the transmission of policy-relevant knowledge' (Haggard and Webb, 1993, p. 156). The widespread attempts at liberalisation in the 1980s were largely motivated by such a transmission, for example, that outward orientation is seen as conducive to economic growth. In the future, this role can involve the transfer of knowledge on policy implementation and institution-building (section IV). In this section we explore the roles of GATT and the World Bank.

An observation provides a link between the role of the GATT and World Bank. The GATT has explicitly permitted protection in LDCs either to foster infant industries or because of balance of payments crises under Article XVIIIi and XVIIIiii respectively. Moreover, Part IV of the Agreement has absolved LDCs of a reciprocity commitment. The IMF has long had responsibility for stabilisation, but this really only addressed short-term responses to payments crises. As SALs are intended to improve economic efficiency, increase growth and render the economy more flexible, they should facilitate a long-term response to payments crises. Such crises will not be eliminated, but the rationale by which they exempt LDCs from GATT discipline will be undermined. This will be increasingly important as a principle of graduation appears to be enshrined in GATT 1994: LDCs with a per capita income above $1000 will not be excused from compliance with GATT discipline. Successful adjustment, given the emphasis on minimising government interventions, would also undermine the infant industry argument. Hence, the Bank has promoted unilateral trade liberalisation in LDCs and, through adjustment, is helping to foster conditions in LDCs which will allow them to be brought under GATT discipline (whence the WTO can assume its intended responsibility for trade liberalisation in all countries). Whether the ultimate result will be greater and sustained trade liberalisation depends on the relationships between the Bank, GATT and LDCs.

Yarbrough and Yarbrough (1992) set out to offer an explanation for why historically liberalisation has taken different organisational forms. If we confine attention to the post-war period, they observe that liberalisation was predominantly multilateral (through GATT) until the 1960s. There followed a period where much 'new' liberalisation resulted from bilateral negotiations (the US, in particular, tended to go its own way in the 1980s); by the 1990s, the dominant form of liberalisation initiatives appeared to be minilateral, by which they refer to the increasing prominence of preferential trading arrangements with formal supranational enforcement mechanisms, in particular the European Union and to a lesser degree NAFTA. While their approach is useful, and we will make use of aspects of it, it is deficient in two respects for our purposes. First, it offers little insight into how global institutions can proactively promote trade liberalisation.[7] Secondly, the approach is more applicable to developed countries in general and says little about the specific circumstances of LDCs. These, of course, are the two issues with which we are concerned and are integrated into our discussion of the approach in this section.

The strategic organisational (SO) approach to the forms of trade liberalisation focuses on relation-specific investments, representing assets which, after the investment, have limited alternative uses. This builds on the work of *inter alia* Williamson (1985), who identified asset specificity as a fundamental element of transactions costs and hence a determinant of the institutional form of a relationship. Williamson pioneered the application of transactions costs to explaining the organisation of firms, and it is especially relevant to multinationals (MNEs). It also applies to states, among whose functions is determining the terms of foreign access to their market, which requires the state to 'trade' access with other states and corporations. At the root of the institutional approach is the view that the identity of trading partners matters; trade here does not take place in an abstract environment of full information and perfect markets, but in one of uncertainty, strategic behaviour and repeated interactions between agents who have incomplete knowledge about each other. Of fundamental importance is whether either or both parties have assets specific to the relationship: if they do, they are to some extent locked in; if they don't, they are more free.

Consider the case of trade between two countries. If each party can easily find alternative partners and there are no specific assets, the cost to either party of withdrawing from the trade relationship is minimal. Consequently, there is no incentive for opportunistic behaviour by either party (such as taxing exports to increase welfare at the expense of the partner) because the other could withdraw costlessly from the relationship. This is analogous to a situation of perfect competition where the market institution of liberal trade is stable and optimal. No country will gain by imposing trade barriers. This view of international trade is also implicit in the arguments for liberalisation, as eliminating protection will enhance efficiency and increase welfare.

In the situation depicted there would be no need for any supranational body to monitor trade relationships and offer third-party enforcement of liberal trade. In reality, we observe the use of trade barriers by many countries. A number of explanations can be suggested. It may simply be that governments are not aware of, or do not believe, the true economic costs of protection, or that they are willing to accept these costs because protection achieves domestic political economy objectives. The role of the Bank in promoting trade liberalisation has been to convince governments that the costs of protection are too high, and that the reward from liberalisation will be faster economic growth. The GATT does not have a direct role in this, but assumes importance when countries liberalise and wish to ensure that others also liberalise. A more fundamental explanation for trade interventions by government is when they believe the market is imperfectly competitive. In particular, we consider the case where there is asset specificity.

If assets are specific to a relationship there will be costs to one or both parties from withdrawal, and there will be incentives for opportunistic behaviour. An example may be where a country has few sources for important imports (such as oil or precious metals) so that a tax on exports can be fully shifted forward. Alternatively, a country with only one export market may have to absorb part of the burden of tariffs on its products. It is difficult to find real cases of such specificity. However, the notion becomes more relevant when we realise that most trade is between, if not within, companies rather than countries. The SO approach is most readily applicable to relationships between LDCs and multinational enterprises (MNEs). For example, if a foreign company invested in designing a computer keyboard for Hindi, it will have assets specific to trade with India, and the country may perceive gains from opportunistic behaviour, which could take many forms, such as tariffs (if these are expected to be borne by the producer) or requiring production in India (MNE–host relations are discussed in section IV). The point is that when there are specific assets 'self-help through unilateral withdrawal no longer provides adequate safeguards' (Yarbrough and Yarbrough, 1992, p. 121). Bargaining between the parties becomes central, and the need for enforcement determines the institutional form of the relationship.

If there is no effective external (third party) enforcement the parties have to rely on bilateral agreements, whereas the establishment of external enforcement can stabilise the relationship, in principle benefiting both parties, and can facilitate multilateralism. 'The primary task of institutions then becomes one of supporting and signalling the parties' continuing commitment to the ongoing relationship' (Yarbrough and Yarbrough, 1992, p. 122). In this context, states choose not only their stance on free trade but also the forum through which (mutual) trade liberalisation will be negotiated, monitored and enforced. The SO approach does not address the active role that global institutions can play, but the analysis allows us to distinguish the institutional roles of the Bank and GATT, the former as facilitator and the latter as enforcer.

The Bank, under the auspices of SALs, has assumed the role of convincing LDCs of the desirability of trade liberalisation and, through conditionality, of trying to enforce compliance. The Bank bargains with a 'carrot and stick' approach (Greenaway and Morrissey, 1993). The carrot is, most obviously, the external financing associated with the SAL (and trade liberalisation); in principle, this could be extended to providing direct support in the design and implementation of reforms (see section IV). The stick is the threat of withholding funds or not lending in the future to countries that fail to implement reforms. As this institutional relationship is one of bargaining, the outcome is uncertain, hence the degree to which countries liberalise has been varied. Furthermore, while this relationship may be adequate to convince LDCs to liberalise in a world where there is no asset specificity, it is not adequate in situations of specific assets as the Bank does not act as a third party enforcer. In these situations, the GATT has a role. In providing so many loopholes, GATT was unable to fulfil its role as a third-party enforcer of liberal trade by LDCs. LDCs did engage in bilateral bargaining with the Bank, which was able to encourage trade liberalisation (to varying degrees). This should allow LDCs to be brought fully into the WTO, and thus a full party to multilateral negotiations.

IV   SOME APPLICATIONS

What are the prospects for enhanced and sustained trade liberalisation in
LDCs? In the previous two sections we have highlighted the important
institutional roles of the Bank and GATT. In this section we will consider
how these roles can develop by addressing four distinct issues. First, we
examine the experience of GATT's TPRM and consider the ability of this
instrument to increase transparency and support enforcement. Second, we
consider how the erosion of special and differential treatment under the
Uruguay Round enhances the potential for enforcement. Third, we address
one of the new issues brought within GATT under the Uruguay Round in
order to highlight the difficulties arising when there are asset-specific
relations between firms and states. Finally, we consider the role of the Bank,
in particular what it can do to assist the implementation of reforms and
expand the institutional capacity of LDCs, and how this could be (implicitly)
co-ordinated with the WTO.

Credit and Tariff Bindings

One of the key devices, perhaps the key device, which GATT has utilised to
effect third party enforcement on industrialised countries has been tariff
binding. Once a tariff is bound under GATT it cannot be increased
unilaterally. Under various 'special and differential' arrangements developing countries have been exempted from binding. One very important
outcome of the Uruguay Round has been to change this, and to do so rather
dramatically. Specifically, the proportion of developing country tariffs which
are bound has increased from 21 per cent to 65 per cent. Even allowing for
the fact that some developing countries are binding in some 'water' in the
tariff, this is significant. Not only does it impose a constraint on unilateral
changes, it also places these tariffs on the table for negotiation in future
rounds.

How was this secured? A key factor in the Uruguay Round negotiations
was the skill of the Secretariat in linking bindings to developing countries
being given credit for liberalisation they had already undertaken as a
consequence of adjustment lending programmes.

Trade Policy Review Mechanism (TPRM)

Instrument substitution is a relatively common by-product of liberalisation.
In other words, a trade reform programme commits to reducing nominal
tariffs, but a wide range of exceptions are subsequently introduced, thereby

facilitating an increase in implicit tariffs. This *may* have been a contributory factor to the apparent failure of some liberalisations. Clearly if it occurs, it frustrates the process of eroding the influence of pro-protection lobbies and empowering pro-export interests. Under existing arrangements, it is not easy to monitor. The TPRM which came out of the Montreal mid-term review in 1988, and which has been endorsed by the Uruguay Round Final Act, provides a vehicle for independent audit of a country's trade policy.

The TPRM process involves the GATT Secretariat preparing an instrument by instrument evaluation of trade policy. Table 8.4 sets out the heading of a typical TPRM report. A key feature of the process is that it takes place on a regular basis – every two years in the case of the big three (EU, US

Table 8.4   Structure of Trade Policy Review Reports

I   Economic Environment of the Contracting Party

II   Trade Policy Regime: Framework and Objectives
• General framework
• Structure of trade policy formulation
• Trade policy objectives
• Trade laws and regulations
• Trade agreements

III   Foreign Exchange Regime and Foreign Direct Investment
• Exchange rate regime and policy
• Foreign direct investment

IV   Trade Policies and Practices by Measure
• Overview
• Measures directly affecting imports
• Measures directly affecting exports
• Measures affecting production and trade

V   Trade Policies and Practices by Sector
• Overview
• Agriculture
• Mining and energy
• Industry

VI   Trade Disputes and Consultations
• Dispute settlement under GATT and related arrangements
• Dispute settlement outside GATT

and Japan), up to every seven years in the case of the smallest contracting parties. According to the Secretariat, the TPRM 'is not ... intended to serve as a basis for the enforcement of specific GATT obligations or for dispute setlement procedures, or to impose new commitments on Contracting Parties'. However, it also states that 'The objectives of the TPRM are to contribute to improved adherence by all Contracting Parties to GATT rules, disciplines and commitments and hence to the smoother functioning of the multilateral trading system, by achieving greater transparency in, and understanding of, the trade policies and practices of Contracting Parties.' Thus, the GATT seems to regard the TPRM as fulfilling an information function, rather than being an enforcement device. It is inevitable, however, that the greater transparency which it brings to trade policy creates the potential for use as an enforcement mechanism. Moreover, the commitments in the Uruguay Round to biennial ministerial conferences and closer co-operation with the World Bank and IMF increases the likelihood that it will be used in this way. Liberalisation commitments within SALs are the outcome of bilateral bargaining between the World Bank and a developing country government. Arrangements for implementation and enforcement have tended to be weak due to the fact that monitoring arrangements are poor and ultimately, since the *raison d'être* of the Bank is to lend, it often lacks effective sanctions. Since the TPRM provides *independent* monitoring services it is ideally placed to evolve as a third party monitoring device. Moreover, as the scope for special and differential treatment within GATT is eroded (as it is by the Uruguay Round) and as the proportion of tariffs which are bound increases (again an outcome of the Uruguay Round), the incentive for the WTO Secretariat to develop and enhance the mechanism is obvious.

Is this a 'good thing' or a 'bad thing'? From the standpoint of the trading system in general, and developing countries in particular, it must be a desirable development. In the short term it can assist in giving greater credibility to unilateral liberalisation; in the longer term it can assist in giving the panoply of rules and disciplines greater credibility.

Erosion of S and D

The principle of special and differential treatment for LDCs is well established, both in its 'right to protect' and 'right to access' forms. The former manifests itself in various ways – through Article XVIII and Part IV, for instance; the latter through the GSP (see Whalley, 1991). The various right to protect provisions have offered developing countries the opportunity not only legitimately to maintain relatively high barriers, but *unilaterally* to vary these fairly freely. The effect of this is then reinforced by the reciprocity waiver, which means that when *multilateral* negotiations come round, there is no obligation to reduce their barriers. Since GATT (1947) has no explicit graduation criteria, this is in effect an open-ended commitment.

The Uruguay Round changes this situation quite dramatically. Although the various Uruguay Round Agreements affirm the legitimacy of S and D, they repeatedly make a distinction between the least developed and other developing countries. For example, for purposes of implementing and enforcing the new export subsidy arrangements, the distinction between the two is set at a GDP per capita of $1000. For most other purposes, least developed are defined as the UN set of (37) least developed countries plus: Bolivia, Cameroon, Congo, Ivory Coast, Dominican Republic, Egypt, Ghana, Guatemala, Guyana, India, Indonesia, Kenya, Morocco, Nicaragua, Nigeria, Pakistan, Philippines, Senegal, Sri Lanka and Zimbabwe. This group only remains on the list however until (nominal) GDP per capita reaches $1000.

This is an important constitutional change. At a stroke it dramatically constrains the conditions under which recourse to S and D is permitted. It is inevitable that implementation of this new policy will increasingly involve the WTO in third party enforcement of GATT disciplines. It provides a mechanism which one contracting party can use against another to challenge the use of a wide range of instruments beyond a given level of 'development'. Moreover, it is bound to interact with the TPRM process in highlighting whether or not individual developing country members are complying. Thus, although the changed position on S and D may appear to be superficial, it will in practice turn out to be quite a profound reform.

Trade-Related Investment Measures (TRIMs)

Our analysis also has implications for some of the new issues brought into GATT under the Uruguay Round. We will limit attention to TRIMs, but the arguments can be applied to disciplines in intellectual property. Broadly speaking, TRIMs are any performance measures required of MNEs operating in an LDC which, through their effect on the MNE, distort the trade flows of the LDC (Morrissey and Rai, 1995, provide an extensive discussion).

Trade-related investment measures take many different forms. What they have in common is that their use by states in the area of foreign direct investment (FDI) may distort the flow of international trade in goods (and the flow of international investment). There are many reasons why MNEs may wish to engage in FDI in developing countries. The most obvious, perhaps, is the commercial search for profitable investment opportunities. Access to large host markets may also prove attractive; if protectionist regulations prohibit direct importing, tariff-jumping FDI may result. Another reason is that the target host state may offer incentives to attract FDI. The MNE decision of *where* to locate is based on weighing up the benefits and costs of one location over another (and of one form of investment over another). The host state is usually keen to encourage FDI as a source of potential benefits, such as employment, demand for locally produced inputs, improved balance of payments and technology transfer. Often these benefits do not materialise to the degree expected by the host. One reason may be that the MNE engages in restrictive business practices (RBPs), whose fundamental nature is anti-competitive. Such RBPs include transfer pricing and various ways of restricting the trade of the subsidiary (e.g. import from or export to the parent). TRIMs are imposed to counter these perceived RBPs.

Examples of TRIMs with fairly direct trade effects are: local content requirements, which limit imports as the subsidiary must purchase a certain amount of inputs from local suppliers; direct restrictions on imports; export requirements, stipulating that a certain share of output must be exported; foreign exchange and trade balancing requirements, which limit imports to the value of exports. As these distort trade they fall within the remit of GATT and have been brought under GATT discipline in the Uruguay Round. They are to be dismantled, although LDCs are given at least five years to abolish TRIMs, and the least developed will benefit from an exemption.

Foreign Direct Investment (FDI) is specific to a bilateral relationship where the two parties, the investing MNE and host state, do not share a mutually accepted legal enforcement mechanism. While *ex ante* alternative hosts (MNEs) are available to the MNE (host), FDI creates a specific bilateral relationship *ex post*. If TRIMs are effective in creating local linkages and other benefits to the host, the host, and especially local suppliers, become more dependent on the MNE (initial concessions can actually strengthen the bargaining position of MNEs). Thus there are many aspects to the bilateral bargaining between MNEs and LDCs.

The incorporation of TRIMs into GATT can be seen as introducing third party enforcement to stabilise a widespread bilateral relationship. More generally, third party enforcement is a necessary condition for multilateral agreements where there are relation-specific investments. However, although the SO approach predicts that multilateral negotiations will occur when both external enforcement and relation-specific investments are present, it does not explain why external enforcement (and multilateralism) can be imposed in respect of some issues, such as TRIMs, but not others, such as investment measures and RBPs. When there was no external enforcement, negotiations had to be bilateral and each party had two instruments: the host offered investment measures and imposed TRIMs; the MNE offered FDI but could have recourse to RBPs. Subjecting TRIMs to external enforcement weakens the position of hosts. The only way to balance this is to provide third party enforcement against RBPs or, failing that, to strengthen hosts' ability to identify and counteract RBPs so that we can create a situation where both parties act in good faith and accept that the other acts in good faith.

It follows that LDCs may feel unfairly treated: MNEs, to the extent that they can lobby the government in the parent state to bring a complaint (against TRIMs), have recourse to third party enforcement in a manner not available to LDCs (in respect to RBPs). One possible avenue of removing this bias is to ensure that the WTO addresses investment measures in general and associated RBPs, an intention enshrined in the Uruguay Round and in Article IX of the TRIMs Agreement. (Morrissey and Rai (1995) suggest a way in which this could be done utilising UNCTAD Codes on restrictive business practices.)

The World Bank and Institution-Building

Economic policy reform requires the administrative capacity to implement reforms and also often involves a change in institutions. For example, privatisation implies shifting from a public sector mode of production to a private market mode; the two are very different and the institutions required to support them, such as capital markets and property rights, are also different. In order to be able to privatise, a country must first create the required institutions. More generally, it is clear from policy accounts across a very large number of reforming countries that initial conditions matter. The success or otherwise of a particular liberalisation episode depends very much not only on initial economic conditions but on the infrastructural context against which the reforms are implemented. Where this is weak, the probability of failure is higher. The process of institution-building is not well understood; while there is a considerable body of literature analysing the efficiency of various types of institution and discussing the evolution of institutions, there is only limited analysis of the process of institutional change (Lin and Nugent, 1994). This is an important area where the Bank can offer assistance to LDCs; as we suggested earlier, institution-building can be an important carrot in encouraging reform and a vital ingredient in facilitating reform.

Institution-building can be assisted in a number of ways. The most basic level is training and technical assistance for the administration required to implement reforms in LDCs. Weak administrative capacity can often be a major constraint on implementation; for example, inadequate training and poor resources lead to collection inefficiency which can undermine tax reforms. On a broader level is assistance in the design and sequencing of a reform programme (Levy, 1993), which should account for political circumstances. A particular example is where the Bank sponsors studies of the impact of reform, such as the case of trade liberalisation discussed in section II, the results of which (assuming they demonstrate the gains from reform) can help in building political support for the reform programme. At an even higher level is assistance in creating new institutions, such as capital markets to support privatisation or agricultural markets to replace government marketing boards.

There is also potential for institution-building at a global level. As the World Bank has expanded its remit from project finance to economic reform programmes to political conditionality and institution-building, its form as a global institution changed, as did the nature of its relationship with clients. Similarly, the post-Uruguay Round GATT has a broader remit and the WTO will be a different institution. A better understanding of the role these institutions can play will facilitate greater trade liberalisation, by persuasion against the inefficiency of protection and by offering third party enforcement for fragile relationships between trading partners.

V CONCLUSION

One aspect of SALs we have not mentioned so far is that widespread privatisation has been advocated in LDCs. To the extent that this occurs, it will lead to an increase in FDI, both because LDCs need foreign investment and because domestic capital markets and the private sector are insufficient to absorb widespread privatisation. For example, of eight agricultural parastatals in Tanzania that had been privatised by 1992, four were sold to foreign companies and three were established as joint ventures with foreign companies (Due, 1993, p. 1983). It follows that MNE–host relations will remain an important issue for the future. Both the Bank and GATT can play a role. The TRIMs Agreement in GATT (1994) acknowledges that regulation of TRIMs should take into account both the presence of investment incentives and the need for a competition policy to monitor if not regulate the behaviour of MNEs. The WTO can assume the role of a global institution to address these issues. An appropriate role for the World Bank would be to complement UNCTAD in providing assistance to LDCs in their dealings with MNEs, in particular regarding the design of competition policy.

The general point is that the World Bank can sponsor trade liberalisation and build institutional capacity in LDCs, allowing LDCs to be brought fully into the WTO. The WTO may be able to use TPRMs to monitor and enforce liberalisation. If the scope for enforcement in relations involving asset-specific investments is extended from TRIMs to investment measures, RBPs and intellectual property protection, then third-party enforcement can be applied to MNEs and hosts, facilitating multilateral liberalisation. The scope of TPRMs could also be extended. The more comprehensive set of issues to be covered by the WTO (in contrast to GATT) and its more legalistic foundation, mean that its third party enforcement function will be enhanced. Although all of our discussion has focused on the implications which this has for liberalisation in LDCs, it must be noted that it also has important implications for the ability of LDCs to influence behaviour in developed countries. Stronger third party enforcement in the context of developed countries, and especially MNEs, is likely to be even more important than in developing countries.

ACKNOWLEDGEMENT

This paper was prepared for a Festschrift in honour of Jagdish Bhagwati, at Lancaster University, December 1994. An earlier version of the paper was presented at the Western Economic Association Conference, Vancouver, 2 July 1994. The authors are grateful to Jagdish Bhagwati, Vijay Joshi, Sajal Lahiri, Sheila Page, Alasdair MacBean, Doug Nelson, William Kaempfer and Rick Harper for comments. Remaining deficiencies are the responsibility of the authors.

Financial support from the Ford Foundation is also gratefully acknowledged.

NOTES

1. The GATT, World Bank and IMF are organisations, in the sense that they are entities with formal status. We are primarily concerned with the manner in which they interact with, and try to influence, LDCs – essentially, the nature of their bargaining relationship with LDC governments. In this sense we are more concerned with their institutional than their organisational form. We are using the broad interpretation of institutions as the rules constraining and governing interactions and expectations between agents (here countries and organisations). We combine insights from the organisational approach to trade liberalisation of Yarbrough and Yarbrough (1992) and the applications of institutional analysis to economic development (Lin and Nugent, 1994).

2. We abstract from measurement problems since they are not central to this paper. None the less, the reader should be aware that liberalisation is not straightforward to measure. Broadly speaking, one can take either, or both, of

two approaches. First, policy accounts. The key difficulty here is that actual trade reforms may differ from intended trade reforms, due to slippage from commitments and/or instrument substitution. The second approach is to measure outcomes, by reference to some relative price ratio, like Krueger's (1978) bias index. Problems here relate to data availability and reliability. In practice both are used, as for instance is the influential multi-country study of Papageorgiou, Michaely and Choksi (1991).

3.   Of course, once introduced such measures generate rents and are difficult to remove. Nevertheless, they can be important in encouraging a more efficient allocation of resources as a country tries to move away from protection. Greenaway and Morrissey (1994) also point out that export subsidies can result in the trade stance being more neutral, and many commentators equate trade liberalisation with a more neutral trade bias.

4.   In many of the countries concerned there does appear to be an association between liberalisation and subsequent growth. However, econometric analysis using both structural break and smooth transition analysis casts doubts on the role of liberalisation in stimulating growth. See Greenaway and Sapsford (1984) and Greenaway, Leybourne and Sapsford (1994).

5.   The basis for this goes back to the pioneering work of Bhagwati (1958) on optimal intervention analysis.

6.   Compensation can be of various forms. Social welfare payments and guaranteeing employment to a portion of workers in industries being privatised are examples of direct compensation, the costs being budgetary and that such industries will be less attractive to private investors. Indirect compensation arises where complementary reforms provide economic opportunities to the losers, such as increasing wages to compensate workers for cuts in food subsidies. The potential cost here is that the effect of the original reform may be undermined. The argument that an improved economic performance resulting from reform will ultimately improve the welfare of everybody could be described as implicit compensation, but may not be very convincing to losers in the short run.

7.   Yarbrough and Yarbrough (1992) argue that the US had sufficient hegemonic power, at least in respect of asset-specific investments, in the first few decades after the war to secure multilateral trade liberalisation through GATT. This power had been significantly eroded by the 1970s: the US was unwilling and unable to maintain the momentum of GATT and became increasingly protectionist. Multilateralism was infeasible as third party enforcement (previously through the GATT backed by the US) was weak, and countries increasingly had recourse to bilateral negotiations on trade concessions. By the late 1980s, these bilateral negotiations had broadened to groups of countries forming preferential trading arrangements. The formation of the European Union with supranational enforcement marked the advent of minilateralism. However, the approach does not adequately explain *why* these changes occurred when they did, and does not allow for global institutions with an active role.

REFERENCES

Bhagwati, J.N. (1958), 'Immiserizing Growth: A Geometric Note', *Review of Economic Studies'*, vol. 25, pp. 201–5.

———— (1988), 'Export Promoting Trade Strategy: Issues and Evidence', *The World Bank Research Observer*, vol. 3, pp. 27–58.

———— (1990), 'Multilateralism at Risk: The GATT is Dead, Long Live GATT', *The World Economy*, vol. 13, pp. 149–69.

———— (1991), *The World Trading System at Risk*, (Hemel Hempstead: Harvester Wheatsheaf).

Bhagwati, J.N. and Ramasurami, V. (1963), 'Domestic Distortions, Tariffs and the Theory of the Optimum Subsidy', *Journal of Political Economy* vol. 71, pp. 44–50.

Dean, J., Desai, S. and Riedel, J. (1994), 'Trade Policy Reform in Developing Countries Since 1985: A Review of the Evidence', mimeo (The World Bank).

Due, J. (1993), 'Liberalisation and Privatisation in Tanzania and Zambia', *World Development*, vol. 21, pp. 1981–8.

Greenaway, D., Leybourne, S.J. and Sapsford, D.R. (1994), 'Modelling Growth (and Liberalisation) Using Smooth Transitions Analysis', *CREDIT Research Paper 94/10* (University of Nottingham).

Greenaway, D. and Milner, C. (1993), *Trade and Industrial Policy in Developing Countries* (London: Macmillan).

Greenaway, D. and Morrissey, O. (1993), 'Structural Adjustment and Liberalisation in Developing Countries: What Lessons Have We Learned?', *Kyklos*, vol. 46, pp. 241–61.

———— (1994), 'Trade Liberalisation and Economic Growth in Developing Countries', in S. M. Murshed and K. Raffer, eds, *Trade Transfers and Development*, (Aldershot: Edward Elgar).

Greenaway, D. and Sapsford, D.R. (1994), 'Exports, Growth and Liberalisation', *Journal of Policy Modelling*, vol. 14, pp. 165–86.

Haggard, S. and Webb, S. (1993), 'What Do We Know about the Political Economy of Economic Policy Reform?', *The World Bank Research Observer*, vol. 8, pp. 143–68.

Krueger, A.O. (1978), *Liberalization Attempts and Consequences* (New York: NBER).

Levy, B. (1993), 'An Institutional Analysis of the Design and Sequence of Trade and Investment Policy Reform', *The World Bank Economic Review*, vol. 7, pp. 247–62.

Lin, J. and Nugent, J. (1994), 'Institutions and Economic Development', in J. Behrman and T. Srinivasan, eds, *Handbook of Development Economics: Volume 3* (Amsterdam: North-Holland).

Morrissey, O. (1993), 'Compliance and Conditionality: The Sustainability of Adjustment in Turkey', paper presented to the Working Group on Aid and Conditionality at the EADI Conference, Berlin. Forthcoming in O. Stokke, ed., *Aid and Conditionality* (London: Frank Cass for EAD).

———— (1994), 'Political Commitment, Institutional Capacity and Tax Policy Reform in Tanzania', University of Nottingham, CREDIT Research Paper 94/4; also in *World Development*, vol. 23, no. 4.

Morrissey, O. and Rai, Y. (1995), 'The GATT Agreement on Trade Related Investment Measures: Implications for Developing Countries and their Relations with Transnational Corporations', *Journal of Development Studies*, vol. 31, no. 5, pp. 702–24.

Papageorgiou, D., Michaely, M. and Choksi, A. (1991), *Liberalizing Foreign Trade* (Oxford: Basil Blackwell).

Thomas, V. and Nash, J. (1991), 'Reform of Trade Policy: Recent Evidence from Theory and Practice', *World Bank Research Observer*, vol. 6, no. 2, pp. 219–40.

Whalley, J. (1990), 'Non-discriminatory Discrimination: Special and Differential Treatment Under GATT for Developing Countries', *Economic Journal*, vol. 10, pp. 1315–28.

Williamson, O. (1985), *The Economic Institutions of Capitalism: Firms, Markets, Relational Contracting* (New York: Free Press).

Yarbrough, B. and Yarbrough, R. (1992), *Cooperation and Governance in International Trade: The Strategic Organisational Approach* (Princeton, NJ: Princeton University Press).

161–68

Global
LDC's
F13
L41
O19

9 Possible Developing Country Impacts from a Competition Policy Negotiation[1]

Carlo Perroni and John Whalley

I INTRODUCTION

The relationship of competition policy to the GATT has been discussed recently in a number of papers (Hoekman and Mavroidis, 1994; Levinsohn, 1994; Lloyd and Sampson, 1995; and Grey, 1994). All of these set out what a potential competition policy negotiation might involve and examine the relationship between the GATT/WTO and competition policy. In this literature there is little discussion of the possible impacts of a competition policy negotiation on the developing countries.

The aim of this paper is to begin to fill this gap. We discuss what a competition policy negotiation might entail for the developing countries, and attempt to delineate the developing countries' position in such a negotiation *vis-à-vis* developed countries. We then outline the various implications of competition policies, both for domestic economic efficiency and their impacts on international trade-flows. We also set out the considerations involved in any international effort to co-ordinate competition policies and outline the channels through which developing countries could either gain or lose from such an effort. Finally, we summarise some back-of-the-envelope calculations we present elsewhere, which attempt to quantify possible developing country effects.

II THE CONTENT OF A POSSIBLE GATT/WTO COMPETITION POLICY NEGOTIATION

The current interest in a global competition policy negotiation reflects a number of concerns. Foremost is the US view that vertical ties between production and distribution in Japan, reflected in the *Keiretsu* system,

161

represent a barrier to US exports. The belief is that these arrangements are supported by weak application of anti-trust laws in Japan. A competition policy negotiation has been seen in the US as a way of limiting these practices, and hence as a means of obtaining improved access for US suppliers to Japanese markets.

Along with this have come concerns over the application of anti-dumping duties and the growing realisation that anti-dumping can in itself be an instrument of protection. A global competition policy regime is seen as one possible way of dispensing with anti-dumping. Anti-dumping petitions are now widely seen as the most convenient vehicle for domestic producers to seek protection and to harass foreign competitors even if no meaningful dumping is present. In some trade areas, such as the European Union, competition laws have been integrated, and countries and firms abide by community statutes interpreted by European courts and also enforced. As a result, anti-dumping duties have been dispensed with for trade across national borders of the trading area. Some observers argue that the same direction would be desirable globally in international trade, and suggest that such an outcome should be an objective for competition policy negotiation.

A further argument is that anti-dumping duties can support a non-competitive domestic market structure, thereby generating their own competition policy problems. When dumping petitions occur, and negotiated withdrawals of petitions are arranged with accompanying price undertakings by the supplying foreign companies, in effect a collusive arrangement is being supported by anti-dumping duties and their administration. Some, such as Grey (1994), have argued strongly that competition policy issues are created by trade policies in this way. Once again, the implication is that anti-dumping duties should by replaced by more broad-ranging global competition policy arrangements.

Another growing argument that is taken by some further to underscore the need for a competition policy negotiation is the recognition that the influence of policy on trade is not limited to border-related measures, but extends to any policy intervention that indirectly affects trade through impacts on production and consumption. Within this broader perspective, domestic competition policies are a particular source of concern because they can have effects on trade, and to some extent can be used as a substitute for border measures for the purpose of restraining or promoting trade, potentially weakening the effects of previous multilateral trade liberalisation efforts.

Fuelled by these concerns, the process leading towards a multilateral trade-related competition policy negotiation is now moving ahead. In all probability such a negotiation is likely to involve two distinct components:

1. The first reflects concerns over trade-related aspects of competition policy, specifically anti-dumping. The objective here will be to achieve international agreements in the competition policy area, which eventually will remove the need for anti-dumping statutes. This may prove an unrealistic goal, but the motivation reflects the desire to replace an existing inefficient policy instrument by one which is less inefficient.

2. The second goes substantially beyond trade-related aspects of competition policy, focusing instead on international differences in competition policy regimes, both in terms of the statutes and their application, and their effects on trade. Negotiations here could cover domestic anti-trust laws, including rules on vertical restraints, domestic regulatory regimes for natural monopolies and, more generally, any form of domestic regulation relating to business practices, such as rules on advertising, safety standards and other forms of consumer protection.

At present, the prospects for the inclusion of either of these topics on the agenda for the next round of GATT/WTO negotiations remain far from certain. In both areas, harmonisation could proceed through several stages of negotiation, much as with trade liberalisation such a process could hinge on the application of key principles to international application of competition policies, such as MFN and bindings of existing competition policy arrangements. Their impacts involve the following.

Trade-related Aspects of Competition Policy

Any form of non-competitive behaviour which creates wedges between domestic and international prices can have impacts on trade-flows. Examples are discriminatory pricing between domestic and export markets, vertical links between large domestic producers and retailers, import and export cartels, and more generally, any form of concentration which affects market power of importers and exporters in international markets.

Competition policies which change domestic market structures also impinge on market access and hence trade. It follows that they can also be used as a substitute for trade policies. For example, by relaxing rules on concentration applying to large exporters, a country can create conditions in which there could be export dumping by domestic producers, with similar results in their effects on trade and on aggregate national welfare to those resulting from the use of export subsidies in a perfectly competitive setting.

This raises the question of whether protectionist competition policies, either partially or wholly, can replace pre-existing border measures, nullifying trade liberalisation efforts. The potential for competition policies to be used as substitutes for trade polices, even if imperfect ones, seems considerable. Since protection achieved through relaxation of domestic competition policies would be achieved at a cost of introducing further domestic distortions, this new form of protectionism could involve larger efficiency costs than traditional border measures. The possibility exists, if importing countries fell victim to protectionist pressure from domestic producers and used competition policies to offset reductions in pre-existing trade barriers, trade liberalisation could result in a global efficiency loss.

Competition Policy Aspects of Trade Policies

The other side of the argument that competition policies can be used as a substitute for trade policies is that trade policy itself is a second-best instrument of competition policy. From a global point of view, it would be more efficient to deal with predation directly through competition policy than by using anti-dumping policies, although this clearly involves international co-ordination of both competition rules and enforcement. In this case trade policy (anti-dumping) is second-best competition policy.

There are also a number of ways in which competition policy problems are directly created by trade policy implementation. Price undertakings resulting from anti-dumping petitions, in effect, allow a form of collusion around a focal point, the price floor at which the foreign supplier is forced to enter the market. It is common for petitions to be filed, examined and then subsequently withdrawn after negotiating an undertaking with foreign supplying firms. The general argument is that it is possible to eliminate competition policy problems and simultaneously generate efficiency gains. Nowhere is this idea more common in current policy debate than in proposals to replace anti-dumping mechanisms by competition policy.

A significant gain following from such co-ordination could be the rationalisation of domestic industries. With fixed costs and scale economies, generally speaking it is beneficial to have a smaller rather than a larger number of firms in an industry. Within national economies there is typically some optimal size of firm, reflecting scale economies, although exploitation of these have to be traded off against costs of monopoly associated with concentration. If competition policies can be designed to deal with issues such as predation, but still allow non-discriminatory arrangements which allow foreign firms the right of entry into domestic markets, then rationalisation gains on a world-wide basis could be achieved.

Rationalisation gains from trade policy reform are emphasised in numerical literature on the effects of trade liberalisation, in particular in the Cox and Harris (1985) analysis of the potential gains from a Canada–US free trade agreement, and subsequently from NAFTA. Here domestic pricing involves collusion around a focal point given by the world price, gross of the tariff. Under trade liberalisation, rationalisation occurs within the domestic market as firms move down their average cost curve, and the number of firms falls.

Other International Aspects of Competition Policies

Even abstracting from direct links between competition policies and trade, there are a number of other domestic features of competition policy where international co-ordination could also bring substantial benefits. With globalisation over the last 20 years, it has become ever more apparent that an uncoordinated approach to competition policy can be ineffective. In particular, domestic regulators can be left impotent against multinational producers owing to a lack of extra-territoriality in the application of competition policy rules and to the difficulty of monitoring foreign activities of residents.

One example arises with the design of anti-collusion policies. Collusion is one of several restrictive business practices which are generally thought to be inherently undesirable. Hence an object is to limit them through competition policy. Collusion, however, can combine with other considerations, including rationalisation, to support an optimal firm size within an economy. Hence collusion need not necessarily be undesirable on efficiency grounds, depending on the net outcome. The idea of an international negotiation on competition policy as a way of restraining collusion may seem attractive, especially as it operates across national borders. But if large suppliers outside of the economy are colluding on pricing and other policies in markets which they jointly supply, domestic competition policy rules may have little effect. Internationally co-ordinated competition policy, on the other hand, could effectively restrain such activities.

III DEVELOPING COUNTRIES AND COMPETITION POLICY

Assessing the impact of a competition policy negotiation on developing countries is difficult. On the one hand, is the concern that their ability to constrain foreign companies operating in their own economies may be limited. On the other hand, access benefits to markets abroad and more efficient domestic economies may follow. Thus, a number of considerations would enter a developing country position on a possible competition policy negotiation.

Importantly, such a negotiation could help protect the results achieved by developing countries in the Uruguay Round with respect to market access in developed countries. Also, relatively small suppliers, developing countries are potentially vulnerable in the event of an international competition policy war among developed countries and affecting both developed and developing countries. This may be restrained by such a negotiation.

It is the possible replacement of anti-dumping duties by competition policy where developing countries could also benefit. The possibility of construed predation against small suppliers is small, thus benefiting developing countries. The mirror image of the same argument is the fact that many developing countries become entangled with anti-dumping practices through such nefarious devices as cumulation, where the cumulative damage is calculated in a large country market (e.g. the US) including all previous shippers to the market, with the incremental effect of the further small developing country then added, even though, if taken on its own, the country would represent only a small effect. Thus, were anti-dumping mechanisms removed and new internationally co-ordinated competition policy arrangements put in place, arguments of predation and rationales for restraints on foreign suppliers would almost certainly apply mainly where large suppliers ship into large developed country markets, rather than to small suppliers.

A further source of benefit could come from stronger enforcement of competition policy laws against foreign producers. With a small industrial base in key sectors, some developing countries are susceptible to non-competitive practices of foreign suppliers. And if this is the case, their power to constrain foreign firms is often limited, given that domestic competition policy rules in developing countries are weak and usually have limited extra-territorial reach. Benefits for developing countries from an agreement to extend the extra-territorial reach of domestic anti-trust laws could be substantial.

A final source of benefit would be unilateral benefits of increased competition within developing country economies that a competition policy negotiation could induce. In many developing countries there is substantial concentration in the manufacturing sector, along with restraints on inward investment flows and establishment. These restraints serve to raise prices for domestic consumers, but also increase the costs of exports from these countries. Benefits would thus accrue to developing countries as domestic rationalisation occurred in parallel with a fuller integration within the global economy.

Along with these benefits, however, could come a series of costs, represented most notably by the disciplines which would be imposed on the actions of developing countries against externally directed restrictive business practices. Thus, if developing countries wished to take action against collusive supplies into their countries, such as by increasing a tariff on an imported product, they might be restrained from doing so by their participation in such a negotiation.

Any attempt to quantify the gains to developing countries from a global competition policy initiative is inevitably heroic in that different model formulations can be used and underlying key parameter values are not known. The gains involved break down into a series of individual components which we attempted to quantify individually in a related paper (Perroni and Whalley, 1995).

The first of these involves firmer guarantees of continuation of access under free trade regimes as a result of competition policy negotiation which restrains competition-related trade measures. The second key element is improved discipline over the use of anti-dumping measures against developing countries. If anti-dumping measures are replaced by competition measures which involve a test of predation, then the presumption is that, being small, most developing countries would not be caught in any such predation test for the use of trade restricting measures. Hence, they would experience gains, both in terms of market access and in GDP terms.

A further component of the gain involves the reduction of markups by foreign suppliers. The presumption is that competition policy measures would restrict the ability of foreign suppliers to exact markups in their markets, with some anti-collusion or extra-territoriality provision. To estimate this component of the possible impact of a competition policy negotiation on developing countries, it is necessary to use evidence on markups by product suppliers in developing country markets, and estimate the value of imports in such markets, as well as the average markup rate. In addition to these come domestic gains from reduced concentration associated with harmonisation on competition policy.

Overall, and on the basis of the estimates presented in Perroni and Whalley (1995), the indication is that the potential gains to developing countries could be quite significant, in the region of 5–6 per cent of national income, perhaps even larger. This would make a competition policy negotiation of potentially more significance to developing countries than the whole of the trade disciplines achieved in the Uruguay Round.

These estimates clearly depend on the extent of concentration in developing countries; and there is limited evidence as to exactly what concentration elements are present. They also depend on available estimates of the average markup by domestic producers in developed countries, although these could be inferred directly from international price differentials (which could provide a more complete global estimate of efficiency gains from removals of such market concentration).

NOTES

1. This paper draws on joint work by the two authors for a project on the impact of The Uruguay Round on developing countries undertaken by UNCTAD and the Centre for the Study of International Economic Relations (CSIER), the University of Western Ontario, London, Canada, and supported by the Ford Foundation. A more complete discussion is available in Perroni and Whalley (1995).

REFERENCES

Cox, D. and Harris, R. (1985), 'Trade Liberalization and Industrial Organization: Some Estimates for Canada', *Journal of Political Economy*, vol. 93, pp. 115–45.

GATT (1993–4) *Trade Policy Review Mechanism Reports* (various countries) (Geneva: GATT).

Grey, R. de C. (1994), 'The Impact of Competition Policy on Trade Policy', mimeo (UNCTAD).

Hoekmann, B. and Mavroidis, P. (1994), 'Competition, Competition Policy and the GATT', mimeo.

Levinsohn, J. (1994) 'Competition Policy and International Trade', mimeo (University of Michigan).

Lloyd, P. and Sampson, G. (1995), 'Competition and Trade Policy: Identifying The Issues After The Uruguay Round', *The World Economy*, September, vol. 18, no. 5, pp. 681–706.

Messerlin, P. (1991), 'The Uruguay Negotiations on Anti-dumping Enforcement: Some Basic Issues', in P.K.M. Tharakan, ed., *Policy Implications of Anti-dumping Measures* (Amsterdam: Elsevier).

Perroni, C. (1994), 'The Impact of the Uruguay Round on Developing Countries: A Survey of Model Results', mimeo (University of Warwick).

Perroni, C. and Whalley, J. (1995), 'Competition Policy and the Developing Countries'. A report prepared for an UNCTAD/CSIER Project on The Impact of The Uruguay Round on Developing Countries.

Part Four
Country-specific Studies

10 Macroeconomic Management in India, 1964–94

Vijay Joshi and Ian Little

India
023,
E65

Jagdish Bhagwati's work on India is surely one of the highlights of his remarkable contribution to economics. As a prescient, searching and constructive critic of India's inward-looking development strategy, he is an intellectual progenitor of the country's current drive to reform. The main focus of his work has been on issues of trade and resource allocation.[1] Indeed, we have several times heard him declare that he is no macroeconomist and, amazingly enough, given the multiplicity of his writings, it seems to be true that he has largely avoided the subject. We have been less wise, but hope that he will consider this essay an appropriate way to honour him.[2]

I THE OBJECTIVES AND INSTRUMENTS OF MACROECONOMIC POLICY

Macroeconomics is the study of large economic aggregates such as the gross domestic product, savings and investment, exports and imports, in both real and monetary terms. Macroeconomic policy is government policy intended to influence these magnitudes.

Everyone, of whatever political persuasion, agrees that one of the functions of government is to supply public goods, that is commodities or services that cannot easily or effectively be supplied by individuals or small groups (including firms) in civil society. A libertarian might say that this is the only proper function of government.

The provision of a stable currency is a public good, which ranks in importance with law and order, and defence. It follows that a primary objective of macroeconomic policy is stabilisation of the price level. In practice this means keeping inflation to levels consistent with money efficiently fulfilling its functions as a means of exchange and a standard and store of value.

However, only an extremist would want to give absolute priority to any one objective if it conflicts with others. Fortunately, the supply of few if any other public goods is competitive with a stable price level. Law and order, defence, public health, public education and various infrastructural investments have nothing to gain from inflation: they can be financed in non-inflationary ways.

Some would argue that the relief of absolute poverty is a public good. Fortunately again, poverty relief, including food for work and employment guarantee schemes, does not compete with a stable price level. Studies of the supply and the financing of these different public goods fall within the demesne of microeconomics.

It is important to note that such employment guarantee schemes as that of the Maharashtra state government bear no relation to the obligation assumed by some governments of industrialised countries in the early post-war period to provide full employment. Such obligations have long since been forgotten. Using only the instruments of macroeconomic policy, all that the governments of predominantly private enterprise economies can do in pursuit of higher levels of employment or output is to increase demand. But at some threshold, which may be far short of any previously defined level of full employment or output, increased demand will cause only inflation. There is, then, no long-run trade-off between employment and inflation.

Defined levels of employment or output cannot therefore be objectives of macroeconomic policy. But this does not imply that measures to stabilise prices should be pursued regardless of the effect of these measures on either aggregate output and employment or output and employment in important sectors of the economy. Certainly not! Indeed it will be part of our critique of macroeconomic policy that deflationary measures triggered by high inflation have, on occasion, been excessive. Further than this, governments should try to use macroeconomic policy to reduce exogenously created fluctuations in output and the demand for labour. But such uses of policy should not endanger the objective of low inflation. Indeed, they cannot be employed if inflation is dangerously high. In this sense, the objective of stabilising output is secondary to that of stabilising the price level.

We have so far been vague about exactly how stable the currency needs to be, or what constitutes a dangerous level of inflation. Instability of relative prices is probably more harmful than any constant rate of inflation, but the higher the rate of inflation the more unstable are relative prices likely to be. The reason why some higher rate than zero may be desirable is that inflation acts as a tax on cash balances. Therefore, if this inflation tax is a good tax compared with others, there is a case for some inflation. The inflation tax has often been castigated as regressive, it being assumed that cash balances are a high proportion of the wealth of the poor. This may not be so. Cash may be mainly held by tax-evaders! In considering inflation in India, one must also note that inflation has often stemmed from a fall in the supply of cereals, the price of which then 'leads' the inflation. Such inflation is bad for the poor. How much inflation is tolerable and even advisable is a country-specific matter. Much depends on history, the structure of production and the distribution of income and wealth. In India, the authorities become alarmed and take action when the annual rate reaches 10 per cent. We have no reason to quarrel with this perception. In view of the tendency for inflation to accelerate as the expectation of rising prices becomes entrenched, we would advocate an inflationary target of not more than 5 per cent (yielding an inflation tax of a little over 1 per cent of GDP).

Before considering the longer-run aims of macroeconomic policy, we should briefly review the instruments. The operation of fiscal and monetary policies requires little comment. In some developing countries there is little difference between the two in that the government cannot borrow domestically except from the Central Bank, thus increasing the quantity of base money. In India, the Reserve Bank of India (RBI) may reduce the effective cash base of the banking system by raising the cash reserve ratio (CRR) that the commercial banks are required to hold. The government also pre-empts loans from the commercial banks by the statutory liquidity ratio (SLR), which stipulates the proportion of their deposit liabilities that must be invested in government (and other 'approved') securities. This helps to reduce government borrowing from the RBI. Some countries are so open to monetary movements that no independent monetary policy is possible. This is not the case in India where exchange controls are still operative, and interest rates may diverge from those in the world's main capital markets.

Apart from fiscal and financial policies, there are exchange rate, and balance of payments, policies to consider. These differ from fiscal and financial policies which devolve inescapably from the provision of public goods. A government need have no policy in the area of foreign payments. It can refuse to deal in foreign currency, letting exchange rates be determined in private currency markets. A stable exchange rate is valuable only in so far as it assists stability in general, both in the short and the long run. Neglect of the balance of payments can also be benign. This may seem strange given the multiple occurrence of balance of payments crises in India and many other countries. But these crises can occur only if the government and its Central Bank are themselves major dealers in foreign assets and liabilities, which they need not be. The extent to which governments *should* borrow abroad and should peg exchange rates remains a highly controversial matter.

Trade and Development

Finally, controls have been used extensively as instruments of macroeconomic policy. India has operated a vast array of controls apart from the exchange controls already mentioned. We can ignore most of them as being concerned with microeconomic matters. Those of major macroeconomic significance include controls over imports, and almost all interest rates, and of the amount of credit extended to the private sector. Many prices have also been controlled: though the objectives were often microeconomic, reducing inflation has also been considered a reason. We should also mention that private investment, both domestic and foreign, has been extensively controlled, but this form of control does not seem to have been used as a macroeconomic instrument. Of all these controls, those over imports have been by far the most important. Together with export subsidies they were frequently used to maintain or bolster the exchange rate.

What about the long-run objectives of macroeconomic policy? First, it must be emphasised that stabilisation in the long run must be an objective as well as the short-run stabilisation towards which fiscal and monetary policy and exchange rate policy are generally directed. It is possible to live in a fool's paradise of year-to-year stability, but with debts mounting which will, in time, lead to a crisis and consequential instability. Indeed the Indian situation in the 1980s was just such a paradise. But is there not some more glamorous objective than mere stability towards which a government should be directing its interventionist arrows? Surely a government can do much to promote growth and development. Two points are important in this connection. First, stability itself is important for growth. This not only accords with common sense, but is also strongly supported by the history of the developing countries in the last 10 years.[3] Secondly, most of the governmental interventions which interventionists nowadays advocate as growth-promoting need not impinge on macroeconomic policy. These may include the subsidisation of particular activities such as education and training, special encouragement of private savings and investment, and various institutional innovations. The same is true of distributional interventions.

However, there are major 'strategies' intended to have a developmental role which are so pervasive that they must be considered to be within the realm of macroeconomics. The two most obvious are autarky and extensive public ownership of the means of production. India, of course, has in the past pinned its faith to both of these. But until 1991, there was no serious change of strategy and it was possible to describe and discuss macroeconomic policy without mention of such long-run fundamental attitudes. Since 1991 there has been a profound change, and stabilisation policy has had to be pursued in the context of a major change of system and the role of government.

II CRISIS AND ADJUSTMENT, 1964–91

The whole period 1964–91 was marked by four crises. The first three were mainly the result of exogenous events, droughts and oil price rises, which presented the authorities with a serious stabilisation problem. They could not have been easily predicted. The fourth and last crisis, that of 1991, was very different. It resulted from the pursuit during the 1980s of unsustainable policies, that is, of policies that were destabilising in the longer run. It was easily predictable.

In this section we describe the course of the first three crises (causes, policy reactions and immediate outcomes) and the genesis of the fourth crisis.[4] In sections III and IV, we give an assessment of short-run and medium-run macroeconomic management. In section V we discuss the resolution of the crisis of 1991: this raises some special issues since stabilisation has to be combined with the transition to a less regulated and more open economy. Section VI is devoted to political economy issues.

The Crisis of 1965–7 (The First Crisis)

The crisis was triggered by two severe droughts in succession. Foodgrain output fell by 20 per cent in 1965–6, and recovered by only 1.7 per cent in 1966–7. There was no buffer stock of foodgrains and foreign exchange reserves were minimal. Famine was avoided only by foodgrain imports, largely financed by aid. Despite these imports, food availability per head fell by 10 per cent from average levels in the first half of the decade. Wholesale prices rose by more than the critical figure of 10 per cent, and cereal prices by 18 per cent (by far more in some parts of the country). The severity of the crisis was all the greater because the droughts hit an economy with low reserves and unresolved tensions in a state of 'quiet crisis'. Agricultural output was growing only very slowly, and exports not much faster. But public fixed investment under the Third Plan had risen by 11.2 per cent a year from 1961/2 to 1965/6, and current expenditure had also risen rapidly partly as a result of the war with China in 1962. Despite tax increases, the consolidated government fiscal deficit rose from 5.6 per cent of GDP in 1960/1 to 6.7 per cent in 1965/6. The balance of payments was contained by import controls severe enough to hinder production and exports (a state of affairs we call 'import starvation'). Even so, the current account deficit increased from 43 per cent of exports in 1964/5 to 84 per cent of exports in 1966/7.

The Aid Consortium formed the view that India was in an impasse in 1964. The government reluctantly accepted a World Bank mission headed by Mr Bernard Bell, whose diagnosis was in line with the description of tension given above. There was no official disagreement with this diagnosis. One of the main recommendations was a major shift of inputs, investment and high level attention to agriculture. This was pushing at a door that was ajar, and was readily accepted. But the other main recommendation, a devaluation, also reluctantly accepted in July 1966, was a political disaster.[5] It was intended not so much to cure the current deficit but as part of a long-term reform designed to achieve balance at a higher level of exports and imports with a much more limited and less distortionary set of controls. It is to be noted that the diagnosis and the recommendation came before there was any hint of drought or crisis. But as a result of inevitable political delays, the reforms comprising the devaluation, removal of export subsidies, reduced tariffs and loosening of controls on imports of materials and components were made after the onset of the crisis but before it was known that there would be a second monsoon failure. The timing was unfortunate and more related to political chance than to economic reasoning. The devaluation was not a crisis measure, but the droughts that were the immediate cause of the crisis also nullified the benefits expected from the devaluation. It was not long before the trade liberalisation measures were reversed.

Since the devaluation was basically unrelated to the crisis we may return to the fiscal measures that were a response to the crisis.[6,7] In August 1965 prices were rising alarmingly and there was an emergency budget which, however, only raised taxes modestly. The fiscal year 1965/6 was one of high pressure of demand with real government expenditure on both investment and consumption rising strongly as real GDP fell due to the drought (agricultural GDP fell 13.5 per cent, but non-agricultural GDP rose modestly by 3 per cent). The WPI rose $11\frac{1}{2}$ per cent over the course of the year. By the time of the February 1966 budget the extent of the drought was fully known. Taxes were again moderately raised, but they were accompanied by large cuts in public investment which fell by 13 per cent in real terms over the year 1966/7. Despite this, with GDP virtually unchanged due to the second successive drought, the consolidated public deficit actually rose slightly as a percentage of GDP. The WPI and CPI each rose by 14 per cent. In February 1967 there was a general election, and Morarji Desai became finance minister. Taxation was once again moderately raised, but the overall fiscal stance became much more deflationary than in the previous two years. Public fixed investment fell by another 8 per cent, other public expenditure rose little, and the consolidated fiscal deficit was reduced to 5.5 per cent of GDP. There was a bumper kharif harvest, and prices began to fall in the autumn of 1967. Although annual inflation of the WPI was nearly 12 per cent (i.e. comparing 1967/8 with 1966/7 as a whole), from March 1967 to March 1968 there was no rise at all. The crisis was over, but it cast a long shadow ahead. The manifest dependence on food imports, and the feeling that the US and the World Bank had imposed the unpopular policy of devaluation, reinforced an existing belief in self-sufficiency or autarky. Partly as a result, fiscal policy remained deflationary for about $2\frac{1}{2}$ years after inflation had ended and agriculture had recovered: public fixed investment in particular did not recover its previous level for many years. There was a slowdown in industrial growth.

The Crisis of 1973–5 (The Second Crisis)

The oil price rises of 1973 and 1974 were a major shock to many developing countries. The change in the terms of trade as a proportion of GDP was quite small for India but the effect on the balance of payments was more serious. The current account deficit went from $445 million in 1972/3 to $951 million in 1974/5. But this could be quite easily handled. Reserves were quite high in 1973, and India borrowed from low-conditionality IMF facilities. There was also a substantial increase in aid which had fallen to a low level in 1972/3 as a result of the war with Pakistan. Of course, the deterioration in the balance of payments would have been worse without internal measures to counter the concurrent inflation which, however, was predominantly due to drought, not to the oil price rise. The fall in capital-intensive public investment reduced the volume of imports, though food and fertiliser imports were allowed to rise. Admittedly, other imports controls were tightened. Nevertheless, the crisis would have been a minor affair if it had not been for the droughts in 1972/3 and 1974/5.

The price of foodgrains (in terms of year-on-year average) rose 16 per cent in 1972/3, 19 per cent in 1973/4 and 38 per cent in 1974/5 – a horrific rise for India of 90 per cent over the three years. The WPI was not very far behind, rising by a cumulative 66 per cent. Inflation began before the oil shock. The influx of refugees from East Bengal in 1971, and the brief war with Pakistan put a strain on government expenditure. Fiscal policy was thus expansionary in 1971/2 and monetary policy was also very lax; M1 growth increased from 11 per cent in 1971/2 to 17.5 per cent in 1973/4. The drought of 1972/3, which reduced agricultural GDP by 5.6 per cent and foodgrain production by 8.2 per cent, thus hit an already extended economy. The rise in the price of oil added to inflation (but not by very much since import costs are a small proportion of total cost in India). The inflation might have been considerably reduced if food supply had been better managed. Food imports were unnecessarily and much delayed, when the world price was rocketing. Domestic stock management (unlike in 1965/6 there was a domestic buffer stock) was also mishandled, ending with the brief populist nationalisation of the wholesale wheat trade.

As in the 1965–6 crisis the main reaction to the inflation was fiscal. But on this occasion, monetary policy was also used. However, it was only in the middle of 1973 that the government began tentatively to respond, reducing its own expenditure and tightening monetary policy. In the event the consolidated fiscal deficit was reduced by almost 1 per cent of GDP in 1973/4. There were also, as usual, modest tax increases in the regular budget of 1974. But by this time there was serious civil disorder, and a rail strike involving 2 million workers was threatened. In June 1974, governmental action became dramatic, even brutal. The rail strike was broken, and in July extremely tough fiscal, monetary and incomes policy measures were introduced. These included tax increases, a wage freeze, dividend limitation and increases in interest rates. The fiscal and incomes policy measures were estimated to reduce disposable incomes by 2 per cent in a full year, and there was a severe monetary squeeze, M1 actually falling by 5.7 per cent in the quarter July–September 1974.

Only two months after the July package, prices began to fall; the WPI fell 3 per cent by the end of the year, and food prices by 4 per cent. Wholesale prices were then roughly stable for three years, while foodgrain prices fell by about 25 per cent. This speed of reaction is somewhat puzzling especially as the kharif harvest of 1974 was already known to be bad. It seems as if the causes must be looked for at least partly in the deflationary measures taken before the dramatic July measures, including the monetary tightening.

The period until the next crisis in 1979 was tranquil in economic, though disturbed in political terms. In particular there was a dramatic turnaround in the balance of payments after the large deficit of 1974/5 with export growth in dollar terms of 17 per cent p.a. over the next three years. This can be attributed to a depreciation of the real exchange rate, which resulted initially from the sterling peg (until September 1975) and later from India's near zero inflation from 1974 through 1978. Unlike in the aftermath of 1965–7 the cuts in public investment were quickly reversed. GDP grew fast by Indian standards (5.8 per cent p.a. from 1974/5 to 1978/9) despite a drought in 1976/7. Large stocks of both foreign exchange and foodgrains were accumulated, so that the government was widely criticised for not being expansionary enough.

The Crisis of 1979–81 (The Third Crisis) and its Aftermath

The shocks which triggered the crisis, the drought and oil price rises of 1979, were very like those of 1973/4. The drought was the most severe since Independence, agricultural GDP falling by 13.4 per cent and foodgrain production by 16.8 per cent in 1979/80. The terms of trade deterioration was slightly less than in 1974. The current account deficit of the balance of payments deteriorated from $347 million (4 per cent of exports) to $2.7 billion (26 per cent of exports). However, as in 1974/5 this was easily financed by loans from the IBRD, IDA and low conditionality IMF facilities. Reserves were high at the onset of the crisis, and fell only slightly in 1979/80 and 1980/1. Unlike 1973/4 there was no resort to tightening import restrictions. Indeed, one cannot say that there was a balance of payments crisis at all.

The crisis was thus essentially an inflation crisis, as was indeed the case with both previous crises. The WPI rose 17–18 per cent in both 1979/80 and 1980/1. Foodgrain prices rose rather less than industrial prices and non-food agricultural prices. This was largely because cereal stocks were high and the government could make large sales. Thus the inflation on this occasion was quite largely a cost–push inflation (there was a recession in private manufacturing), resulting from the rise in the price of oil and of agricultural raw materials, and also wages (the real wage in organised manufacturing rose 14 per cent in 1978/9): this was probably exacerbated by the very poor condition of Indian infrastructure, leading to power and transport bottlenecks. That the inflation was not wholly the result of the drought of 1979 is also shown by the fact that prices started rising in February 1979 well before the failure of the monsoon became evident around August. The effect of the rise in import prices was surely magnified by the high liquidity of the economy, resulting from a rapid rise in the quantity of money in the previous two years.

The government's supply response was much better than in previous crises, though not above criticism (it could early on have allowed increased imports of food other than cereals, and some raw materials, since foreign exchange reserves were ample).

Fiscal and monetary policy was only mildly restrictive in 1979/80 and 1980/1. It was determined that the deflationary policies of 1973/4 would be avoided and a progressive adjustment set in motion. In particular no cuts were made in public investment. Inflation would come down when agricultural output recovered. Negotiations for a large IMF loan which would permit expansionary policies to continue began at the end of 1980. The budget of February 1981 was quite tough partly because inflation was still continuing, but also because it was anticipated that the IMF conditions would necessitate a reduction in the fiscal deficit. However, public investment was still maintained although the central government fiscal deficit for the year 1981/2 was reduced to 5.4 per cent of GDP (from 6.5 per cent). The inflation, and the crisis, was over by August 1981. Prices fell from then to March 1982. The IMF loan of SDR 5 billion was approved in November 1981. It was a precautionary loan intended to support the policy of expansionary adjustment. The conditions were no more stringent than the

Indian authorities intended anyway. India terminated the loan in May 1984 after drawing SDR 3.9 million.

There was certainly expansion through the rest of the 1980s. Public investment was maintained at a high level of 10–11 per cent of GDP, which grew rapidly in the 1980s compared with previous decades. Manufacturing in particular grew at 6–7 per cent p.a. compared with a little less than 5 per cent in the 1970s. There was some successful import substitution in oil, but otherwise little reform or liberalisation on the supply side. The deterioration in the terms of trade in 1980 would have warranted a depreciation of the real exchange rate. Since India's rate of inflation was higher after 1979/80 than those of its trading partners this would have required a nominal devaluation, still a politically difficult operation. In fact the real exchange rate appreciated by about 15 per cent in 1980/1 and 1981/2 and then remained stationary until 1984/5. Exports stagnated. The current account worsened, almost without remission throughout the decade. This was not surprising in view of the sharply rising fiscal deficits. The consolidated government fiscal deficit rose from 6.7 per cent of GDP in 1981/2 to 10.4 per cent in 1989/90. In view of India's failure to adjust, it can be argued that the IMF should have tried to impose stronger conditions. The counterfactual, if negotiations had then collapsed, is too difficult to assess.

The Crisis of 1991 (The Fourth Crisis)

This was a severe but unexceptional crisis. In June 1991 the foreign exchange reserves were down to about a fortnight's imports, and falling fast. India was on the verge of default. This was easily predictable. In the year just passed, the current account deficit was $9.9 billion, about 3.5 per cent of GDP and 44 per cent of exports. At the end of March 1991, external debt reached $70 billion constituting 29 per cent of GNP and 275 per cent of exports (up from 12 per cent of GNP and 140 per cent of exports in March 1980). The debt service ratio was 29 per cent. In these circumstances only a spark was needed. It was provided by the temporary rise in oil prices following the Iraqi invasion of Kuwait. India suddenly ceased to be creditworthy and was unable to borrow. This loss of confidence was clearly also related to the domestic political turmoil of the previous six months which inhibited measures to restore some element of fiscal probity.

The crisis had been in the making throughout the 1980s, especially in the second half. Exports rose rapidly from 1985 helped by an active depreciation of the rupee. The external environment was also favourable since oil prices collapsed in 1986. Nevertheless the high and rising government and public sector deficits made a large current account deficit inevitable. The crisis simply arose as a result of the 'unpleasant arithmetic' of deficit financing. The stable and (for India) quite high growth of the 1980s was based on an apparent failure to appreciate the dynamics of rising debt and interest payments (internal as well as external) which made her growth path unsustainable and hence unstable in the longer run.

There was no drought on this occasion, and the external shock would have been negligible if the macroeconomy had been in reasonably good shape. It is to be noted, however, that inflation was over 10 per cent and rising despite good harvests for the past three years (and despite the current account deficit). Clearly the economy was experiencing excess demand.

III SHORT-TERM STABILISATION POLICY, 1964–91: AN ASSESSMENT[8]

An economic crisis usually means a payments crisis. A country (or a person for that matter) has debts it cannot pay; and no one will lend it money. Or drastic action has to be taken to avoid such a situation which will, if allowed to develop, lead to severe disruption of trade, loss of output and unemployment. The drastic action must include measures which will sufficiently relieve the balance of payments for creditors and traders to continue to do business.

The first three Indian 'crises' examined above were not crises in the above sense. Default was not threatened. India was not yet a major borrower and trade was tightly controlled. They were all primarily inflation crises. Inflation was what moved the government to emergency action. The primary cause of the inflation in all cases was drought. There were secondary causes, some generalised excess demand on each occasion, and a rise in import prices on the second and third occasions. But these were minor disturbances compared to the declines in agricultural production, especially of cereals.

Droughts are essentially temporary disturbances, which however are known to occur from time to time. In these circumstances it should be possible to avoid a crisis. Sufficient reserves of grain and foreign exchange, as well as reserves of credibility which permit a rise in borrowing, should be maintained. The years 1965/6 and 1973/4 were crisis years because reserves were very low and commercial borrowing was not then easy. But, it may be argued, ample reserves were held in 1979, and yet there was a crisis. Of course, a difficult and unpleasant situation must arise when there is a fall of 17 per cent in foodgrain production and a big rise in import prices (50 per cent from 1977/8 to 1980/1). It would be impossible, even undesirable, to avoid any increase in prices in such circumstances. In fact the WPI rose about

17 per cent in 1979/80, with cereals prices rising by a similar amount with a normal lag of about a year. Macroeconomic policy was not bad, but it could have been better. As we have seen, a large monetary expansion had been permitted in the late 1970s, and the supply side could have been handled better in 1979/80. With better handling, inflation might have been kept to a non-crisis level. Our main point is thus that a very severe double exogenous shock could be met with only a temporary and not too alarming inflation, and no severe deflationary fiscal or monetary action (probably none would have been needed if monetary growth had not already been excessive).

It follows, of course, from the above argument that the severely deflationary monetary and fiscal policies of 1966 and 1975 could have been avoided if adequate stocks had been built up (stocks especially in the 1960s were regarded as a waste of scarce resources, which should be used to create heavy-industrial capacity). But this does not imply that monetary and fiscal measures were wholly inappropriate. It could, however, be argued that they were, on the ground that the demand for food is extremely income-inelastic. We do not take this view, for two reasons. First, there was some general excess demand. Secondly, a fiscal (or incomes policy) attack on incomes will have a small but nevertheless significant effect on food prices, helping to reduce the effects of inflation on the poor. But the design on the fiscal measures was wrong, especially the cuts in investment, which would have virtually no effect on prices. Also the deflationary measures were both delayed, and then maintained for too long, especially after 1965.

The first three crises thus arose primarily from drought-induced inflation. But the balance of payments aspects, though secondary, were not unimportant. Each crisis was marked by a large current account deterioration. In the first crisis, this arose from the drought itself (which reduced exports and necessitated increased imports). In the second and third crises, the cause was external, namely, a sharp deterioration in the terms of trade due to a rise in the price of imported oil.

The difference between balance of payments adjustment in the second and third crises is noteworthy. The current account turned round very quickly after the second crisis; indeed it went into a large surplus. After the third crisis, however, the current account showed no improvement. The role of the exchange rate was critical. In both crises, current account adjustment required a real depreciation. In the second crisis, policy was compatible with this requirement. The nominal exchange rate was pegged to sterling and depreciated with it. Consequently, during the crisis itself, the real exchange rate changed little in spite of high domestic inflation. In the aftermath of the crisis, the real exchange rate depreciated substantially. While luck played a large part in this, one can at least say that policy-makers did not fight the real depreciation. In contrast, in the third crisis, the nominal exchange rate was allowed to appreciate slightly despite rapid domestic inflation, so that there was a large real exchange rate appreciation. After the crisis, the real appreciation was not reversed. This goes a long way to explaining the export boom during and after the second crisis and the export stagnation during and after the third crisis.

Elementary balance of payments theory tells us that a devaluation is a necessary condition for improving the current account, not a sufficient condition. It cannot succeed without a reduction in the gap between investment and saving, which normally requires supporting macroeconomic measures. In this respect too, the policy reactions after the second and third crises were very different. In the aftermath of the second crisis, fiscal policy was prudent; after the third it was imprudent. Indeed, the imprudence soon gave way to downright irresponsibility and produced the fourth crisis.

IV   MEDIUM-RUN MACROECONOMIC MANAGEMENT

Macroeconomic policy cannot be guided by purely short-run considerations even though these may well predominate during crisis episodes. In this section, we examine India's macroeconomic policies from a medium-run perspective.[9]

Fiscal Policy

Stabilising output, or more precisely avoiding both excesses and deficiencies of demand, is the traditional role ascribed to fiscal policy in Keynesian economics. We have tested whether Indian fiscal policy was output-stabilising in this sense by using conventional procedures. The standard criteria regard fiscal policy as stabilising if the cyclically adjusted 'fiscal impulse' is negatively correlated with the movement of output in relation to trend. In this sense, fiscal policy was destabilising in no fewer than 22 years in the period 1960–90. This result has to be interpreted with some care. Output may be below trend because of a drought. A positive fiscal impulse can do nothing about that, but it can alleviate the induced fall in industrial output and in aggregate consumption. Such a policy would, however, have been possible only if the economy had possessed greater stocks of foreign exchange reserves and commodities, especially foodgrains, the use of which would have reduced inflation by increasing supplies, and would have either ameliorated or financed a deterioration in the balance of payments. In the first two crises, the coincidence of a negative fiscal impulse and below-trend output can be explained by this condition not being met. Apparently more puzzling are the many instances of positive fiscal impulse and above-trend output. We explain this by our observation that inflation in India is inversely correlated with the fiscal impulse, indicating that inflation was taken as the main guide for fiscal policy. This is understandable. Changes in most important prices are known immediately; changes in output are known for sure only with quite long delays. Nevertheless, while it is understandable, reacting mainly to prices can lead to serious mistakes. Inflation may be low during a boom for special reasons such as a run of good harvests or rising balance of payments deficits financed by external borrowing. In such circumstances, an expansionary fiscal policy can be destabilising both cyclically and in a long-run structural sense. This is an important element in the story of the 1980s.

It goes without saying that one of the requirements of a satisfactory fiscal stance is that it should be intertemporally sustainable. In the 1980s, the primary deficit of the non-financial public sector rose to about 7 per cent. Our calculations show that public sector deficits of even half this magnitude are unsustainable. During the 1960s and 1970s, the government and the public sector ran primary deficits of around 4 per cent of GDP. This was, however, possible only because of (1) highly concessionary external borrowing in the 1960s, and (2) low or even negative real interest rates maintained by coercion of the banks (and exploitation of the public). In the 1980s these favourable conditions vanished and the position rapidly became unsustainable, in spite of higher growth of GDP (by Indian standards). Fiscal deterioration continued, though even the simplest calculation was enough to show the unsustainability of the fiscal track. India's experience confirms that neglect of fiscal dynamics is a recipe for disaster.

Monetary Policy

In the medium run, the main objective of monetary policy is to maintain a low rate of inflation. In this simple sense, policy has been good. Two points are relevant. First, monetary policy has been restrictive or at least non-accommodating whenever exogenous shocks have resulted in inflationary bubbles.[10] (Our econometric model shows clear evidence of such a policy reaction.)[11] Low coverage of indexation arrangements has also helped. Secondly, monetary policy instruments, particularly reserve ratios, have been actively used to prevent fiscal deficits from spilling over into monetary expansion.

But the system created longer-run problems. It involved forcing banks to hold cash and government securities at significantly below market rates. This in turn kept deposit rates low and lending rates to the private sector high. The effect of mild financial repression on private financial savings has not been adverse, suggesting that the effect of low interest rates was outweighed by the 'spread of banking' effect. But the growth of savings has shown clear signs of levelling off in the 1980s, suggesting that this could now be a serious problem. The system of 'forced capture' of private savings had further deleterious effects. First, the apparent ease with which government could borrow induced complacency about fiscal deficits. Secondly, it inhibited the development of open market operations as a genuine instrument of policy. Last, but not least, it undermined the financial strength of the banking system to the point where emergency action had to be taken after the crisis of 1990/1.

Trade and Payments Policy

The microeconomic shortcomings of import controls in India have been analysed in depth by Jagdish Bhagwati.[12] But Indian experience shows that import controls are also inefficient as a macroeconomic device. The argument in favour of import restrictions is their certainty of operation in improving the current account. This makes them attractive to policy-makers as a way of reconciling internal and external balance if reserves are low and exchange rate devaluation is dismissed on the basis of 'elasticity pessimism' or because of its presumed inflationary consequences. These objections to devaluation are largely inapplicable in the Indian context. Moreover, import restrictions have serious shortcomings as a macroeconomic instrument (except in the very short run). They reduce the relative price of exportables and the incentive to export, so that in the medium run, current account improvement is eroded. While removing the competitive advantage of a variable exchange rate, they also remove the anti-inflationary anchor that is the main advantage of a fixed exchange rate. As import controls are progressively tightened, they can result in a fall in domestic production due to shortages of essential inputs ('import starvation'). They lead to delays and administrative bottlenecks that reduce the elasticity of supply of exports and more generally the speed and flexibility with which the economy can respond to unfavourable (and indeed even to favourable) shocks.

The heyday of the use of import controls to manage the balance of payments was the period from the mid-1950s to the mid-1960s, and it clearly bears out the above points. Though the crisis of 1965/6 was triggered by severe droughts, the import control regime played a significant part in creating the weak balance of payments situation and the inflexible economic structure that turned shock into crisis. An interesting commentary on how import controls can impede benefits from favourable changes is provided by the experience of 1975–8. During these years, partly due to luck and partly due to policy, the balance of payments improved dramatically and it would have been both anti-inflationary and growth-promoting to increase import-intensive investment. But this option could not be considered because a radical change in the import control regime was not on the agenda. Import controls must therefore take part of the responsibility for both the loss of momentum in public investment and the rapid money growth during these years and therefore for the inflation that followed in 1979–81.

India's macroeconomic performance has been handicapped by a reluctance to vary the nominal exchange rate actively. We base this judgement on three considerations. First, the current account is responsive to variations in the real exchange rate. 'Elasticity pessimism' stands refuted by empirical evidence.[13] Secondly, a change in the nominal exchange rate *does* translate into a change in the real exchange rate. India is a large country with a small traded goods sector and low indexation of wages. Her inflation is driven mainly by agricultural production and the monetary/fiscal situation, not by the exchange rate. Hence, using the exchange rate as a 'nominal anchor' makes little sense in the Indian context. Thirdly, it follows that if there is an adverse real shock (e.g. a rise in the price of oil) which is expected to be permanent, devaluing the nominal exchange rate would be desirable, even essential. It would be fanciful to expect that adjustment could be achieved via a fixed nominal exchange rate putting downward pressure on prices.

The two periods when the reluctance to devalue was most in evidence were 1960–5 and 1980–5. In the former period, payments balance was maintained by import restrictions and concessional borrowing, with consequences outlined above. From 1980–5, the reluctance first to devalue at all and then to devalue sufficiently led to stagnation of exports and to persistent current account deficits. This time, import controls were not tightened, nor was investment cut. Payments balance was maintained by a sharp increase in non-concessional foreign borrowing from the IMF and commercial sources. The rapid build-up of debt sowed the seeds of the crisis of 1990/1. Leaving aside 1980–5, however, the overall trend in the 1970s and 1980s has been towards a gradual depoliticisation of the exchange rate instrument. Macroeconomic adjustment would have been even less smooth and growth lower without this flexibility.

Controls

A fashionable view of Indian economic policy is that it was unsound microeconomically but sound macroeconomically, and further that these phenomena were positively linked – in other words, the controls that led to microeconomic inefficiency made it easier to attain macroeconomic stability.[14] Can this dichotomy between macroeconomic and microeconomic management be maintained? Were the controls really needed for macroeconomic management? We argue that, on balance, they were not only not needed but were actually counterproductive.

We showed in section IV how controls on international trade, together with reluctant use of the exchange rate, impeded good macroeconomic management, reducing output and growth. We also pointed to long-run damage to the banking system and other deleterious effects of the highly controlled financial system.

The damage caused by controls goes deeper. They result in black markets and present innumerable opportunities for both tax evasion and corruption. This has contributed to the serious breakdown of tax morality on the part of the public and fiscal discipline on the part of the government. The fiscal problem has been exacerbated in yet other ways. Trade controls with an overvalued exchange rate result in a loss of tax revenue and a need for export subsidies: and by keeping agricultural prices low they have led to huge countervailing subsidies. Finally, both import controls and industrial controls over investment and production have reduced the flexibility with which output can respond to changing circumstances and the levers of macroeconomic policy.

Price and distribution controls in the food market merit special attention. Their objective was originally to supply rationed quantities of food at subsidised prices through the public distribution system, rather than to stabilise prices. In recent years with a succession of good monsoons the 'procurement' prices paid to farmers for these supplies have become support prices. However, the stabilisation of food prices by buffer-stock operations is an essential part of India's anti-inflation policies. But this can be achieved without controls by buying and selling in the market, building up stocks in good years and running them down in bad years in order to moderate any rise in food prices. When the government buys for the buffer-stock it is, of course, supporting the price. This support need not necessarily be at a pre-announced price, but it has become so. It is widely accepted that such pre-announced support prices, by reducing uncertainty, have a beneficial effect on output.[15] But there is a danger. In some recent years the strength of farm lobbies has led to large rises in procurement prices. Thus they may become an element in cost–push inflation. The buffer-stock and its provisioning while insuring against large inflationary rises in food prices after a drought may in other years ensure that food prices always rise somewhat. The experience of other countries shows that support prices often also lead to wastefully large stocks. Indeed cereal stocks are probably excessive in India now.

Whatever the policy on buffer-stocks and food price stabilisation, the provision of subsidised food can continue, but not for everyone. Rising food subsidies threaten the use of cheap food as an anti-poverty device. They must be limited by targeting the very poor.

Finally, while we believe that most controls hinder sound macroeconomic management in the medium run, the transition to fewer controls is a task of some delicacy. We have not considered the question of sequencing because radical liberalisation of controls was not seriously on the agenda until 1991. Since then, it has become a live issue. We comment on one important sequencing problem – that concerning the liberalisation of external capital flows – in the next section.

V   STABILISATION AND STRUCTURAL REFORM, 1991–4

The first priority of the new government which took office in July 1991 was to avoid default with all the immediate consequences of trade dislocation, and long-term damage to India's credit-rating. However, the dramatic measures undertaken to restore credibility were, from the outset, combined with first steps towards a basic long-term reform of the whole economic system. Quite suddenly it seems that a swathe of the educated public had become convinced that India's autarkic highly regulated system must end. It had taken a long time. There has been much inconclusive debate about whether stabilisation should precede reform, or whether the two can march together. The arguments in favour of prior stabilisation seem to be mainly relevant to countries with very high inflation. The Indian inflation though troubling by Indian standards was not very high: moreover, Indian inflation is not established in the sense of there being a permanent expectation of inflation (though there will be if it is not soon brought down to zero as it has been on several occasions in the past). There was thus no need for an exchange rate and price freeze to break expectations. Moreover, the planned reforms, and structural adjustments, though both wide-ranging and profound, were to be gradual. We shall not deal with the detail of the reforms here, discussing them only when reform and stabilisation have been in conflict.[16]

The drastic action of July 1991 made use of all the usual instruments. Taxes were raised and expenditure cut. Import controls were severely tightened; and the rupee was devalued by 22 per cent, which permitted export subsidies to be abolished. Some of the measures taken were clearly not in tune with the structural changes planned. These included the tightening of import controls, and increases in already highly distortionary excise taxes. But import controls began to be dismantled as soon as the reserves rose to safer levels, and have by now been almost eliminated except for consumer goods. The excise tax increases have also been moderated and made less distortionary, though a lot remains to be done.

The major tension has been between the need to reduce the fiscal deficit and the need to reform the trade regime and the tax system. A good start was made with the central fiscal deficit in 1991/2 and 1992/3 when it was brought down to 5.7 per cent of GDP from 8.4 per cent in 1990/1. But although export subsidies were eliminated and there was some reduction in the large fertiliser subsidy, this was achieved too much by cutting public investment (the old story!), which is especially undesirable given the poor state of much of India's infrastructure. In 1993/4 the fiscal deficit grew to 7.3 per cent of GDP against a budget estimate of 4.7 per cent. Comparing 1993/4 with 1990/1, the central fiscal deficit had fallen by only 1.1 per cent of GDP, comprising a fall in revenue of 0.9 per cent, in current expenditure of 0.2 per cent and in capital expenditure of 1.8 per cent. The fall in revenue of 0.9 per cent was more than accounted for by a fall in tax receipts of 1.3 per cent. This latter was due mainly to a fall in customs and excise.[17]

The reforms have required a fall in customs duty and will require a further fall. As at present levied excise taxes are highly distortionary. Reforms are taking place, but one should not expect any offsetting increase (as a proportion of GDP) until a concurrent national and states' VAT can be put in place. There is clearly tension here between indirect tax reform and the macroeconomic need for a reduced fiscal deficit. Furthermore a case can be made for increasing public investment, and social sector expenditure (this latter has been done in the last two budgets). The two candidates for relieving this tension are raising direct tax collection, which is abysmal by any standard, and reducing 'non plan' expenditures, especially on subsidies, defence and general administration. Of course, this is easier said than done and the Finance Minister, Dr Manmohan Singh, is walking a tightrope.

The second important tension is between freeing inward capital movements on the one hand, and inflation or exchange rate appreciation on the other hand. Freeing capital movements has gone faster than trade reform (bearing in mind that consumer goods imports are still banned with few exceptions), reforms of the tax system and industrial policy reform. Restrictions on direct foreign investment have been greatly reduced and portfolio investment now faces fewer hurdles. These measures together with the 'push' factor of lower US interest rates, the 'pull' factor of the profit opportunities opened up by India's reform process and some bandwagon effects, mixed up in unknown proportions, have resulted in a large inflow of private capital by Indian standards. The inflow was about $5 billion per annum in 1993/4 and 1994/5, about three-quarters of which was portfolio capital. This inflow has created an acute dilemma for macroeconomic policy.

If the inflow is 'permanent', in other words, can confidently be expected to continue for a long time, the appropriate response would be to allow the nominal exchange rate to appreciate sufficiently to produce a current account deficit equal to the capital inflow. (Real exchange rate appreciation could also be secured with a fixed nominal exchange rate but would be an inferior alternative since it would involve increased monetary expansion and a higher price level.)

If the inflow is 'temporary', matters are not so simple. Allowing the nominal exchange rate (and hence the real exchange rate) to appreciate would reduce exports and increase the current account deficit. But these developments cannot be regarded as benign if the inflow is not secure. Exports, once discouraged, cannot easily revive, being subject to lags and hysteresis effects. Moreover, an exchange rate appreciation would create resistance to import liberalisation, an important aspect of the reform process. A pronounced exchange rate cycle could also destabilise the financial system. A further point is that even if the inflow is reasonably long-lasting, it is important that the associated widening of the current account deficit should reflect an increase in investment, not a reduction in saving. The absorption of foreign inflow into investment is less likely to be held up by infrastructural shortages if it takes place at a measured pace rather than in a rush.

It is presumably on considerations such as these that the Indian authorities chose to react to the capital inflow by keeping the nominal exchange rate fixed and accumulating reserves. Unfortunately, this strategy brings about real exchange rate appreciation by another route since it results in an increase in the quantity of money and in prices. If the inflow is 'temporary' or at least if the authorities are unsure that it is long-lasting, it therefore becomes important to investigate possibilities of 'squaring the circle' by keeping the nominal exchange rate fixed while breaking the link between the capital inflow, the money supply and inflation.[18] It should be noted here that a reduction of the fiscal deficit, which is in any case desirable on other grounds, would help in this context. It would reduce monetary expansion in so far as the fiscal deficit is financed by printing money. It would directly reduce the pressure of demand in the goods market. In addition, by reducing interest rates, it would deter those capital inflows which are caused purely by the inappropriate fiscal–monetary policy mix in India.

If a sharp reduction in the fiscal deficit is not feasible, both sterilisation and capital controls may have to be employed in the short run, even if they run contrary to the liberalising thrust of the reform programme. Of course, there will be some costs involved. Pure sterilisation by the sale of government bonds involves a quasi-fiscal cost since the interest rate on government securities is higher than that on foreign exchange reserves. Other methods of immobilising the monetary base such as increasing the CRR do not involve a fiscal cost but do reduce bank profits. All these methods hold up domestic interest rates and preserve the incentive for inward capital flows. It follows that in these circumstances, a 'big bang' relaxation of controls on inflows would be unwise.

Capital flows into India in 1993/4 and 1994/5 were about 2 per cent of GDP per annum. Assuming a 7 per cent differential in the interest rate on government bonds and foreign exchange reserves, the cumulative fiscal cost of sterilisation of the entire inflow by open market operations would have been about 0.3 per cent of GDP. (The fiscal cost would have been lower still if methods other than pure sterilisation (such as a rise in the CRR) had been employed.) This cost may well have been worth paying. It would also have been wiser to have instituted earlier than was done measures such as (1) reducing interest rates on non-resident foreign currency deposits, and (2) asking Indian companies to hold newly borrowed funds outside the country until they were willing to undertake productive investment. As it happens, the government did not pursue sterilisation policies aggressively enough so that the money supply grew by 18 per cent in 1993/4 and is expected to rise at a similar rate in 1994/5. Not surprisingly, inflation is running somewhat higher than 10 per cent per annum. Since inflation in the rest of the world is very low, this has implied an appreciation of the real exchange rate.

Surges in capital inflow have created dilemmas for policy in many reforming countries. We are echoing here the view that external financial liberalisation should not run ahead of real sector liberalisation.[19]

VI   POLITICAL ECONOMY AND THE FISCAL PROBLEM

For a long time, the balance of payments was considered to be the key macroeconomic problem faced by developing countries, including India, in their drive for development. We believe, on the contrary, that the fiscal problem is central, and that this is particularly true of India and other countries that see a very large and necessary role for the public sector in promoting development while at the same time suffering from a narrow revenue base. If the public finances are in good shape, and the exchange rate is flexible, the balance of payments and inflation will rarely be a major problem.

Fewer controls and greater reliance on the price mechanism, which the present economic reforms encourage, will help the fiscal problem, though not necessarily in the short run. But far more is needed. Fiscal laxity is a danger whatever the system of regulation. Indeed, it is a danger whatever the political system. It is often supposed that the pressures that may lead to fiscal laxity are more keenly felt in a democracy. As against this, elections have to be won and inflation is unpopular. Autocratic governments may be more insulated from pressure groups, but this has not stopped some charismatic autocratic rulers from initiating wild bursts of public expenditure.

Until the 1970s, India may have had the best of both worlds. It was effectively a genuine one-party democracy. The Congress could mediate conflicting claims through its own internal democracy. Although it had little fear of losing elections, the Gladstonian traditions of the civil service and the austerity and high-mindedness of the first generation of post-Independence politicians were effective restraints on inflationary finance.

This system has been progressively weakened. Some dissolution of such a convenient kind of democracy was perhaps inevitable as a result of 'political awakening', the increasing self-assertion of groups that were not part of the narrow post-Independence elite structures. But along with political awakening there has been 'political decay', the erosion of institutions which manage conflict.[20] The mediating role of the Congress Party has been lost along with the atrophy of its grassroots organisations. The institutions of restraint, such as the civil service, including the Ministry of Finance, and the Reserve Bank, have become more subject to political pressures. Politics has consequently become more populist: claims on the state are settled to a greater extent outside the political process, by handouts or by measures that reduce tax or non-tax receipts.

Economic stability in a democracy would seem to require a stable centre insulated from excessive demands. This is not a problem that can be answered by economic liberalisation as such. India must somehow rediscover her fiscal prudence.

NOTES

1. Bhagwati and Desai (1970) and Bhagwati and Srinivasan (1975) are widely regarded as landmarks in the analysis of India's trade and resource-allocation policies.
2. This paper draws on the comprehensive critique of Indian macroeconomic policies in Joshi and Little (1994).
3. See Little et al. (1993).
4. For a more detailed treatment see Joshi and Little (1994), chapters 4–7.
5. The rupee was devalued by 36.5 per cent. See Bhagwati and Srinivasan (1975) for an exhaustive and illuminating analysis of the devaluation.
6. Other noteworthy aspects of the policy response were (a) supply-management through increased aid-financed imports, and (b) income-support policies in famine-affected states like Bihar.

7. There seems to have been no independent monetary policy during the crisis years. M3 rose quite steadily at about 10 per cent p.a. over the crisis period.
8. See Joshi and Little (1994), chapter 8.
9. A more extended treatment will be found in Joshi and Little (1994), chapters 9–14.
10. This is not to say that the conduct of short-term monetary policy has been above criticism. It has been blunt, erratic and overactive.
11. See Joshi and Little (1994), chapter 10.
12. See Bhagwati and Desai (1970) and Bhagwati and Srinivasan (1975).
13. See Joshi and Little (1994), chapter 11. Our econometric work shows that the medium-run price elasticity of demand for exports in India is around 3 and the medium-run price elasticity of supply of exports is in excess of 1 (and that 80 per cent of the demand and supply effects come through within three years). We also note various reasons why these estimates may be biased downward.
14. For a devastating critique of India's micro-control system, see Bhagwati (1993). Bhagwati does not espouse this fashionable view.
15. The Indian government cannot support the world price of wheat or rice. In the unlikely event that the landed price falls below the support price, a variable levy would be required to bring the landed price up to the support price; continued canalisation of the trade would not be necessary.
16. The topic is treated in greater detail in Joshi and Little (1993a) and Joshi and Little (1993b), both of which are reprinted in Cassen and Joshi (1995). See also Joshi (1994).
17. Due to lack of recent figures we discuss only the central deficit, though ideally we should be considering the whole public sector. However, the two deficits are closely correlated. The primary fiscal deficit of the Centre in 1993/4 was 3 per cent of GDP. It can be shown that fiscal sustainability requires that the primary fiscal deficit of the Centre should be brought down to around zero (see Joshi and Little, 1993b). Thus the quantity of fiscal adjustment has been insufficient. As noted in the text, the quality of fiscal adjustment has also been less than adequate. Much of the cut in the central deficit can be attributed to a retrenchment of capital expenditure and thus of public investment in infrastructure. The current revenue deficit in 1993/4 is in fact larger than it was in 1990/1. Though lack of data makes it difficult to make definite statements on the issue, it is also virtually certain that consolidated centre and state real social expenditures per head have fallen.
18. See Joshi (1994).
19. For example, see Mckinnon (1991).
20. We owe the terms 'political awakening' and 'political decay' to James Manor. See Manor (1983). Our discussion is also influenced by the work of Bardhan (1984) and Kohli (1990).

REFERENCES

Bardhan, Pranab (1984), *The Political Economy of Development in India* (Oxford: Basil Blackwell).
Bhagwati, Jagdish (1993), *India in Transition* (Oxford: Clarendon Press).

Bhagwati, Jagdish and Desai, Padma (1970), *India: Planning for Industrialisation* (Oxford: Oxford University Press).

Bhagwati, Jagdish and Srinivasan, T.N. (1975), *Foreign Trade Regimes and Economic Development – India* (New York: National Bureau of Economic Research).

Cassen, Robert and Joshi, Vijay, eds. (1995), *India: The Future of Economic Reform* (Delhi: Oxford University Press).

Joshi, Vijay (1994), 'Macroeconomic Policy and Economic Reform', *Exim Bank Annual Lecture* (Bombay).

Joshi, Vijay and Little, I.M.D. (1993a), 'Future Trade and Exchange Rate Policy for India', *Economic and Political Weekly*, vol. 28, no. 31, pp. 1599–605 Reprinted in Cassen and Joshi (1995).

———— (1993b), 'Macroeconomic Stabilisation in India, 1991–1993 and beyond', *Economic and Political Weekly*, vol. 28, no. 49, pp. 2659–65 Reprinted in Cassen and Joshi (1995).

———— (1994), *India: Macroeconomics and Political Economy, 1964–1991* (Washington DC: World Bank; and Delhi: Oxford University Press).

Kohli, Atul (1990), *Democracy and Development* (Cambridge: Cambridge University Press).

Little, I.M.D., Richard, N., Cooper, W., Corden, M. and Rajapatirana, S. (1993), *Boom, Crisis and Adjustment: The Macroeconomic Experience of Developing Countries* (New York: Oxford University Press).

Manor, James (1983), 'The Electoral Process amid Awakening and Decay', In Peter Lyon and James Manor, eds., *Transfer and Transformation: Political Institutions in the New Commonwealth* (Leicester: University of Leicester Press).

Mckinnon, Ronald (1991), *The Order of Economic Liberalisation: Financial Control in the Transition to a Market Economy* (Baltimore: Johns Hopkins University Press).

11 Trade Policy in Transition: The China Story

Alasdair MacBean

This story is a modest attempt to follow in the tradition of the seminal work of Jagdish Bhagwati (1978) and Anne Krueger (1978) in assembling evidence on the effects of trade policy on economic and social progress in many developing countries. It also follows on from Jagdish Bhagwati's recent book, *India in Transition: Freeing the Economy* (1993), where he draws attention to the changing perceptions and reality about the relative progress of the two Asian giants (pp. 6–17).

China's main economic reforms began with the declaration of 'The Open Door Policy'. Since then both China's economy and its policies towards trade and investment have been in a continual state of transition, not always in one direction, but with a general trend towards a more open and market-directed economy.

The growth of China's exports, the influx of foreign investment, the sheer growth of national product, all testify to the success of China's Open Door Policy. But that success can only be understood in the context of the other main areas of reform. Without the gains from agricultural and rural enterprise liberalisation the impact of trade policy would have been much less. But equally, the trading opportunities, the foreign exchange earned, management know-how, technology transfers and jobs achieved by the Open Door Policy have been the motor of change in China. Explaining China's success in exporting and attracting foreign investment requires at least a minimal grasp of reform in other sectors. This paper looks first at China's economic performance before and after the pivotal year of 1978, when real reform began. Next the main reforms in agriculture, industry, pricing and other changes in commodity and factor markets are set out. Then these are related to the principal reforms in international economic policies in trade and finance. Finally, some implications are drawn for further reform in China and Eastern Europe.

CHINA'S SPECTACULAR PERFORMANCE

Even though no laggard before 1978, China's growth rate increased dramatically during the 1980s decade of reform. National income growth

195

rose from an average 5.7 per cent per year between 1953 and 1978 (Nolan, 1990, p. 9) to over 9 per cent from 1980 to 1991 (World Bank, 1994). Although the government reacted to rising inflation at the end of the 1980s with a credit crunch which squeezed growth down to 3.7 per cent in 1989, the economy bounced back to a 9 per cent rate in 1990 (IMF, 1991a), and has exceeded 13 per cent in the 1990s, but is once more threatened by 28 per cent per year inflation (*Financial Times*, 18 November 1994). Population growth was reduced from 2.2 per cent to 1.3 per cent per year in the 1980s. Absolute poverty was cut from 17 per cent of rural households in 1987 to 13 per cent in 1988 (World Bank, 1990). Agriculture, the largest sector, was sluggish under Mao; its net material product grew at only 1.9 per cent per year in 1953–78, but surged to 6 per cent in 1978–87. Rural incomes doubled in the six years 1978–84 contributing demand as well as materials, investment and labour to the rest of the economy. Industry, the favoured sector in pre-reform China, kept up its 10 per cent annual growth, but with more emphasis on light industries, while construction, transport and commerce in the 1980s doubled or tripled their past rates of growth (Nolan, 1990, p. 11). Total private consumption in 1980 constant yuan rose from 215 billion in 1978 to 488 billion in 1989 (World Bank, 1990, Table 1.2). The improvements ran through every physical indicator from grain to cloth, but are particularly marked for housing space and durable goods like watches, bicycles, radios and television sets (Nolan, 1990, Table 1.3) and for social factors like life expectation, infant mortality and adult literacy (*Beijing Review*, 1995, p. 18).

The foreign trade ratio (exports plus imports over national income) at 5 per cent was low even by the standards of large countries. In the 1980s it tripled. Merchandise exports rose from $18.2 to $52.5 billion, and China's share of world trade expanded from a mere 0.97 per cent to 1.7 per cent (World Bank, 1990, Table 1.1).

Compared with India, the material progress in China since 1980 has been outstanding. On most criteria China has outstripped India. Even on the UNDP Quality of Life Index, China's progress is almost double that of India. Table 11.1 sets out comparative data on the two economies. There are problems with China's statistics, but the overwhelming impression from both data and observation is of very rapid material progress. Against this should be weighed various environmental problems which are only beginning to be appreciated and tackled by the Chinese authorities.

THE PRE-REFORM ECONOMIC SYSTEM (1949–78)

The birth of Communist China in 1949 came after 30 years of political instability and war. There was hyperinflation. Output of steel, coal and

Table 11.1   Recent Data and Trends on Economic and Social Indicators for China and for India

	China	India
Population (1992)	1162 million	883.6 million
GNP per capita (1992)	470 (1910)*	310 (1210)*
Growth per capita GNP (1980–92)	7.6	3.1
Life expectancy at birth (1992)	69.0	61.0
Adult illiteracy % (1990)	27.0	52.0
Growth of GDP % per annum 1980–92	9.1	5.2
Growth of Agriculture % 1980–91	5.7	3.2
Growth of Industry % 1980–92	11.1	6.5
Growth of Exports % per annum 1970–80	8.7	4.3
Growth of Exports % per annum 1980–92	11.9	5.9
Debt Service % of Exports 1980	4.3	9.3
Debt Service % of Exports 1992	10.3	25.3

*PPP basis US = $23 120.
Source: World Bank, *World Development Report*, 1994 (Extracted from Tables 1–30).

electricity was about 80 per cent, 50 per cent and 30 per cent respectively below their previous peaks. The transport system was in ruins, grain output was 25 per cent down and other major crops much worse (Hsu, 1989, p. 2; IMF, 1991b, p. 2). With substantial Soviet assistance Chinese development policies in the 1950s achieved very respectable economic growth with massive investment in physical and human capital. This heavy investment (over 30 per cent of national income in most years) based almost entirely on domestic savings is a characteristic of most of China's growth up to the 1980s. Efficiency in terms of output per unit of capital or labour was low (Hsu, 1989; Naughton 1989; Nolan, 1990; IMF, 1991b, p. 2). The command system could direct resources into projects but lacked the information and the incentives to become efficient. Moreover, the perceived external political threats led to heavy investments in defence-related industries, to the aim of self-sufficiency in all areas, and to regional dispersion of industry to ensure survival in the event of nuclear or conventional attack. (Despite Chinese denials, it seems certain that China's defence industries had first claim on key inputs including administrative and scientific talent (Naughton, 1989, pp. 19–20).) This, together with its isolationist policies after the break with the Soviet Union in the late 1950s, kept its industries starved of new technology and the spur of international competition. The policy of dispersal of industries and regional self-sufficiency meant that opportunities for gain from specialisation, economies of scale and trade were forgone.

Growth was also interrupted by the follies of the Great Leap Forward in the late 1950s and the Cultural Revolution, which peaked in 1967–8. These did lasting damage to China's ability to manage development.

The early 1950s saw China's attempt to become a fully socialist, centrally planned command economy on the Russian model. The means of production, distribution and exchange were nationalised. Only small family plots and tiny businesses remained in private hands. By 1956 nearly all enterprises were in the public sector.

But the attempt to run a fully socialist economy in the first five year plan (1952–7) swiftly taught China the problems imposed on central control by the lack of information. At its height only some 200 products were controlled by the central authorities. The key industries of coal, electricity, petroleum, machinery, iron and steel, and chemicals were given targets, had centrally allocated supplies and sold their outputs to the state for allocation to end users. Local planning authorities were given wide powers to control output targets and key inputs for non-key industries, and to allocate investment to projects up to a certain value and to control material balances and distribution of finished goods.

Large-scale industry in the 1950s was run on a Soviet pattern with one-man management, piece rates, bonus systems and sizeable wage differentials. Agriculture was organised in collectives. But the Great Leap Forward radically changed both. In the industrial enterprises management passed to committees of party members and workers. Managers lost power and were often humiliated, piece rates were abolished and earnings differentials reduced (Nolan, 1989, p. 6).

In the rural area Mao forced China's 700 500 collective farms into 24 000 rural communes with an average of 22 000 members. These conducted massive, labour-intensive rural public works, especially in irrigation. But they proved largely useless as most projects that could be done by traditional methods had already been done (Perkins, 1969, quoted in Nolan, 1989, p. 7). The private plots largely disappeared and all activities that could be communal were made so. Incomes were equalised. As a result of free-rider problems and lack of incentives, output dropped. The resulting economic chaos and terrible famine in 1959–61 led to a policy reversal.

The smaller collectives were restored, the production team became paramount, the private sector was partially restored and economic incentives were reintroduced. Although the system in agriculture continued to swing between accentuating equity and incentives, no serious institutional changes took place there between 1965 and 1976. The Cultural Revolution largely bypassed the farmers. But at its height Mao imposed collectivist policies on industry. There it had the same ill-effects on management and worker motivation as it previously had in agriculture. The resulting economic problems in the early 1970s led to a swing back to policies much like those of the first Five Year Plan (Nolan, 1990, pp. 5–7; Hsu, 1989, pp. 3–5).

INTERNATIONAL ECONOMIC RELATIONS

Under Mao China sought to make itself as independent of foreign trade as possible. All trade took place through 12 State Trading Corporations organised mainly on product lines. Enterprises were cut off from contact with foreign customers or suppliers. The yuan prices facing exporters and importers had no connection with world prices. Trading was not seen as a way of using resources efficiently by exploiting comparative advantage, but purely as a way of obtaining investment goods and other essential imports. Until the 1970s there was a high correlation between China's investment and imports (Hsu, 1989, fig. 1.1). China gained substantial inflows of capital and technology from the Soviet Union in the 1950s, but after the break Mao placed his confidence in the development of technology within China. Despite a few dramatic successes, this proved illusory and after Mao's death China swung to the opposite extreme in the late 1970s in a desperate race to catch up on Western technology through wholesale importing of machines, complete factories and power plants.

TAX REVENUES

Like many developing countries China's massive investments in heavy industry were squeezed out of the agricultural and mineral sectors. At the beginning of the 1950s this was inevitable as 80 per cent of the population were rural. And it was made easier in that the long wars and inflation had turned the terms of trade against agriculture. By preventing the terms of trade swinging back to agriculture the new leadership in 1949 was able to capture a good deal of the increase in production in the 1950s. This was done by keeping food and raw material prices low relative to prices for producer goods, which in turn were kept low relative to the protected, high prices for consumer goods. As all industrial profits were returned to the central authorities the artificially high profits of state enterprises provided the bulk of the government's revenues. As industry grew so too did this source of revenue. By 1957, it was 50 per cent of government revenue and by 1964 more than 70 per cent. The dangers of the system were that it held down incentives in agriculture, made for a very narrow fiscal base, feather-bedded manufacturing and accustomed urban workers to low food prices. These features were stored up problems for the 1980s.

China achieved much economic and social progress under the leadership of Mao Zedung: per capita growth of at least 3 per cent per year between 1953 and 1978, substantial improvements in nutrition, life expectancy and education. But by the 1970s several factors meant that the economic system was becoming increasingly wasteful. These factors included the long-term effects of the schism with Russia and the Cultural Revolution, both of which deprived China of educated, highly trained administrators, managers and technologists. This lack weakened both Central and Regional planning so projects were wrongly selected, badly implemented and poorly managed. Many were never completed. Decentralisation and regional dispersion were responses to external threats but led to enormous waste, duplication and loss of scale economies. By the end of the 1970s, Chinese planners were struggling to get hundreds of unworkable, poorly designed or incomplete projects into production; in 1977, the stock of uncompleted construction projects amounted to 210 per cent of the value of that year's capital construction. In other words, two full years' worth of investment was 'in the pipeline making no contribution to current production' (Naughton, 1990, p. 28). Barry Naughton claims that over a half of the extra output created by economic growth between 1953 and 1978 was wasted, in written-off construction and/or tied up in excessive stocks and military expenditure. Less than half of the increase in output went to increased consumption or new investment.

LEGACIES OF CHINA'S COMMAND ECONOMY

By 1978 China had passed the first phase of industrialisation. Agriculture's share in national material product had fallen from 52 per cent in 1952 to 28 per cent in 1978 (Nolan, 1990, p. 8). But this was achieved at the cost of neglect of agriculture and huge waste and inefficiency in both sectors. Marginal output to capital ratios fell from about 32 per cent in the first Five Year Plan to 16 per cent in the fourth Plan (1971–5) (Nolan, 1990, Table 1.2). A great deal of the capital stock was worthless. Grandiose plans for a massive leap forward with imported capital and technology, predicated on buoyant exports of petroleum, collapsed as a result of mismanagement and a failure of the petroleum industry to meet expectations. Huge investments based on expected piped gas from Sichuan were largely wasted when it was discovered in 1978 that there was insufficient gas (Naughton, 1990, p. 32).

Chinese assessments in the 1980s blamed Soviet-style centralised planning: 'Such a structure put the national economy in a straitjacket, discouraging initiative in all quarters, causing serious waste of manpower, materials and capital, and greatly hampering the growth of the productive forces. For many years, this was a major cause of the slow pace of the growth of the Chinese economy and the improvement of the living standards of the Chinese people' (Lin and Wang, 1984, quoted in Nolan, 1990, p. 13). But apart from the planning system, China's economy had been damaged by the loss of human capital caused by the madness of the Cultural Revolution and by the great costs of the regional autarky created in the name of defence and equity. It was not just central planning, it was bad planning that produced China's economic problems in the late 1970s.

Nevertheless most of the problems were characteristic of those met by other centrally planned economies. They are clearly summarised in a recent IMF study:

> irrational pricing stemming from controls, over-staffing and inefficiency in industry, an emphasis on product quantity and not quality, and isolation from foreign competition. These failings were exacerbated by biases against individual incentives, markets, and labor specialization. In industry, there was effectively no link between individual productivity and remuneration. The labor market was virtually nonexistent as a result of rigid restrictions on the geographical mobility of labor, the assignment of jobs to labor market entrants, and the system of lifetime employment under which enterprises provided housing, pensions, medical care, and other forms of welfare benefits. (IMF, 1991b, p. 3)

CHINA'S ECONOMIC REFORMS

By 1978, China's leaders had recognised that to use resources more efficiently was vital and that this required market-oriented reforms. But there was no master-plan. Reforms were piecemeal, experimental and pragmatic, and gave local authorities much discretion in implementing them. China's reforms, it has been said, resembled a person crossing a river, moving carefully from stone to stone with little idea where the next stone lies since it is hidden by the water ahead (Nolan, 1990, p. 14). Various reforms were tried in all sectors, but agriculture, aptly, provided the most fertile ground.

Agricultural Reforms

From a system of collectivised farming with procurement through mandatory quotas at low fixed prices there was a rapid and progressive shift to contracts at higher prices and increased latitude to sell surpluses in free markets. In 1979/80 procurement prices for staples were increased by 41 per cent for grain, 62 per cent for oil and 47 per cent for cotton (Weimer, 1990, p. 5). The Household Responsibility System was introduced. This gave family units contracts for their outputs and security of land tenure, initially for periods of 3–5 years, but extended in 1984 to 15 years and even 30 years for tree crops. In 1985, farmers were freed from obligatory contracts and in principle allowed to sell to the market or the state. In practice, pressure to deliver to official organs continued. In 1988, land use rights were made legally transferable. Farmers were further benefited by administered price increases for raw materials (World Bank, 1990, p. 63; Nolan, 1990, pp. 14–15; IMF, 1991b, p. 11).

The progressive moves towards a market-directed system were checked and even reversed somewhat in 1988/9 in the atmosphere of panic-buying, inflation and the massacre in Tiananmen Square. Despite this, by 1991, only an eighth of farming output still sold at government procurement prices (*Economist*, 1 June 1991).

The effects of reform in agriculture were dramatic. Growth between 1978 and 1984 was about 8 per cent p.a. compared to 1.6 per cent over 1971–7. The increases in labour productivity and profits released labour and savings to create or expand rural manufacturing and service industries which, under Mao, had been discouraged as 'bourgeois'. The expansion of demand and the release of resources from food production gave a boost to the development of small to medium, private rural industries and town and village collective enterprises (TVEs).

Agricultural growth slowed to 3 per cent p.a. in 1985–8. This was partly inevitable: the easy options for expanding output were seized first. But also the initial short contracts gave incentives to over-exploit rather than nurture the land, so some early growth was at the expense of conservation, and the maintenance and expansion of common facilities, such as irrigation, flood protection, transport, processing and storage. Also, the attractive opportunities for investment in non-agricultural activities, such as the rural industries and housing, diverted investment from land improvements. From 1987 the government increased state agricultural investment, particularly in irrigation, and on-farm investment was encouraged by the legislation of transfer of land use rights in 1988 (IMF, 1991b, p. 11). 1990 saw a bumper summer grain harvest, which helped ease inflationary pressures (World Bank, 1990, p. 100).

Social Effects of Rural Reform

There have been a number of negative effects from the economic reforms. Inequalities have increased between families, villages and regions. The ending of the commune system has reduced medical and social services, and rural education has suffered as these activities were all financed by the communes. Women may also have lost status. They are once more working in the household as wives and daughters with no right to pay, whereas in the commune system they earned 'work-points' and had some independence (Bettleheim, 1988, p. 28).

Enterprise Reforms

Before reform state enterprises were centrally controlled. Output, prices, sales and investment were all planned. All profits went to the state and losses were covered by the state. Enterprise investments were funded by grants from the state budget. Working capital was supplied partly by grants from the state budget and partly by credits from the banking system. Wage rates were set by a centrally approved scale with little scope for differential and incentives. Workers and managers were often dependent on their work unit for housing, health services and other social benefits. Under the 'iron rice bowl' system, enterprises could not easily dismiss workers for inefficiency or redundancy.

Since so little was under the control of the enterprise, the management could not be held responsible for financial results. Their job was simply to meet physical output targets fixed by the plan. Neither managers nor workers had any incentive to improve efficiency.

The main aims of reforms have been to increase incentives to efficiency by giving enterprises more freedom to manage and more responsibility for their profits and losses. The process of reform has involved trial and error and a gradualist approach.

Main Reforms of State Owned Enterprises (SOEs)

Between 1978 and 1983, enterprises were allowed to produce outside the plan, retain depreciation allowances and a share of profits, and there was a shift in financing from government to banks. Managers were given discretion over labour recruitment and performance-linked wage bonuses were introduced.

These reforms were extended over 1984–6, allowing SOEs to sell surpluses over plan targets at negotiated prices. A major reform replaced profit remittances to the government with direct taxation. Banks were given greater freedom to act commercially.

Between 1987 and 1990 the job of enterprise directors was defined more formally and the Contract Management Responsibility System was introduced. Some 90 per cent of medium and large-scale enterprises had signed management contracts by 1988. A national bankruptcy law was introduced in June 1988, but hardly used (IMF, 1991b, p. 5; Hussain and Stern, 1991, p. 155). According to *The Economist* (1995, pp. 59–60) the state recently granted \$1.2 billion to provincial authorities to prop up SOEs, and in Dalian only one SOE has been allowed to go bankrupt, though 200 firms are listed as candidates for bankruptcy.

A pronounced pause in the reform process followed the events of June 1989, with some attempt to restore central control, but recently government policies seem to have become reformist once more (*Beijing Review*, 1995, pp. 7–15).

Despite the reforms many SOEs' inefficiency has proved relatively intractable. But with average productivity increases of 2.4 per cent between 1980 and 1988 (Chen et al., 1988) SOEs' performance has not been all bad.

Although SOEs have generally been favoured in the allocation of inputs and credit, their output in 1990 grew by only 3 per cent compared with the industrial output of collectives, up by 20 per cent, and of foreign joint ventures up by over 50 per cent (albeit from an admittedly small base). The share of SOEs in China's industrial output fell from 80 per cent in the late 1970s to 54 per cent in 1990 (*Economist*, 1991, p. 18). According to the *Beijing Review* (1995), the share currently stands at 53 per cent. But that probably includes outputs of unsaleable products.

The shift from profit remittance to profits taxation without a properly designed fiscal system has sharply increased China's budget deficits. A uniform profits tax proved impossible because of the unfairness it would involve when there were substantial differences among firms in location, capital equipment, input and output prices. But this meant great scope for bargaining which was exploited by SOEs to reduce their tax liabilities.

Frequently, the results differed little from profit or loss sharing. SOEs have 'soft budget constraints'. Up to two-thirds of them are described as 'chronically in the red' (*Far Eastern Economic Review*, 10 October 1991, p. 77). But losses, particularly in the SOEs in the heavy industries have been partly due to continued price controls on their outputs such as energy and steel (see Singh, 1993).

The existence of different prices (fixed prices, guideline prices and free market prices) for the same products and large differences in profit retention rates between firms led to substantial rent-seeking and corruption among enterprise managers (IMF, 1991a, p. 7).

Despite some experiments with selling shares in SOEs privatisation is not an option being considered in China (Perkins, 1992, p. 20) Future SOE reforms seem mainly to concern improving their efficiency, removing or reducing their social security functions, modernising their equipment and exposing them to competition on a more level playing field (*Beijing Review*, 1995, pp. 7–18).

Township and village enterprises, both collectives and individually owned, have prospered. Restrictions on their activities were relaxed after 1978. They generally operated in a more competitive environment for both inputs and outputs than did SOEs, and their budget constraints were harder. They have proved more flexible and more dynamic. Though often owned by municipal authorities, the latter's needs for revenue forced them to seek maximum profits so at the margin the TVEs operated much like private sector firms (IMF, 1991a, p. 5; Thoburn et al., 1991, p. 45). Their absolute productivity has, however, often been low owing to dated technology and small scale of operation.

PRICES AND WAGES

Before 1979 both commodity prices and wages were controlled by the state and changed rarely. After 1979 there were both administered changes and some price liberalisation. Substantial increases in controlled agricultural prices were made in 1979 and subsequently. A two-tier price system was first introduced in rural areas. Farmers delivered quotas to the state at fixed prices and were then allowed to sell above-quota supplies to the state at negotiated prices, or in the free market. A few SOEs were given similar freedoms, but up to 1984 prices for important consumer goods, industrial raw materials and procurement prices for major agricultural commodities were still set by the state.

After 1984, the two-tier system was extended and more prices became market-determined or negotiable. As negotiations were generally left to local authorities the 'guided' or negotiated prices have tended to follow market prices. The share of trade at state-fixed prices fell from two-thirds of retail sales in 1978 to about one third in 1988. The inflation which recurred in 1987–8 led to a reimposition of some price controls as the authorities sought to combat price increases. But in 1991 large increases in the subsidised prices of cooking oil and grain indicated a return to price reform (*Economist*, 1991, p. 18).

Wage reforms have involved linking wages and bonuses to the value of sales or to profits of enterprises. By 1988 such wage systems covered a third of employees in SOEs. But most enterprises continue to distribute bonuses on an egalitarian basis. Despite taxes levied on excessive bonuses enterprises have significantly increased such payments. Also payments in kind have expanded to avoid tax penalties. Easy access to subsidies and credit in the late 1989s facilitated excessive payments to SOE workers and managers.

Labour was immobile in China. Up to the mid-1980s most jobs were assigned, employment was for lifetime, welfare (including housing, health and pensions) was normally dependent on the work unit, and there were severe restrictions on geographical mobility. Since 1986 SOEs have hired workers on 3–5-year contracts. They have been given more freedom to select employees and, in principle, to dismiss them. In 1987 contract workers were above 8 per cent of the SOE workforce (IMF, 1991b, p. 7). Other measures to improve mobility have included experiments with pooling pension funds between several enterprises, creating unemployment insurance schemes, housing reforms, including private ownership and some easing of restrictions on geographical mobility through a system of temporary residence permits. Despite these efforts mobility remains restricted and under-employment is endemic in the state sector (IMF, 1991a, p. 8). The main social welfare policy seems to remain that of continuing to employ people in unproductive work (*Economist*, 1995, p. 60). But that may be the only way to avoid serious hardship and social unrest at this stage.

OPEN DOOR POLICIES

China's pre-1978 trade policy has been likened to an airlock which sealed the domestic economy from the world. All trade was exclusively controlled by 12 state-owned foreign trade corporations (FTCs), each of which had a monopoly over particular products. The central plan set the levels of exports and imports for the year ahead and implementation of these targets was administered by the Ministry of Trade (MFT), later the Ministry of Foreign Economic Relations and Trade (MOFERT), and now the FTCs bought goods for export and sold imports at their domestic prices which often bore little or no relations to world prices. The FTC's profits were remitted to the state and losses were met by grants from the state budget. Imports were intended only to make up domestic shortages of goods and materials, and to provide these capital goods which could not be produced in China. These imports were financed by exports of commodities such as rice, petroleum, other minerals and processed foods in which surpluses could be generated. The centrally controlled trade plan aimed at balancing China's foreign trade and avoiding international indebtedness.

TRADE REFORM

The basic strategy of the reforms was decentralisation. In 1979 part of decision-making power was distributed to local governments and enterprises. MOFERT became responsible for a foreign trade plan divided into a directive plan and a guidance plan. The first gave mandatory levels for exports of heavy industry such as petroleum and for imports of raw materials and equipment for major state projects.

The guidance plan set targets for the value of exports and imports to ministries and local administrations. They were allowed to form their own foreign trade corporations (FTCs) who have considerable discretion on how to meet their targets. Over the years the number of goods subject to the plans has fallen and licensing, together with export and import duties have become more important in influencing trade.

Since 1984 FTCs have become more responsible for their financial performance, paying taxes instead of remitting their profits to the state. In 1988, most local branches of national FTCs were made independent and responsible for their own finances. The number of FTCs exploded to over 6000 and some domestic enterprises were authorised to engage directly in foreign trade. FTCs were encouraged to adopt the agency system, where they received fees for handling trade instead of acting as buyers and sellers on their own behalf. These various reforms encouraged competition in foreign trade and some increase in the extent to which foreign prices were passed through to the domestic prices of imports and goods for export.

Enterprises were allowed to retain 25 per cent on average of foreign exchange earned for quota sales and 75 per cent above quota. In three sectors – garments, light industry, and arts and handicrafts – retentions were between 60 and 100 per cent. At the same time, subsidies and official allocations of foreign exchange were ended in these industries, making them more or less financially independent. If enterprises or the local authorities with whom they shared exchange retentions did not wish to use their foreign exchange, they were allowed to sell it in new foreign exchange adjustment centres (FEACs) where they could earn on average a 75 per cent premium over the official rate. These moves generated real incentives for enterprises and the provincial or town authorities to earn foreign currency. In the late 1980s and early 1990s there have been several devaluations of the yuan, which have also generally increased incentives to export and reduced the gap between the official and the parallel market rate to about 10 per cent (*Economist*, 1991, p. 18). More recently the two markets' rates have been merged.

The proliferation of FTCs and the incentives to export led to some excesses. It was alleged that competition between FTCs drove up the procurement prices of exportable goods, e.g. silk products, thus cutting the profits of some large state FTCs. More seriously some export contracts were not met and some poor quality products were exported. These damaged China's commercial reputation. The authorities responded by seeking to impose some quality control on the FTCs, withdrawing licences and forcing some mergers.

Further reforms have increased competition among FTCs. State-owned enterprises are now able to choose which FTC to handle their exports and imports and large ones can handle their own foreign trade (*Beijing Review*, 19 November, 1991, p. 13; see also MacBean, 1995, for detail on China's Foreign Trade Companies).

FOREIGN INVESTMENT AND THE SPECIAL ECONOMIC ZONES

The reformers saw attracting foreign investment as a way of gaining foreign technology and capital without adding to foreign debt. To experiment with this and more general economic reforms five special economic zones (SEZs) were set up in 1980 as the main areas for foreign direct investment. Three of these are in Guangdong, the best known being Shenzhen. They offered preferential tax and tariff rates, and tax holidays. In 1984 similar privileges were accorded to 14 coastal cities and Hainan Island. Originally intended to attract joint ventures, especially from Western countries, foreign investors are present in a variety of relationships, from processing and assembly arrangements to wholly owned ventures. In Guandong, Hong Kong businesses have appeared far beyond the SEZs (Thoburn et al., 1990). The relationship with Hong Kong and overseas Chinese has proved enormously fruitful in attracting investment, marketing and managerial expertise to assist China's exports. Hong Kong companies have created 2 million jobs in Guangdong. Output in Guandong grew at 13 per cent per year in the 1980s, in Shenzhen it reached 47 per cent a year. By 1990 Guangdong had attracted over $20 billion of foreign investment, most of it from Hong Kong, while Xiamen in the neighbouring province of Fujian has also been a major success with over $3.5 billion foreign investment, about a third of it from nearby Taiwan (*Economist*, 1991, pp. 17–18).

Recently, the US and Japan have accelerated their investments in China. Japan is a latecomer but is rapidly making up for lost time. In general foreign investments in China are continuing to increase despite some hiccups in payments disputes (*Financial Times*, 1994).

CONCLUSION ON INTERNATIONAL ECONOMIC RELATIONS

China's Open Door policies have been a success. Since 1979 China's foreign trade ratio has soared. The share of manufactures in total exports has risen to over 70 per cent. China's share of world exports doubled (1979–89) (World Bank, 1990, Tables 3.1 and 3.7). The average annual growth of China's exports 1978–89 was 14 per cent. They slowed to 10 per cent in 1989, but surged to 20 per cent growth in 1990 (World Bank, Table 3.3; *Economist*, 1991, p. 18).

There is a risk that China's foreign trade may nevertheless be inefficient given the remaining distortions in the economy: multiple prices, soft budget constraints in SOEs, incentives which vary across industries and regions. This is certainly the contention of John Hsu (1989). Without a detailed set of shadow prices and estimates of the domestic resource costs of China's industries it is impossible to test. But some casual observation of China's exports suggests otherwise. They are the largely natural resource-intensive or labour-intensive consumer goods and light industrial goods which conventional trade theory would predict. A recent study by Alexander Yeats (1991) provides revealed comparative advantage statistics, which tend to confirm that judgement. The rapid growth in manufactured exports has followed a similar path to the other successful Asian economies. The steps which China has taken to offset an import substitution bias have been broadly correct: exports, on balance, are probably little if at all subsidised. Chinese labour seems to be highly thought of by overseas businesses when comparing locations in Asia for overseas investment (*Economist*, 1991). Most of the increase in output and in exports in recent years has come from the private or the quasi-private sector of collectives. They operate in a much more competitive, less subsidised environment than the SOEs.

On the import side there may be greater risks of waste. Eagerness to use up foreign exchange allocations or currency retentions to avoid having to surrender them to the state did in the past lead to excessive imports of particular products and imported equipment being left idle, as Hsu argues. But the opening up of the FEACs must have reduced the incentive to use up foreign exchange surpluses when other enterprises, which really needed imports, were willing to offer attractive exchange rates for foreign currency.

SOME CONCLUSIONS AND IMPLICATIONS

Three basic lessons from China's economic successes since 1978 are the importance of early liberalisation in agriculture and international economic relations and that 'gradualism' at least in some circumstances can work. 'Shock therapy' is not a panacea for economic reform. The combination of financial incentives and family or collective responsibility systems worked wonders in China in stimulating production and exports. The growth of farm production and incomes generated the demand and the resources necessary to stimulate rural, village and township enterprises. These in turn provided the main gains in manufacturing for both the domestic and foreign markets. The Open Door Policy encouraged the overseas Chinese to combine their talents in management, production know-how and marketing with low-cost Chinese labour, especially in Guangdong and Fujiian provinces. The policy was less successful in attracting the hoped for Western technology, but recent changes to rules on foreign investment which allow wholly-owned subsidiaries have proved more attractive to Western multinationals. The 1990s have seen a surge of foreign investment in China. The relative abundance of food and consumer goods in post-reform China helped dampen inflation and is a major contrast with Russia and most East European economies. Probably none of the former Soviet Bloc countries has the great asset of a neighbouring Hong Kong or Taiwan to be tapped for capital and skills, but perhaps several could make more use of exiles who have successful businesses abroad.

The main weaknesses in China's economy are the slow pace of reforms in the state enterprises, the labour markets and taxation. The SOEs remain overmanned and heavily subsidised. Many continue to produce obsolete goods with out-of-date equipment. Reforms resulting in closures or mergers would convert widespread underemployment into open unemployment and naturally meet powerful resistance. Until proper unemployment benefit schemes are in place such resistance is entirely understandable. But it would be wasteful to put increased finance into inefficient state enterprises when similar resources lent to non-state enterprises could create real jobs and earn higher returns. New investment in the state sector should be confined to those activities which it is clear the private sector cannot handle in a more socially efficient manner.

The partial and incomplete nature of China's reforms stimulated particularly divisive forms of corruption. Decentralisation put more power in the hands of provincial and local leaders. These, subject neither to the disciplines of central control nor fully competitive markets, were able to exploit opportunities for buying at controlled prices and selling in free markets, and to exact bribes and favours for granting the various licences and permits needed to do business. Corruption, fraud and increased nepotism seem to have been widespread in the mid-1980s. They were widely reported in the press, and contributed to the discontent of students, teachers and workers on fixed incomes, which led to demonstrations and protests culminating in the Tiananmen Square crisis (Meaney, 1991, pp. 129–38). The initial response of the authorities was to take back responsibility and control to the central authorities, but recent action to free more prices, raise controlled prices, devalue the yuan and widen access to foreign exchange have reduced some of the incentives to illicit arbitrage. More and better trained auditors, together with incentives for 'whistle-blowing', are standard ways of dealing with fraud and other illegal business practices. But in China, when many enterprises belong to the military, relatives of leaders and regional governments, control over corruption, monopolies and illegal practices is particularly hard. With its long history of nepotism, special measures may be necessary in China to ensure that merit rather than connections gain advancement.

Despite some reforms to ease geographical labour mobility, such as temporary residence permits, the present system gives individuals little choice of job or location. But requirements to advertise managerial posts widely, combined with transparent appointments procedures, and easier mobility for higher grade personnel would enhance efficient management. Special arrangements for mobility of key skilled workers such as housing and attractive contracts would also ease bottlenecks. For ordinary workers, mobility between work units can be improved by further social security reforms that transfer pension and health obligations from enterprises to the state. Similarly, existing and new housing should be removed from enterprises and transferred to municipal authorities with a view to developing a proper market for housing which would allow workers to rent or buy accommodation for themselves and their families when they change jobs.

Fiscal reform is a key area. The reduction in revenues from SOEs has to be replaced. In China there may be a stronger case than in most developing economies for the introduction of an income tax as 25 per cent of the labour force are in the state sector. Their incomes in cash and kind are more easily assessed (Hussain and Stern, 1991, p. 177).

China's record under reform shows the dynamism which can be released when families in agriculture and small to medium-sized enterprises in towns and villages are given responsibility and incentives. But it also shows the severe difficulties which face efforts to reform state enterprises. Similar problems have been met in Hungary and other reform-minded East European economies. It would be hard to deny that important lessons for the future of both China and other reforming centrally planned economies can be learned from China's experiences since 1978.

ACKNOWLEDGEMENTS

An earlier version of this paper was presented to a seminar at the University of East Anglia and to a workshop of the Development Studies Association in Manchester (1992) and published in Paul Cook and Fred Nixson, eds., *The Move to the Market? Trade and Industry Policy Reform in Transitional Economies* (London: Macmillan, 1995), chapter 8, and is reproduced here with permission. I have also benefited from conversations with Professor Sumner La Croix of the Economics Department, University of Hawaii. None of the above are responsible for omissions, errors and misinterpretations in this paper.

REFERENCES

Beijing Review (1995), vol. 38, no. 2, 9–15 January.
Bettleheim, C. (1988), 'Economic Reform in China', *Journal of Development Studies* (Special Issue), vol. 24, no. 4, July.
Bhagwati, J.N. (1978), *Anatomy and Consequences of Exchange Control Regimes* (Cambridge, MA: Ballinger).
———— (1993), *India in Transition*: Freeing the Economy (Oxford: Clarendon Press).
Chen, K., Jefferson, C., Rawski, J., Wang, H. and Zheng, Y. (1988), 'New Estimates of Fixed Investment and Capital Stock for Chinese State Industry', *China Quarterly*, vol. 114, pp. 243–66.
The Economist (1991), 1 June issue and Special Survey of 16 November.
———— (1995) 14–20 January.
The Far Eastern Economic Review (1991), 8 August, 22 August and 10 October.
Financial Times Survey: China (1994), 7 November.
Hussain, A. and Stern, N. (1991), 'Effective Demand, Enterprise Reforms and Public Finance in China', *Economic Policy*, no. 12, April.

Hsu, J.C. (1989), *China's Foreign Trade Reforms: Impact on Growth and Stability* (Cambridge: Cambridge University Press).

IMF (1991a), *International Financial Statistics*, August.

IMF (1991b), *China: Economic Reform and Economic Management*, occasional paper no. 76 (Washington DC), January 1991.

Krueger, A. (1978), *Liberalization Attempts and Consequences* (Cambridge, MA: Ballinger).

MacBean, A. (1995), 'China's Foreign Trade Corporations (Export–Import Companies): Their Role in Economic Reform and Export Success', proceedings of a Conference on Management Issues for China in the 1990s, forthcoming in J. Child and Y. Lu, eds., *Management Issues for China in the 1990s – International Enterprises* (London: Routledge).

Meaney, C.S. (1991), 'Market Reform and Disintegrative Corruption in Urban China', in Baum, R., ed., *Reform and Reaction in Post-Mao China* (New York and London: Routledge).

Naughton, B. (1989), 'The Pattern and Legacy of Economic Growth in the Mao Era', a paper for the 'Four Anniversaries China Conference', Annapolis, Maryland, 10–14 September.

Nolan, P. (1990), 'Introduction', in Nolan, P. and Fureng, D. eds., *The Chinese Economy and its Future* (Oxford: Polity Press and Basil Blackwell).

Perkins, D. (1969), *Agricultural Development in China, 1368–1968* (Edinburgh: Edinburgh University Press).

————— (1992), 'China's Gradual Approach to Market Reforms', UNCTAD Discussion Paper no. 52.

Singh, A. (1993), 'The Plan, the Market and Evolutionary Reform in China', UNCTAD Discussion Paper no. 76, December.

Thoburn, J., Leung, H., Chau, E. and Tang, S. (1990), 'Foreign Investment and Economic Liberalization in China', Discussion Paper no. 9104 (Economics Research Centre, University of East Anglia).

Thorburn, J. et al. (1991), 'Investment in China by Hong Kong Companies', *Institute of Development Studies Bulletin*, vol. 22, no. 2.

Weimer, C. (1990), 'Price Reform Stalled', *Journal of Asian Economies*, autumn.

World Bank (1990), Country Study, *China: Between Plan and Market* (Washington, DC).

Yeats, A. (1991), *China's Foreign Trade and Comparative Advantage*, World Bank Discussion Paper no. 141.

Index

215